Leaving Iran

A Glimpse Into The Persian Mind

Isaac Yomtovian

ISBN 978-0-9831300-6-2

Library of Congress
2012900282

Editor
Joanne Fenton Humphrey

Book Design
Ron Humphrey

Windjammer Adventure Publishing
289 South Franklin Street, Chagrin Falls, OH 44022
Telephone 440.247.6610 Email windjammerpub@mac.com

To my wife, Roz

*You are my light! My life has meaning
only because you shine.*

To: Sandy

Dave E. Jont

ACKNOWLEDGEMENTS

It is with deep love that I acknowledge my parents, Ebrahim and Ezat, who did their best to raise seven proud, educated, and God-fearing children; my Kourosh High School friends who have been my life's anchor and inspiration; my great-uncle Asher Nejat, who mentored me for a brief but important time in my life; my siblings, especially my older brother Ruben, who has mentored me throughout my life; and of course, my wife Roslyn; my daughters, Misha, Ezi, Leah and Ariela; and my sister Lydia—all of whom have encouraged me to write this book.

I also wish to extend heartfelt thanks to the scholars and activists from whom I have learned a wealth of information: Dr. Houman and Mrs. Homa Sarshar, the editors of the monumental work, *Esther's Children,* whom I had the pleasure of meeting in person; Bahram Moshiri; Naser Engheta; Professor Ehsan Yasharel; and especially Dr. Manouchehr Ganji, whom I had the privilege of inviting to Cleveland to discuss Iran; Professor Zamani, my literature and history teacher in Iran, who demanded that I learn about the truth and instilled in me an appreciation for democracy; Mr. Dilmani, of the Mashhadi Jewish Community of Iran, who taught me Hebrew and provided me an introduction to Judaism; Dr. Warren (Bud) Veissman, the University of Nebraska, who gave me the opportunity to obtain a graduate degree in hydrology and hydraulics, and consequently remain in America.

My deepest appreciation goes to those who read my manuscript and made constructive criticisms and suggestions: Reuben Mizrachi, Judaic Scholar; Dr. Alan S. Rosenbaum, Professor of Philosophy, Cleveland State University; Mehdi Amjadi, Dr. Farshid Afsarifard, and Dr. M. Valadbeigi, scholars of Islamic Studies and Persian History; Cindy Datzman Friedman, journalist; Brian L. Berger; Thomas P. Slavin, Middle East Scholar; Donna Levine; and Judith Sternfeld. A special thank you to Dr. Mark Lewine, Professor of Anthropology, Sociology and Urban Studies at Cuyahoga Community College who was a great source of inspiration.

A profound thank you goes to my editor, Joanne Humphrey, and to Ron Humphrey, publisher at Windjammer Adventure Publishing.

AUTHOR'S NOTE

This book is based on memories that may or may not be completely accurate. Some of the ideas expressed are my own opinions. There is no intent to invade anyone's privacy or to misrepresent anyone's character, behavior or ideas; I have only relayed *my* understanding of people and events.

I have found the book *Esther's Children: A Portrait of Iranian Jews*, edited by Houman Sarshar, to be the most informative and valuable source of information regarding the history of Iranian Jews. The documents and facts presented in that book are accurate and abundant. For example, *Figure 824* in Sarshar's book shows my great-uncle Mr. Asher Nejat with the members of Esfahan's Jewish group in the ancient Jewish cemetery at Lenjan, standing next to a tombstone with Hebrew letters dated 500 BCE. Almost all the ancient Jewish sites throughout Iran are shown in this book. Most importantly, the Judaic-Farsi documents are presented. I have often used *Esther's Children* as a source for my writings and presentations.

In addition, I have listened to several lectures given by Professor Ehsan Yarshater, the principal author of *Encyclopedia Iranica*. Notes from these lectures have been used as source material.

I have used *Pirkei Avot, Ethics of the Fathers: The Sages' Guide to Living* (Me'sorah Publications, Ltd., Brooklyn, New York) to verify some of the Jewish beliefs related to Jewish practices in Iran, as I remember them.

Information related to the historic treatment of non-Muslims, especially Jews, by the Iranian government, as well as the *Shiah* Muslim population, was obtained from the following sources: *Islam in Iran*, by Eilliapovlowitz Petroshefsky, translated by Karim Keshavarzi; and articles in *Shofar Magazine*, published by the Shofar Foundation, Inc., Yosef Shahery, editor.

I have made an honest attempt to cite factual material (books and internet sources) whenever necessary, though I must apologize if my acknowledgement of sources falls short of expectations.

A glossary has been provided to explain Farsi, Arabic and Hebrew words and phrases.

My deepest hope is that this book might help to unify my fellow Persians—Jews, Muslims, Christians, Zoroastrians and Baha'is. It is a fact that all present day Iranians have inherited the bounty of Persian civilization, and consequently share the richness of a culture which predates the Arab Muslim invasion. Because Iranians all share so much history, literature and music, there must be no designations of inferiority or superiority based on socio-economic, racial or religious differences.

Readers should keep in mind that I lived in an area of Tehran unlike any other in the city: My neighborhood was unusually diverse and my friends were Muslims, Jews, Christians, Baha'is and Zoroastrians. My experiences might have been unique to southern Tehran, where families of average and below average incomes lived in close proximity to each other. Even though it is highly likely that wealthy Jewish and Muslim families who lived in northern Tehran did not share my experiences, I believe that the stories and memories presented here are a true representation of *my* life in Iran—and the lives of most Iranians who comprise the ruling class of today's Islamic Republic.

The children of Adam are limbs of the same body,

Having been created of one essence.

When a calamity afflicts one limb

The other limbs cannot remain at rest.

If thou hast no sympathy for the troubles of others

Thou art unworthy to be called by the name of man.

—*Sa'adi Shirazi*
(1213-1293)

بنی آدم اعضای یک پیکرند

که در آفرینش زیک گوهراند

چو عضوی بدردآورد روزگار

دگر عضوها را نماند قرار

تو کز محنت دیگران بی غمی

نشاید که نامت نهند آدمی

TABLE OF CONTENTS

PREFACE

Eagerly, I informed my Jewish Iranian-American friends that I wrote a book about Iran. Without exception, their reaction was one of alarm. "Don't expose us!" was their typical response. "The mud has settled to the bottom of the pool, why stir it up?" They are afraid of "repercussions," though I don't understand what these repercussions might be, or who might bring them to fruition. The truth needs to be told.

I lived my childhood, through my seventeenth year, in Iran—the land of Persia—homeland of my family for twenty-five hundred years, dating from the reign of Cyrus the Great. It is both daunting and amazing to have a cultural heritage of such richness and duration! In writing this book, I have searched through memories and in so doing I have revisited the land of my birth: its beauty and its terror, for there were always two very different aspects to my experiences in Iran.

Parts I, II, and III of this book are written in the style of a journal, a chronicle of my life experiences and thoughts; each segment or anecdote is set in a particular place and time. If my recollections of childhood were cloudy and indistinct, I relied on the recall of others: my parents, and my older brother Ruben, in particular. I also asked former school chums to help me recall specific details. Whenever possible, I recreated conversations that occurred throughout the years.

In Part IV, I have offered my thoughts and opinions, based on historical facts obtained from sources listed in the References, as to why the Shah fell from power, how the present-day Islamic Republic came into existence, and why the Islamic Republic of Iran behaves the way it does. America and the West must understand Iran's motives and driving principles in order to comprehend Iran's politics and policies of the present.

I invite the reader to take a journey with me back to Iran, to experience the life of a Jewish boy growing up in the multi-cultural neighborhood of a predominantly Muslim country. Hopefully, the reader will learn something about Persian culture and Jewish life in Iran: the sights, smells, tastes and emotions one might experience there. I want the reader to feel the heart and soul of my homeland, with all its love and loyalty, deception and treachery. Writing this book has been a voyage of discovery for me, helping me to understand my confusion and ambivalence towards Iran, as well as my nostalgia and longing for the land of my birth. When all is said and done, I will always be Isaac, son of Ebrahim, grandson of Elyahu, great-grandson of Aghbaba, great-great-grandson of Shelemo, great-great-great-grandson of Yehazghel—otherwise known as Isaac *Pesare' Ebram Johood*: Isaac, son of Ebrahim the Jew.

Isaac (Es,hagh in Farsi) age 8

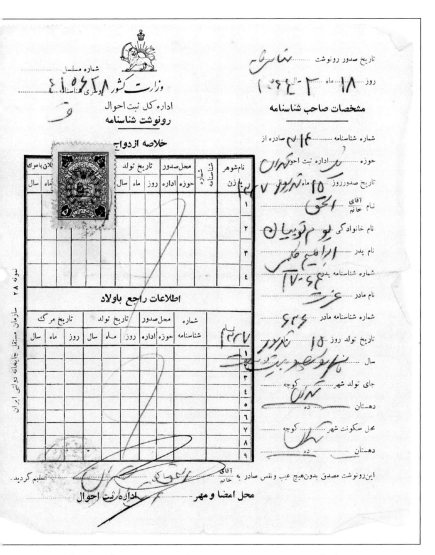

Isaac's Birth Certificate: Copy of Iranian Census Bureau's document; it states, in part, that Isaac's (Es,hagh) father's name is Ebrahim Kalimi, Ebrahim the Jew.

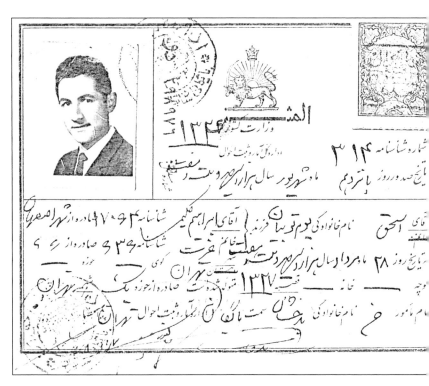

Birth Certificate with ID number and date issued; it states: Mr. Es,hagh Yomtoubian, child of Mr. Ebrahim the Jew (Kalimi) and Mrs. Ezat; and Isaac's parents' birthdates and places of birth. It also states that Isaac was born on the 28th of Mordad, of the year 1327 (August 19, 1948) in Tehran.

Listen to the reed flute, how it tells of separation!
Ever since I was severed from the reed field,
My shrill cries have caused men and women to weep.
My heart is torn open with longing.
How can I explain the pain of yearning?"

Jelaluddin Rumi

بشنو از نی چون حکایت میکند

از جدایی ها شکایت میکند

کز نیستان تا مرا ببریده اند

از نفیرم مرد و زن نالیده اند

سینه خواهم شرحه شرحه از فراق

تا بگویم شرح درد اشتیاق

هرکسی کو دور ماند از اصل خویش

باز جوید روزگار وصل خویش

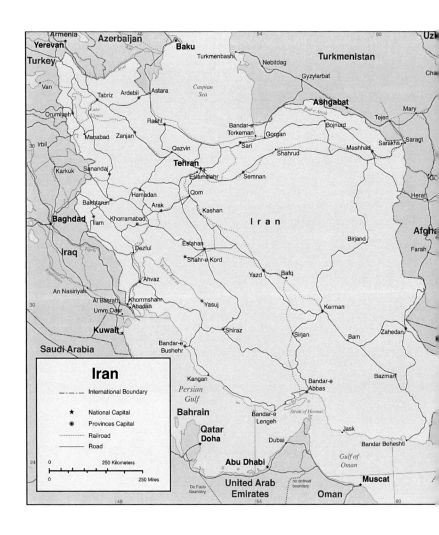

Tehran, Iran
Thursday Morning, August 28, 1966

At 3:00am I was lying on my back staring at the ceiling, unable to sleep. In a few hours I would be leaving Iran, the place of my birth, to live in Israel. I was assailed by the memories of my childhood—some pleasant, some not so pleasant. One episode in particular became as real as the day it occurred. In the darkness of my bedroom, I was transported back to the late summer of 1955, when I was seven years old.

I was playing ball in the narrow street near my house when my friend Ali ran up to me, out of breath.

"Isaac! Come quick! There's a terrible fight! Your father is being attacked!"

I dropped my ball and dashed to my house to alert my mother.

"They are murdering my husband!" she shrieked in horror. She ran to our neighbor's house and pounded on the door with all her might, calling for her friend. "Touran Khanom! Help me! My husband is being murdered! Where is Hassan Khan?" Hassan Khan, Ali's father, was the chief of police in our neighborhood.

While my mother tried to find someone to assist us, I ran down my street, heading south to Sheikh Hadi Street, a short distance away. As I approached the home of Agha Akhoond Abdolah, a well-known clergyman, I saw a crowd gathered in the street. I stopped abruptly near Saghah Khaneh, a small Muslim shrine, and realized that my father was at the center of the chaos. He was trying to fight off a tall, heavy, older man and several young men. I recognized the older man immediately—it was Agha Akhoond himself! The other men I did not know.

My father was a very strong man and he fought like a lion. He tried to fend off the blows as his assailants repeatedly struck him with heavy sticks. Into the melee rushed Hassan Khan. He quickly stopped the assault, subdued the crowd, and removed my father and the clergyman from the street.

"Come with me, Ebrahim Yomtoubian," commanded Hassan Khan

1

house lived a man who was a builder and architect; his three older daughters were schoolteachers. This family was not friendly and kept to themselves, making sure no Jewish children played in front of their house.

Next to our house, to the east, was the home of the Nouryelian family, a Jewish family with five children and a Christian tenant. Soli, the oldest boy, was my age; his younger brother Younai and sisters Mounes and Nasi were the same age as my younger siblings. Touba Khanom, their mother, became my mother's best friend. The two women decided to attend Akaber, an adult class to learn how to read and write Farsi.

Across from our home stood a very large house inhabited by a family whose members belonged to the Baha'i faith. We rarely saw those neighbors, but they were known to be good people.

Further east, on a very short koocheh, was the home of the large Larynejad family; they were Orthodox Mashhadi Jews from the holy city of Mashhad in northeastern Iran. Their household included six children and a number of tenants. When my mother gave birth to my youngest sister Lida, she could not nurse because of a breast infection. At the same time Mrs. Larynejad, called Shamsi Khanom, gave birth to a son named Moeiz. She volunteered to nurse my sister Lida.

Near the end of our koocheh resided a Russian Christian family that included Parviz, a very tall, handsome son, and his beautiful sister Mehry. Across the alley from them lived an attractive prostitute and her only child, a daughter, who played with the neighborhood girls.

At the end of our koocheh, at the intersection of the main street, Sheikh Hadi, there was Shahrokh, a Muslim elementary school for girls that three of my sisters attended. From our house we could hear the happy sound of students playing in the schoolyard.

As I mentally scanned my neighborhood, I remembered other neighbors, including the families of two military officers who lived in modern houses. Several extremely observant, conservative Muslim families lived near the officers in a large rambling house. The women in that household wore black chadors, exposing only their eyes. There were also families we would rarely see—we were told they were members of the Zoroastrian faith.

Going south on Sheikh Hadi, the main street, lived an Assyrian Christian family; they made and sold alcoholic drinks in their house. Across from their house was a small corner grocery store, Baghali, which was frequently visited by the neighborhood children who bought chewing gum there. My Muslim friends, Akbar Shikhol Islami and Masseod Islami lived in this area. Akbar's father was a rich bazaarie (shop owner and merchant in the Tehran Bazaar) and Maseod's father was a poor janitor.

Further south on Sheikh Hadi, on the east side of the street, stood a small Muslim shrine, Saghah Khooneh. Inside there was a pool of drinking water, to be used only by Muslims. The moist walls of the shrine smelled of mold. The stagnant pool of water, with a metal cup chained to it, emitted a metallic smell because Muslims threw coins into the pool after reciting a short prayer; these coins were for charity. Next to that site lived a well-known mullah, Akhoond Agha Abdolah Mohamadi, and his large family. He was a big, heavy man whose stomach constantly rumbled, causing him to belch incessantly. He always wore an ammamreh (a turban) and a long black garment, known as a ghaba. We would often see that stern-faced mullah on his way to prayers, carrying his tasbe'eh (prayer beads).

Continuing to walk south on Sheikh Hadi Street, I would end up at Sepah Street, one of the oldest streets in Tehran, where a large public Muslim girls' school, Nue Bavegan e Zarabie, was located.

Heading north on Sheikh Hadi there were many small houses and shops, including a large teahouse that served as a restaurant for the local laborers. Only Muslim men were allowed to eat there. The most popular item on the menu was deezi, a stew prepared with cooked beans, onions, lamb fat, and small pieces of meat. During the winter season, chickpeas and lima beans served with vinegar and spices and oven-cooked beets (laboo) would be added to the menu. The food was served with fresh bread (sangak), and raw scallions and was reasonably priced so that construction workers and laborers could afford it. Short-legged wooden, bed-like platforms (takht) were arranged along two walls of the teahouse. These platforms were covered with Persian rugs;

especially difficult during mealtime when she had to carry heavy pots of rice, soup, sauce, vegetables and meat to the living room. Following the meal, she had to carry all the dishes back down to the kitchen to be washed.

Upstairs there were three rooms. The most beautiful of those rooms was the domain of the eldest son, my brother Ruben. Also, there were two more rooms upstairs that were rented out when my grandparents no longer lived with us; these two rooms had their own tiny kitchen and toilet. There was also a large balcony upstairs from which I could view the courtyard while enjoying soft breezes. . .

With each minute that passed, I became acutely aware that the plane was taking me farther and farther away from everyone and everything I had ever known. My entire world—my entire universe—had been centered on my home and my neighborhood.

My beloved home! Would I ever see it again?

Isaac's father served two years in Reza Shah's army before his marriage.

Isaac's mother, Ezat Mazloumian Yomtoubian, standing in the courtyard of her home in the Jewish Ghetto of Tehran, in 1944.

Isaac's parents, Ezat and Ebrahim, 1949. This photo was taken about one year after Isaac was born.

Ebrahim, Isaac's father, and Isaac skinning a lamb in the courtyard of their house on Koocheh Sharaf, shortly before Passover, 1956.

Isaac posing with his violin in the courtyard of his home, sometime during the winter of 1961. (He attended the Tehran Institute of Art and Music; his teacher was the famous violinist Habiballah Badiei.) The windows on the upper left side belong to the formal, Western-style dining room; the upper window on the right side belong to Isaac and Hertzel's bedroom; the open basement window on the extreme left corresponds to the basement storage room; a stairway by the middle basement window is the way to the bathroom; the basement window on the extreme right belongs to the kitchen. The decorative pool is covered for the winter and the flowerbed is empty.

A family portrait taken in the Alborz Photography Studio, Tehran, circa 1956. (Left to right) Homa; Ezat, holding Shahnaz; Hertzel (standing behind Shahnaz); Isaac; Ruben, standing behind Isaac; and Ebrahim, holding Sorayah. (Lida was not yet born.)

PART ONE

MY ANCESTRAL HOME

Alas, in later days I look behind
And with remorse I only find
Zestful youth, unaware and blind
To passage of time, fate of mankind.
　　　—Rubiyat of Omar Khayyam

افسوس که نامه جوانی طی شد

و ان تازه بهار زندگانی دی شد

آن مرغ طرب که نام او بود شباب

فریاد، ندانم ، که کی آمد کی شد

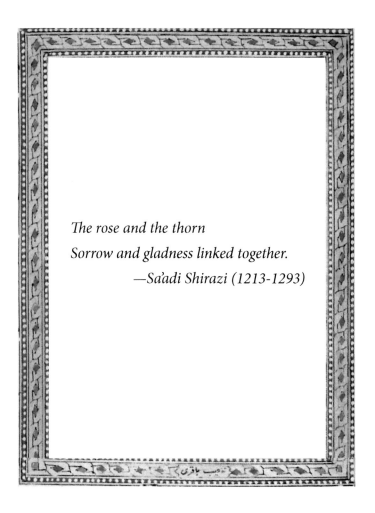

The rose and the thorn
Sorrow and gladness linked together.
　　　　—Saʾadi Shirazi (1213-1293)

#24 Koocheh Sharaf
Tehran, Iran
Late Spring 1952

It was a quiet morning. The sun blazed in a cloudless sky and the hot, parched air radiated off the brick walls of the courtyard. Suddenly the silence was broken by the unmistakable sound of an object falling into water.

My pregnant mother, busily at work preparing the noon meal, heard that sound and feared the worst. Seconds later, before I could cry out, my mother ran up the stairs from our basement kitchen, sprinted across the courtyard, and hurled herself into the deep underground cistern—to rescue me!

Neither of us knew how to swim. She struggled to hold me above her head as she rose, sunk, and then rose again. Whenever she surfaced to swallow a breath of air, she shouted for Ruben, my older brother, to run and get help. Barely seven years old, Ruben understood the seriousness of the situation and dashed immediately to our tenants on the second floor, screaming as he ran, "Help! Help! Mamon and Isaac fell into the water! Help!"

The neighbors were skeptical. Why would a grown woman jump into the large, deep underground water storage pool?

"You must come! You must come!" my brother shrieked. The panic-stricken look on his face must have been very convincing because the tenants rushed down the stairs to the courtyard. Strong hands wrenched me from my mother's grasp and placed me on the ground. As everyone's attention turned to rescuing my mother, I began to vomit.

"Here, put some salt in his mouth," said someone whose voice I didn't recognize.

"Cover him with this towel," advised another tenant.

There I sat, soaked and shivering, the object of everyone's attention.

"Ezat Khanom, you picked an unusual way to cool off on such a hot day," exclaimed Mr. Hakim, the male tenant, laughing. "But you are a very brave woman," he continued, in a more serious tone of voice. "You don't know how to swim, and yet you jumped in to save your son."

"I did what I had to do," Mother shrugged as she hugged me close to her chest. "Isaac, Isaac," she whispered in my ear, " *Ghorbonat beram*! You are a lot of trouble for a four-year-old." She was too relieved to be angry with me.

At dinnertime, father returned from the day's work at his fabric store. The *sofreh* was already spread over the Persian carpet on the living room floor and a large plate of bread had been placed in the center. Smaller plates were set out for my parents, my brother Ruben, sister Homa, and me. Father, Ruben and I were sitting on the floor, eagerly waiting for our dinner. My mother hurried into the room carrying a large bowl of *khoresh ghormeh sabzi*, a vegetable and meat stew. The scent of turmeric filled the air.

"Homa, go back to the kitchen and bring the *sangak*," ordered my mother. As Homa hurried away to get the bread, my mother took a large spoon and began to serve food.

"Ruben already told me that Isaac caused quite a bit of trouble today, Ezat Khanom," my father announced, as he scooped food into his mouth.

"*Waay bar man*! What am I going to do with him, Ebrahim?" responded my mother, looking heavenward. "May God give Isaac a *sheitoon*, a troublemaker like himself, for a son. He took years off my life today and frightened everyone in the house."

"Thank God you are both safe," offered my father. "Isaac will prove to be a good son, I promise you, Mamon Joon."

"Father, I want to ask you for something," I boldly spoke up, sensing that my father was in a grateful and vulnerable mood. "I would very much like to have a tricycle!"

"*Ghorbonat beram*! Do you really think you deserve such a big gift?" asked my mother.

"Yes! I am a very good boy—most of the time."

"I'm not going to buy you a bike, Isaac Joon. You don't deserve it," said my father. "Just eat your dinner."

"But I promise to help Mamon sweep the floor every day. And I'll polish your shoes, father. Mamon, tell him I should have a tricycle. I *want* one!"

My mother shrugged her shoulders. "Your desires mean nothing. Everyone wants something."

Realizing that I had no allies in this struggle, I made a fateful decision. I pushed my plate away and declared that I would not eat another mouthful of food until I received a tricycle. Then I stood up, walked to the door, put on my shoes and walked outside.

At first my parents ignored me. "*Velesh kon*, leave him alone," said my father. "He will be back for his dinner."

But I did not eat my dinner. By breakfast time the next day I was very hungry. I watched as my brother and sister ate yogurt with cucumber and bread and butter, but I remained resolute. My mother become anxious and did not remove my full plate, hoping I would relent and eat eventually. I did not. Hours later, when my father sat down for the evening meal, he commanded me to eat and tried to put food in my mouth. I clamped my jaws tightly closed.

On the morning of the second full day of my hunger strike, Ruben and Homa tried to force feed me to no avail, and my mother started to cry. By the time my father arrived home in the evening, I was quite ill and my mother was frantic. The drama reached a crescendo.

"Agha Joon, do not kill my son! Ebrahim! Do not kill my son!" pleaded my mother. "Buy him the tricycle. If he dies you will never forgive yourself!"

My father picked me up and held me in his strong arms. "Isaac, if you eat all your food right now, I will buy you a tricycle," he promised.

"What color?"

"How about green?"

"It's a deal! I will drink some juice now and tomorrow, when you bring the tricycle, I will eat."

"*Ey pedar sagg!*" My parents laughed at my audacity and cleverness.

The next morning I heard my father's familiar whistle. I ran outside to see him riding his bicycle down our narrow street, balancing a beautiful green tricycle on his right shoulder. Clearly, I was learning the art of negotiation and compromise!

For many days I kept the tricycle in the house and would only ride it in our courtyard. Later, I brought it out to the alley in front of our house and offered rides to my playmates. During my childhood, none of my siblings or friends had toys—we played with mud and sticks and if someone owned a ball, it was a great luxury. Suddenly every boy on the street became my best friend and I realized what it meant to have power and status. I learned an important lesson that became valuable to me years later in business: to possess what others need and to provide services that others desperately desire.

My father's parents lived with us, inhabiting a room on the second floor. My grandfather, whom we children affectionately called *Baba Joon*, was an integral part of our daily life. We lovingly called our grandmother *Mani Joon*. She, however, was usually sick and confined to bed due to a variety of serious ailments that included diabetes and extremely high blood pressure. Doctors often came to the house to treat her. They used leeches to bleed her and they also practiced the ancient art of cupping to alleviate her symptoms. (In cupping therapy a partial vacuum is created inside cups, either by means of heat or suction, which are placed on the skin; this increased blood flow in order to promote healing.)

Early one warm morning in late spring, the entire household was awakened by the cries of my father and grandfather. As I jumped out of bed and quickly dressed, I also became aware of my uncles' wailing voices. "Mamon! What has happened?" I anxiously asked my mother in the hallway. She was trying to run, but since she was eight months pregnant, she had great difficulty.

Tears streamed down my mother's face. "Your grandmother died in her sleep last night," she informed me.

"Mani Joon is dead?"

"Yes. Now try to stay out of the way."

I peeked into the living room. My grandmother's body had been placed in the center of the room, covered by a large white sheet. My father left the house to make the burial arrangements. Meanwhile my grandfather and uncles discussed the preparations for the *shiva*, the seven days of mourning.

My mother set out a tray of dates, bread and cucumbers, and prepared tea. Then she gathered all of the children in the back room; when all of my little cousins began to arrive, she made sure they were sent to join us, because only adults were allowed to stay in the room with Mani Joon's body.

Around 9:00am my father returned with a group of Jewish men and a Jewish *mullah* (the term *mullah* was also used by Jews as a title for learned clergy) from the city of Yazd, Mr. Yedidiya. His name meant "God's Friend" in Hebrew. He was a short, dark skinned man who wore a huge hat and smelled of cigarettes. Mr. Yedidiya had been called because he knew the necessary Hebrew prayers and the religious customs of burial. He knew exactly what needed to be done.

Mr. Yedidiya asked all the men to sit on one side of grandmother's body, and all the women to sit on the other side. He ordered the caretakers he had brought with him to bring in the stretcher, which had four handles for lifting, and set it on the floor. My grandmother's covered body was placed on top of the stretcher. The *mullah* declared that all those who could not travel to the cemetery should say their goodbyes to Mani Joon quickly, in the next five minutes, and then wash their hands and faces after the body left the house. Meanwhile, the rest of us were told to walk down to Sheikh Hadi Street where waiting cabs would take us to the Jewish cemetery located about twenty kilometers east of Tehran.

As the wooden stretcher holding grandmother's body was raised from the floor, the cries of all the family members filled the house. Ruben and I joined my father, grandfather and uncles in the procession behind the body. As we entered our *koocheh,* the crowd of neighbors was so large that we could hardly move. Many of our Jewish neighbors joined the column of mourners led by the *mullah* and his helpers. When we reached Sheikh Hadi Street, my uncles, my brother Ruben and I were pushed into a cab while my father and grandfather were placed in a van with the body. All of the women in my family, along with the Jewish neighbors, were asked to take separate cabs.

The long line of cabs followed the van north on Sheikh Hadi Street, stopping briefly at the Kourosh Synagogue, where my grandfather and his sons got out of their cabs and joined hands for a moment of prayer. After reboarding the vehicles, we all headed east to Beheshtieh (a Farsi word meaning "heavenly") Cemetery.

When we arrived, the body was quickly moved to a building where it was washed and prepared for burial; we were not allowed to enter that building. Our crowd of mourners slowly moved toward the gravesite. I became aware of other families who were experiencing similar losses: They, too, were standing near open graves, lamenting the loss of their loved ones with heartbreaking wails and sobs.

Around noon, my grandmother's shrouded body was quickly buried, without a casket, as was the custom. After the last shovel of dirt was thrown, all my family members sat down on the ground in a circle around the grave. They tore their clothes and poured handfuls of dirt on their heads, crying, "*Khak bar saram!* May dirt be upon my head!" There was great anguish. My father fell on top of the grave and hugged the earth, crying like a small boy. All of this was very frightening to me.

After everyone had regained their composure, my grandfather and his sons recited the *Kaddish,* the Hebrew prayer of mourning. The *mullah* gave a short speech referring to verses found in the Book of Ecclesiastes about the meaning of life and death. Next he recited the 23rd Psalm and then asked us all to leave the grave and walk to a large dining room at the edge of the cemetery, just outside the fence.

Inside the dining room, we were told to recite the blessing for hand washing as we ritually cleansed our hands. The huge glass doors of the room faced south, allowing the warmth of sunshine to penetrate the interior. Hard-boiled eggs, bread, vegetable quiche (*kooku sabzi*), and cucumbers were placed on the table, along with pitchers of cold water. The Jewish *mullah* invited all the mourners to join him in reciting the blessings for the fruit of the trees, the fruit of the earth, and bread. He demanded that the immediate family eat together, even though no one was hungry. After the meal, my father was asked to announce the times for the three daily services which would occur at our home during the seven days of "sitting *shiva*"— 7:00am, 1:00pm, and 7:00pm.

Finally we returned to our home. Pitchers of water, a large basin and a pile of clean towels were placed in our hallway for hand washing. We covered all the mirrors and removed all portraits that hung on the walls—except for Mani Joon's. I knew that pictures of live people should be turned from viewing, because looking at them was a bad omen. The *shiva* means "seven" in Hebrew. For seven days no one in our house would go to work or school—or for that matter, leave the house. No one could take a shower, shave, or even listen to the radio. All meals were prepared in our home by my pregnant mother and the wives of my four uncles. My cousins and aunts, however, slept in their own homes, with permission from my grandfather.

During the morning, midday and evening prayers numerous relatives, friends and neighbors joined us. Many of them stayed for a meal. Members of the synagogue also attended our services, which further complicated the food preparation. All of the pots used to cook food were very large; hot coals were arranged on top of the lids to ensure that the food remained hot throughout the day. In between the meals and the prayers, we were expected to talk about our memories of the deceased.

street near the corner of Koocheh Sharaf and Sheikh Hadi Street. All of a sudden, a jeep that was heading to the demonstration careened around the corner and knocked Amir into the gutter. Amir, bruised and bloodied, lay sprawled out in the street. I was shocked and frightened and didn't know what to do. Luckily, Amir was taken to a clinic and survived his injuries.

#24 Koocheh Sharaf
Tehran, Iran
Autumn 1953

Jalaal and I were about five years old when we began to play together in the *koocheh* in front of my house. We loved to play marbles. Other times we took dirt from the street, added murky water that flowed in the gutter down the center of the *koocheh*, and built little structures from the mud. Jalaal hated to lose when we played soccer or other competitive games, and would ruin our fun by throwing a tantrum.

Jalaal was from a very poor Muslim family that had moved from Sedeh' Esfahan, a small town known for its terrible anti-Jewish incidents. Jalaal's father was a *Seyad*, (or *Sayed)* a direct descendant of the Prophet Mohammed, and was therefore authorized to wear a green sash over his long vest; he proudly wore the sash all the time. Sayed was a tall, heavy, muscular man who always had a sad look on his unshaven face. Jalaal's mother was a *Sadaat,* a title bestowed on her because her parents both were supposedly descendents of the Prophet Mohammed. I was never sure exactly how many siblings Jalaal had—there were several older and several younger than him. His mother always seemed to be nursing a new baby, while his father spent most of the time sleeping. Jalaal's family lived in the back of their small store. They sold fresh vegetables in the summer and winter fruits in the cold months.

Ali, my next-door neighbor, often joined us. He was an only child until he was seven years old, when Fachry Khanom, his mother, gave birth to a daughter. Hassan Khan, Ali's father, was the local police chief who required his children to stand in a line and salute him in a loud voice saying, *"Salam, Hassan Khan!"* when he returned home from work. Ali's father had two wives, Touran and Fachry. Touran was the first wife. She was tall and plump, with a lovely presence—but she could not have children. Fachry was younger and very skinny. She spoke in a very quiet voice and would only talk if asked a question. The understanding was that Touran would raise the firstborn son of Fachry; thus we all were told that Touran was Ali's mother.

Often, after Ali and I spent a morning playing together, Touran prepared a sandwich for Ali and my mother prepared a sandwich for me. Even though Touran and my mother liked each other, Ali and I were not allowed to share our food with each other. I did not understand why that was so, because our mothers did not explain the reason.

One summer afternoon, I innocently offered Jalaal my half-finished ice cream cone. He happily accepted it. A few minutes later, when he and I were playing marbles in the street, his father came outside to watch our game. Jalaal informed his father that I had given him some of my delicious ice cream.

"Allah, help me!" Seyad screamed, roughly grabbing Jalaal. "You ate food that was first eaten by a Jew?"

Jalaal's eyes opened wide with terror. "Yes, but he is my friend!"

"He's a dirty *Johood! Najes!* Unclean! Dirty!" yelled Seyad. He held his son in a headlock and forced his fingers down the boy's throat. Jalaal vomited. "Never eat food that a Jew gives you! If a Jew touches food, it is contaminated! Don't you know that *all* Jews are *najes*?"

Jalaal and I got the message. But what about Ali? Did he know about *Najes*? The next day when Ali came out to play with me, I told him what Jalaal's father had said.

"Ali, you must go ask your mother if it's alright for you to play with Jewish boys," I advised him. He took my hand and we rushed off to see Touran Khanom.

After a moment of thought she said, "Since you boys are just children, and no one sees you touching each other, I think it's alright for you to continue playing together. But when you grow up it will be recognized that Ali is Muslim and you, Isaac, are a Johood." She put her hand on my head with affection, and pushed back my hair with a maternal gesture. "Isaac, you are the same to me as Ali, but we have to be careful of the neighbors. You can continue to play with Ali, and even eat in our house, but the Muslim neighbors must not find out."

How could we remain friends when Muslims claimed to be pure and clean and I was labelled a dirty Jew? It all made no sense to me because I knew that my family was more hygienic than either Jalaal's or Ali's family: My mother demanded that we wash ourselves daily, wear only clean clothes and shoes, and keep our rooms clean. She bought only kosher food, so as to be sure it was clean.

On the other hand, Jalaal lived in the cramped, dirty room in the back of a store with his entire family. His family always wore the same unwashed clothes day after day. They ate the rotten food that their father could not sell. There was no bathroom in the store and Jalaal's poor mother had to take the younger children to the mosque across the street to use the toilets. She had to wash the children in the green, foul-smelling water in the pool located in the mosque's courtyard. Once I watched Jalaal's father preparing to pray one of his five daily prayers: He took an *aftabeh* (pitcher), which the family used in the toilet to clean themselves after bowel movements, and dipped it in the fetid water of the mosque's pool, intending to cleanse himself before prayers. The same pitcher would be used to collect water to use in their daily cooking. None of this made any sense to me.

A few days after Jalaal's father cursed me in the street, I refused to allow Jalaal to ride my beautiful green tricycle. Jalaal became very upset, as he usually did when denied something he wanted. He began to curse me and call me names. I hit him several times, until his face was bloodied. When Jalaal's father found out what happened, he was furious that I had beaten a Muslim. He summoned his wife and all his other children to find me and beat me. They found me at the Nouryelians' house, my next-door Jewish neighbors. Seyad kicked in the door! Jalaal's entire family rushed into the house yelling my name. I ran toward a ladder that led to the rooftop and began to climb as fast as I could. Jalaal's mother reached the ladder and screamed curses at me as she tried to shake me off. Fortunately I made it to the roof. By running along the roof I made it home, breathless, to the protection of my family. For several months I avoided walking close to Jalaal's family store. By the time Jalaal and I were seven years old, he was no longer allowed to play with me.

#24 Koocheh Sharaf
Tehran, Iran
Winter 1953-54

It was a chilly Thursday, laundry day, and I was bored. Most of my friends—and my older brother and sister—were in school. Old Khadijeh Khanom arrived at our house to help my mother with the laundry. I followed her down the steps to the basement kitchen at the back of the courtyard where my mother was already boiling a huge pot of water on the *peermouce*, the largest of her kerosene burners. I watched as the women scrubbed our sheets, pillowcases and clothing by hand, one piece at a time. As the work progressed, the clean items were hung on ropes that were strung back and forth over the courtyard. When the women were ready to wash my mother's bras and underwear, I was told to go somewhere and play. Appropriately, those private articles of clothing would be hung to dry in the basement, hidden from public view.

I stayed out of the busy women's way until I was called for lunch. Thursday's lunch was always more basic than the lunch served on the other days of the week; my mother was too busy doing the laundry to cook a rice dish, so she prepared a *deezi* (stew) in a large pot. Onions, potatoes, chickpeas, white beans, lamb meat and dried lemon were cooked together and served with fresh bread, *sabzi* (green vegetables and herbs such as mint, basil and tarragon), and onions.

After lunch I decided that I needed to use the toilet, which was in a basement room, not too far from the kitchen. In those days, toilets in our neighborhood did not have either running water or sewers. We would carry an *aftabeh* (pitcher) into the toilet in order to clean ourselves. The human waste fell into a deep well. Since tenants and family members lived in our house, my father frequently cleaned the bathroom with boric acid.

My childhood curiosity was always apparent—and it annoyed my mother and father. They knew I would investigate anything and everything, so they placed the large bottles of boric acid in the hallway of the main house, on top of the highest cabinet. For months I had been wondering why those mysterious bottles were kept out of reach. On that particular laundry day I was both bored and curious—a dangerous combination. I decided to investigate and began to climb the curtain that covered the cabinet's shelving. The bottles of acid fell on my head and broke.

My mother heard the sound of breaking glass and knew immediately what had happened. "Isaac, shut your eyes! Shut your eyes!" she yelled with all her strength. Seconds later she grabbed me and put me under running water from the outdoor faucet. "Isaac, keep your eyes shut tight. I will get you to a doctor." Fortunately, the cold water stopped the burning sensation. My entire body felt numb.

My mother ran, with no shoes and wearing soiled clothing, to the office of Dr. Refouah, one of our local Jewish physicians. I was vaguely aware of her voice shouting, "*Waay bar man!* Woe is me! My son broke bottles of acid on his head! *Khoda margam bedeh!* May God give me death! Help him, please!"

I lost all of my hair, even my eyelashes and eyebrows, and a large portion of my skin—but my eyes were saved. For several months my father covered me in oil and removed the dead skin from my body. As he gently took care of me he would quietly pray, "*El na refa na la!* I beg God for healing!" That was the prayer that Moses used when he begged God to heal his sister Miriam of leprosy.

"May God give you a child like yourself, so you may understand what you are doing to us!" declared my exhausted mother.

My father raised his arms to the heavens and exclaimed, "God, why are you punishing me? Please, give my children some wisdom!"

Touran Khanom, Ali's mother, came to our home one bitterly cold winter day, wrapped in her black *chador*. She was looking for me. My mother greeted Touron with hugs and kind words, as prescribed in Persian etiquette.

"My dear Touran Khanom, welcome. *Ghorbanat beram*! May I be your sacrifice!"

"You are too kind. I am not worthy of you," Ali's mother replied.

"Welcome, may your steps be upon my eyes! My home is your home, my friend. Please treat it as your own house," my mother declared with a smile.

Touran entered our house and immediately removed her *chador*. My mother nodded approvingly.

"Of course I feel comfortable here, Ezat Khanom. You and your children are *mahram,* like family members."

My mother ushered Touran Khanom into our formal, Western-style dining room. The room was furnished with a large table and chairs and the most expensive Persian carpets that we owned. Always the attentive hostess, my mother set the table with fruit, cake and an assortment of nuts. After the women chatted a while, my mother called for me to come and greet our guest.

"*Salam*, Touran Khanom. Where is Ali?" I queried upon entering the room.

"Ali is not here, Isaac. He's in the hospital," Touran Khanom replied as she rose to hug me. "I came to get permission from your mother to take you to the hospital to visit Ali."

"What's wrong with him?" I asked, very worried.

"Well, you see Ali is now six years old. He reached the age of circumcision, and so his father and I took him to a doctor, but something went wrong! Ali has been asking me to bring you to see him."

"Of course, Isaac may go with you to the hospital," my mother declared.

Touran rose from the table and put on her *chador* while I grabbed my warm jacket. The three of us walked to the front door.

Again the two women embraced. "May your shadow remain over our head," offered Touran Khanom, with a smile.

"May your shadow never be shortened," replied my mother. "Your steps are always welcome in our home."

We walked to the bus stop, Touran Khanom holding my hand as if I were her own child. Throughout the bus ride to the hospital I kept thinking how lucky I was to have been circumcised at eight days old!

As soon as I entered the ward in which Ali was confined, he reached out his arms. I sat down at his bedside, and he grabbed my hand. "How was your *khatneh*, your circumcision?" he asked. "Did you suffer like this?"

"I don't remember it at all, Ali. Jewish boys are circumcised when they are only eight days old. It is called *brit millah*."

"Boy, are you lucky!" he laughed, then winced in pain. "Tell me all about our friends and what is going on in the neighborhood."

I did my best to fill him in. Finally it was time for me to leave. A week later Ali returned home with a bloodstained, white cotton fabric wrapped around him like a girdle. He was not allowed to play with us for over a month.

Elsewhere in the world in 1954:
-U.S. Senator Joseph McCarthy conducts nationally televised inquiries into communist infiltration of the U.S. Army.
-Nasser becomes premier of Egypt.
-Algerian War of Independence against France begins.

#24 Koocheh Sharaf
Tehran, Iran
Summer 1954

There was no refrigeration in our homes so each day someone in the family had to go purchase the fresh ingredients for our meals. I was now responsible enough to do some of the shopping for my mother. Besides buying vegetables and cheese, I was entrusted with the task of obtaining our daily bread, *sangak*, at the large *nanvai* (bakery) on the northwest corner of the intersection of Sheikh Hadi and Jami Streets. (*Sangak* is rectangular, whole wheat, sour dough bread that is baked on hot stones in a brick oven. It is flat bread, dimpled by the stones on which it bakes, and it can reach a length of two feet or more.)

I loved the aroma of bread as it baked. I liked to watch the dough makers prepare the dough and then hand it to the sweaty *shater* (baker). The *shater* thrust the flat pieces of dough into the huge oven. Each day I quietly entered the bakery and stood meekly, with my head lowered, waiting for my turn to purchase bread. Unfortunately, all the Jewish customers had to stand and wait until all the Muslim customers had been served. If ten more Muslims entered after me, I had to wait until they, too, had been taken care of. Why did they wait on customers who were behind me in line? This second-class service made a deep impression on me. I did not understand why I was treated so unfairly.

As the baker filled each order for his Muslim customers he addressed them politely: "*Mokhlesam*, I am your humble servant, your friend." When it was finally my turn, the *shater* would brusquely shout, "Isaac, son of Ebrahim the Jahood, it's your turn! Hurry up!"

I grabbed the bread and walked to the front of the store, to the cashier. "Make sure you give me the exact change," he reminded me. He stretched out his hand, a piece of paper resting in his up-turned palm. I carefully placed my coins on the paper and breathed a sigh of relief when he handed me the bread. I knew that the little piece of paper protected him from touching money that had been touched by a Jew. The concept of *Najes* was deeply rooted in the soul of those Muslims.

I brought the bread home as quickly as I could, entering my *koocheh* from Sheikh Hadi Street. The aroma of Persian rice with saffron and the smell of garlic assailed my nostrils. A large number of boys were running back and forth kicking a small ball, ignoring other boys playing a game of tag. As I approached my house, I noticed that a heavy rope hung across the alley was being used as a volleyball net. Eager to play, I gave the bread to my mother and hurried back outside.

I became so involved in the volleyball game that I was oblivious to the noises of heavy traffic coming from Sheikh Hadi Street. I barely heard the *azan*, call to prayers, shouted from the neighborhood mosque. Several hours later, however, I heard my older brother and sister screaming for me to come home for lunch. They were very insistent because our mother would not serve the meal until the entire family was seated. I rushed home to eat.

A typical lunch at my house consisted of chicken soup made with dried lemon, rice with dill and other vegetables, and lamb stew made with tomatoes and potatoes. Of course fresh bread was served. Fruit was saved for dessert, and sweets were presented on occasions when guests sat at our table. In Tehran, those less fortunate than my family would cook pots of chickpeas and beans in large pots with lamb fat and water.

After lunch I hurried back outside to play.

#24 Koocheh Sharaf
Tehran, Iran
Early September 1954

"Isaac-Joon *badomi*, my dear almond, today is a big day for you!" sweetly cooed my mother.

"What's so special?" I inquired warily. Her obsequious tone of voice immediately put me on guard.

"Today is your first day of school, my darling son," she answered, preparing for an argument.

"I don't want to go to school." I sat down on the living room rug and crossed my arms in front of my chest. My lips began to quiver.

"Of course you must go. It is time for you to learn to read and write and become educated, Isaac."

"But Hertzel and Soraya and Shahnaz don't have to go to school, Mamon."

"They are still babies, but when they are older, they will go to school, too," she assured me.

"Will I go to school with Homa and Ruben?"

"No, they attend a private Jewish school, called *Kourosh*. You will attend a public Muslim school, called Shahriyar; it's very close to home," my father informed me. "I can't afford to send you to Kourosh, Isaac Joon."

"I am not going alone. I'm not going!" I began to cry.

Father crouched down and looked into my eyes. "I know that you are strong enough to handle going to the Muslim school, Isaac Joon. I have great confidence in you."

"Stop this behavior at once, Isaac. You must let me wash you and put on your school clothes," my mother stated matter-of-factly.

I began to wail. I'm certain the neighbors thought I was receiving a beating.

"*Waay bar man*! Ebrahim! Ebrahim! Come and talk to your son."

"What seems to be the problem, Isaac-Joon?" asked my father as he hurried to my mother's aid.

"I'm not going to school!" I insisted with tears flowing down my face.

"Of course you are going," my father responded. My mother held out a handkerchief and he gently wiped my face.

"No! No! I'm staying home!" I turned my head away from him.

"Look, Isaac, let's make a little deal." My father was becoming exasperated. "If you listen to your mother and get dressed like a good boy, I will give you my own attaché case to take with you."

"Your beautiful blue, wooden attaché case that is lined with silver fabric? The one that no one is allowed to touch but you?" I asked incredulously.

"Yes. It will be a special gift for you," father promised as he emptied the attaché case of its important papers and a few valuable items.

I was hooked. "Alright, I'll go to school," I announced, wiping my eyes with the back of my hands.

My father placed a notebook, a pencil and a blue plastic cup inside the attaché case. He explained that I needed to bring my own cup because I was not allowed to use a cup used by Muslims, otherwise they would become very upset with me.

First I was scrubbed, and then I was dressed in a white shirt, gray pants, and shiny black shoes. The last article of clothing I put on was a gray jacket; it had a white plastic collar sewn on over the fabric, to keep the material clean. As I looked approvingly at myself in the mirror, my mother placed a clean white hanky in my pocket. I patted the top of my head to feel the peculiar sensation of my almost-shaved hair.

My father walked me to the school. I stood nervously in the schoolyard, clasping the attaché case with all my might, as an administrator steered me toward the line of first-grade boys: The shortest boys were in the front, the tallest in the back, and I fit somewhere in the middle. While the superintendent, Mr. Ghahreman, looked on from the second-floor balcony, the teachers walked up and down the lines of students, inspecting fingernails, shirt collars and neatness. I was relieved that my shirt was tucked into my pants because there were punishments for even minor infractions.

After the inspection, Mrs. Nezami, the principal, addressed us from the balcony. She wore a gray skirt, white blouse, and a tailored jacket—no *chador*. "Good morning students! Welcome to another year of study. You must all arrive each day before 8:00am. You must be properly dressed and clean. Remember, cleanliness is next to godliness. You must bring your pencils, notebooks, and reading book. If you bring fruit or a snack, you may eat it during the break, but do not litter."

Next on the agenda was the recitation of the morning prayer, not a particularly religious prayer, but rather a "bless the day" benediction, followed by the pledge of allegiance to the flag. Then our first grade teacher Mrs. Samson, wearing a tailored suit like that of the principal, guided us across the courtyard and down four steps to our windowless classroom. We were sorted by size and instructed to sit, three children to a bench, at our assigned wooden desks.

My career as a student had begun.

When 11:45am arrived, it was time to go home for lunch. I ate quickly and returned to school. At 4:30pm school was over for the day and I hurried home, ready to play with my friends.

"So, the scholar is home," said my mother as she hugged me. "What did you learn today?"

"I'll tell you later, Mamon. I'm going outside to play ball with Ali, Sali and the others," I declared as I left my newly acquired attaché case in the foyer, near the front door. "Call to me and let me know when Ruben gets home from school." It was wonderful to run and shout with total abandon after being on my best behavior all day.

An hour later I heard my mother shout, "Ruben's home!" I abandoned the soccer game and ran home. I dashed up the curved, meandering stone staircase that wound to the second floor. On the north wall, directly above the entry door of the house, there was a large window that allowed us to look down onto the *koocheh* to see who was at the door. On the west end of the hallway there was a spacious room with two large windows. Our most luxurious room (except for the Western-style dining room) was located at the southern end of the hall. One of its walls was covered in a mosaic created with pieces of mirrored glass. There was also a beautifully carved wooden ceiling in that room and exquisite Persian carpets on the floor. This was Ruben's room, but on occasion the entire family would gather there.

"I'm glad you're home, Ruben. I had my first day of school and I'm very excited about it."

"Let's go outside and talk," suggested Ruben. The entire south wall of his room was constructed with tall glass doors that opened onto a long, wide balcony. We both stood on the balcony, peering down at the cherry trees and flowerbeds. We watched the pretty red fish swim in the decorative pool below. "So, what do you think of school?" he asked.

"I think I might like it, after all. I was assigned a seat next to a very nice boy named Bijan Maghbooleh. We will sit next to each other for the entire year. Guess what, Ruben?"

"What?"

"Bijan is a Jew, just like I am! I think he and I will become very good friends."

Oh friend, for tomorrow let us not worry
This moment we have now, let us not hurry
When our time comes, we shall not tarry
With seven thousand-year-olds, our burden carry.
                    —*Rubaiyat of Omar Khayyam*

ای دوست بیاتاغم فردا نخوریم

وین یکدم عمر را غنیمت شمریم

فرداکه از این دیر فنا در گذریم

با هفت هزارسالگان سر بسریم

Shahriyar School
Bazargan Street, northeast of Jami Street
Tehran, Iran
Late Autumn 1954

It was a chilly morning. My teacher, Mrs. Samson, greeted us at the classroom door. She was a plump, middle-aged woman who always wore a white shirt with a dark skirt and jacket and black high heels. Bijan and I, along with a couple of other bright students, proceeded to our benches at the front of the room. We did not remove our jackets because our seats were the farthest from the *bochary*, the coal burning stove which stood at the back of the room. The lazy, unmotivated students were assigned seats in the back of the room where they had the advantage of sitting nearest to the heat source. The heat radiating from the *bochary* made them very sleepy and they paid little attention to the teacher. The school had no central heating.

I became aware that my bench-mate Bijan was squirming and crossing his legs in obvious discomfort. In desperation, he raised his hand. He was ignored. Again he raised his hand and again he was ignored. In desperation he raised his voice and quietly appealed, "May I be excused to use the bathroom?"

"You shall wait until the break," responded the teacher with a loud voice and penetrating look.

Poor Bijan knew he could never wait until 10:30am for the mid-morning break. Quivering with shame, he realized that a trickle of urine was slowly accumulating on the floor beneath the bench. I, too, noticed the growing puddle and the look of despair on Bijan's face. I didn't know what to do or how to help him.

"Bijan Maghbooleh!" The teacher's voice rang out and we all jumped reflexively. "Look what you've done! You must leave school immediately! Go home!"

Bijan silently slid to the end of the bench and stood up. Without raising his head to look at anyone, he hurried out of the classroom in dripping wet pants. The children were silent. No one laughed or made fun of Bijan; we were all embarrassed for him. Soon the caretaker arrived with a bucket of sawdust to absorb the puddle, and the morning lessons continued without further interruption until it was time for recess. The odor remained.

At break time we all ran outside. Along one wall of the courtyard there was a row of toilets for the students' use; along another wall there was a row of water faucets at which we could drink. A wooded area with lovely shade trees and a decorative pool beckoned some of the children, while others gravitated to an open area with benches.

Those of us who had brought a snack were allowed to eat it now. I soon learned that there was a strategy involved with choosing your snack: Oranges and tangerines had a pungent smell that quickly attracted other children, requiring you to share. Apples had a much more subtle aroma, much less noticeable, therefore you would be less likely to draw hungry beggars. Bananas, an expensive luxury obtained only by the rich, could be counted on to attract a large group of admirers. I never had bananas to bring. Cookies were also a luxury. Very often, Muslim and Jewish boys shared their snacks—until Mr. Azimi, a Jew-hater, or some other Muslim adult, intervened. Most days, I eagerly reached into the pocket of my jacket and grabbed a handful of raisins and shelled almonds my mother had given me. Other days she gave me fried chickpeas with raisins or slices of apple and cucumber. I always enjoyed the treats my mother prepared for me.

After the morning recess, we returned to our classrooms for more instruction. At 11:45am we were lined up in the schoolyard according to the streets or alleys on which we resided. The older children, the sixth graders, would lead each line of students, stopping traffic for us on busy Jami Street, and then walking each of us as far as the entrance to our *koocheh*. Besides the fact that the younger children felt protected and safe, walking home with our classmates was fun. The homeward bound group of boisterous, rambunctious boys fostered a feeling of great camaraderie—and we learned who lived where!

A typical noon meal (except on Thursdays, my mother's laundry day) consisted of a rice dish and a meat dish. Rice was the staple; various ingredients were added to the rice depending on what was available at the market, for example: rice with lentils, rice with green beans, rice with dill, or rice with shredded carrots. Rice was usually seasoned with saffron or turmeric, unless it was prepared with something sweet, such as raisins or orange peel, in which case it would be seasoned with cardamom or cinnamon. My mother would also prepare a meat dish: ground meat mixed with spices, made into balls and fried, or sometimes fried chicken. Fried eggplant or fried tomatoes would accompany the meat, and *sabzi* (fresh green vegetables and herbs) and fresh bread were always placed at the center of the *sofreh* (tablecloth). In the summer we drank fresh carrot juice.

All students had to report back to school by 1:45pm for the continuation of the school day. After the last class of the day was over, we all walked home together—following the same "lining up routine" we performed after lunch. My friend Bijan lived on the opposite side of the school from me and we were never in the same line for walking home.

Bijan (left), Isaac (standing), and Fereidoon. These three Jewish boys began their friendship in 1954 in the first grade at Shahriyar Muslim Elementary School.

#24 Koocheh Sharaf
Tehran, Iran
December 1954

Winter in Tehran is often very cold. Most of the city's precipitation occurs in the winter, in the form of snow. Tehran's semi-arid climate is the result of the formidable Alborz Mountains to the north and the central desert to the south.

It was common for large families to live in one or two rooms; these rooms would be used as living room, dining room, and bedrooms. Usually the parents would sleep in one of the rooms and the children in the other. The girls would share their blankets and mattresses and the boys also shared blankets and mattresses. My family was more prosperous than many families and our house had four rooms on the first level and three rooms on the second. In our house, my brother Hertzl and I shared a tiny room. We also shared a metal double bed, a desk and two chairs, and several extra blankets. We also had a radio. As I've said before, Ruben had his own room on the second floor. He had his own radio and a large, ornate clock. My four sisters were all together in one room; Homa had her own bed, and the other three shared a bed. My parents shared a room. In the winter the family would gather around a kerosene heater and eat and play around it. We would also spread our mattresses and heavy blankets around the heater if the cold weather was extreme.

Homes in Tehran were not insulated and were very drafty. During extremely cold days a kerosene heater was insufficient. The most effective method of keeping warm was the use of a *korsy,* a homemade creation. A *korsy* featured a very large square table with short legs that was covered with a big down-filled blanket. A large, deep metal tray holding pieces of hot coals was placed under the table. Members of the family would sit around the *korsy* with their legs under the table, while their backs rested against a stack of pillows. Outside of the blanket the air was uncomfortably cold, so the children would try to keep their shoulders and arms under the blanket, too. When dinner was served on top of the *korsy* the children's hands would dart out to grab the food, then return to the warmth under the blanket. Once we were sitting on the floor under the blankets of the *korsy*, it was very difficult to get up!

When the family was ready to sleep, enough coal was placed in the metal tray to last throughout the night. My family slept around the *korsy* only when the weather was extremely cold; otherwise, we all slept in our beds. The most miserable part of a winter night was extricating ourselves from the warm *korsy* to walk outside, across the courtyard, and down the stairway to the basement to use the toilet.

It was a cold, dreary morning in late December and I was reluctant to leave the warmth of the *korsy*. As I wriggled out from under the blissfully toasty down comforter, I heard my mother's voice in the hallway. My mother was always awake much earlier than the children. By the time we woke up she would have boiled water, to which we would add a little cold water so we could wash our face and hands without burning ourselves. By the time we had washed, mother had spread the *sofreh* and set out the plates and utensils in preparation for the morning meal—and, of course, the *samovar* was already boiling water for tea. On winter mornings she insisted that we swallow a spoon of fish oil flavored with lemon, as a tonic.

"Time to get up, Isaac-*Joon*! Everyone, wake up! Your father is preparing breakfast today."

"His special eggs?"

"Yes, I think so."

I dressed quickly, happily anticipating my father's egg sandwiches.

My mother spread the *sofreh* on top of the *korsy* in preparation for the meal. I ran through the courtyard to the kitchen, excited by the deep, freshly fallen snow. I loved to watch my father prepare breakfast.

"Good morning, Agha Joon," I greeted him. I watched him crack open two dozen eggs, separating the yolks from the whites. The whites went into my mother's cooking pot to be used later in the preparation of e*spenaj* (spinach) or *sybe zamini* (potato) *kookoo* (omelet). The yokes were beaten with sugar in my father's bowl. "Put in lots of sugar, Agha Joon," I urged. "And some cocoa powder, too, please!" He beat the egg mixture until it became very thick, like custard. He would then spread the egg mixture on pieces of fresh warm bread. The raw egg and sugar mixture tasted like cake frosting; usually I would put it between two pieces of bread, but sometimes I spread it on one piece and then rolled it up. I drank hot tea with it, or hot milk. A perfect start to a cold winter morning!

"I'm glad it snowed last night, Agha Joon!" I said to my father.

"Snow makes a lot of work. I've already been up on the roof to shovel off the snow," my father replied.

The homes in Tehran all had flat roofs; many of them were made of mud and straw, so removing the snow was very important. After a snowfall, all the neighborhood men would be up on the roof with wooden shovels, shouting greetings to each other and throwing the snow into the channel that ran down the center of the *koocheh* below. The more it snowed, the higher the pile of snow in the middle of the *koocheh* would become, with only a little room left on either side for people to walk or ride their bicycles.

"Make sure you wear your warm coat, Isaac. And don't forget your hat, gloves, and boots," reminded my mother. And remember, today is December 21st, the shortest day of the year. We will celebrate *Shabeh Chelleh,* the festival of Yalda, tonight."

As I exited the front door of my house I was confronted with a wall of snow. There was just enough space for me to walk. I heard voices on the other side of the snow bank and called out to my friends, even though I could not see them, "Amir! Asghar! Is that you?"

From the other side of the snow mountain came the answer, in unison, "We are here, Isaac! We'll meet you on the corner." As my friends and I continued on our way to school, we constantly looked up at the towering snow barrier. It looked huge to us, impenetrable.

On Sheikh Hadi Street we heard the sound made by chains on the tires of the cars and buses. We jumped out of the way to avoid getting splashed by the slush they sprayed onto the sidewalk.

"I think we have all the snow in the entire universe here in Tehran!" I exclaimed. And so it seemed.

Bijan and I, as always, sat together on one of the benches in the first row, and Feridoon Nazarian sat directly behind us. The three of us were far from the indolent students who were napping uninterrupted in the warmth generated by the stove at the back of the room. We sat through our morning reading lessons. At lunchtime I hurried home for a hot meal of potatoes and fried eggplant. Back at school, I couldn't wait for the afternoon lessons to be finished. Everyone in Iran, Muslim and non-Muslim alike, was excited about the upcoming evening's celebration of *Shabeh Chelleh*.

On the way home we played in the snow until we were chilled to the bone. "Does anyone have any pennies?" asked Kamran. We searched our pockets and between all of us, we came with ten cents—enough for a plate of boiled red beets from a street vendor. We happily shared our warm snack, eyeing the hot lima beans with lemon being sold by another vendor near by. We shared our food with each other when grown-ups were not present; Jews being *najes* was not discussed among us boys.

Shabeh Chelleh always occurred on December 21st and was celebrated as the longest, coldest night of the year—the winter solstice. We were very fond of our grandfather Eliyahu. We lovingly called him *Baba Joon*, a term of endearment. Grandfather sometimes joined us for our evening meal (he no longer lived with us since the death of his wife) but tonight, because it was *Shabeh Chelleh*, he would entertain us after dinner with a story.

And not just any story! The solstice celebration required him to recite the *Shanameh*, the heroic saga of Persia's past, written by the great poet Ferdowsi around 1000CE. *Shahnameh* literally means "Book of Kings." It is structured according to the mythical and historical reign of fifty Persian kings. Part of the great epic tells the story of the heroes Rostam and Sohrab—and that is the tale our grandfather, the family *morshed* (storyteller) told us. (My grandfather could not read or write using the Farsi script, but he could read and write using the Hebrew alphabet to spell Farsi words.) He learned the *Shahnameh*, more or less, by listening to the *morsheds* who recited the poems of Ferdowsi on the street corners of the cities and towns. Grandfather glibly improvised passages that he could not remember exactly.

The family gathered around the *korsy*. My mother lit candles to help create an otherworldly atmosphere. Father spread a beautiful *sofreh* over the top of the *korsy*, and platters of treats were laid out: slices of watermelon and *kharbooze*, a very sweet, large melon that was traditionally served on this holiday. Farmers knew there would be a great demand for watermelons and *kharbooze* in the winter, so they stored the fruit, covered with straw, in underground rooms. There were also grapes, oranges, apples, dried peaches and apricots, almonds, pistachios and cashews—and of course my mother made sure there was an endless supply of hot tea to drink.

To begin, my grandfather said a prayer thanking God for the previous year's blessings and another one asking for prosperity in the coming year. Then he cut the watermelon and the sweet melon and gave everyone a piece. The cutting symbolized the removal of sickness and pain from the family. A plate of pomegranates dusted with *gol-par* (angelica powder) and a plate of *ajil-e shab-e yalda*, a combination of nuts, raisins and pumpkin seeds, were passed around.

"We're ready for the story, Baba Joon. Tell us about Rostam and Sohrab!" we cajoled him.

"Oh, I don't think I feel like storytelling tonight, little ones," he teased. "I think I'm too tired now. Maybe some other time."

"Please, Baba Joon, please!" we pleaded with loud voices.

"Well, alright. I'll tell a little bit, but don't expect the entire saga." He popped a handful of almonds into his mouth, chewing slowly and thoughtfully while we children waited with great anticipation. Finally he began: "My children, many, many years ago, *Yeki bood, yeki nabood; ghiraz khoda kasi nabood*"—"There was one and there was not one—except for God, there was no one. The donkeys were in the pasture and the spiders were busy weaving their webs. Load up the donkeys with all of the lies and take them to each and every town, from one town to another. If the inhabitants want to buy the lies, don't sell them. If the inhabitants don't want to buy the lies, don't bring them back!"

"You always begin your stories saying that!" Ruben exclaimed.

"Of course," continued Grandfather, "that is the *only* good way to begin. Now where was I? Ah, yes, near the ancient city of Samargan, Rostam the Persian went hunting. You see, Rostam was a great warrior, known throughout many kingdoms as the fiercest, strongest fighter there had ever been. Yes, his reputation was known far and wide, across many lands. His physical appearance was so impressive that even the flowers in the fields turned their faces to gaze upon him. He was a monumental man, a colossus. When he took a step, the earth quaked and the mountains trembled. He always held his head high, with his back as straight as a cedar tree. His legs were as strong as marble pillars, and his arms were as thick as boat moorings; his muscles bulged and rippled when he flexed them. Do you know what he carried in his right hand?"

"No, Baba Joon, tell us!"

"Of course a warrior like Rostam must carry a weapon. He held a *gorz*, an enormous staff made of special wood. The staff was intricately carved and had sharp animal horns attached to its end. This *gorz* was as heavy as a tree trunk and no other mortal man could carry it. It was encrusted with so many priceless gems that when the sunlight struck it, one had to look away from the dazzling brightness. When Rostam wielded his *gorz* it made the sound of thunder as it cut through the air—his enemies' shields would be destroyed with one horrendous blow! Now, I must ask you, was

Rostam on foot, my children?"

"No, no! He rode a horse!" everyone exclaimed.

"That's right. But Rostam's huge white horse, named Rakhsh, was like no other horse on the face of the earth. His magnificent tail arched high with pride. His long muscular neck held aloft a noble head, with eyes that shot bolts of lightening and ears that stood as straight as spears. Though his legs were as strong as an elephant's, he moved with the grace and agility of a tiger. No other horse on earth was large enough or strong enough to carry Rostam. Surely, Rakhsh was a worthy mount for Rostam. But wait, my throat is dry. Before I continue, I need a sip of tea."

Our mother reached for the small pot of undiluted, strong tea that was kept hot on top of the samovar. She poured some into a glass and added hot water. Grandfather reached for the glass of hot tea with one hand as he placed a sugar cube in his mouth with the other. "Thank you, Ezat, you are very kind," he said to my mother. "Mmm, there's nothing as delicious as Persian tea," he sighed with satisfaction as he slowly sipped.

"Hurry up and drink, Baba Joon. We want to hear more of the story," I pleaded. All of my brothers and sisters nodded their heads in agreement.

Grandfather took several more swallows of tea. He cleared his throat. Finally he continued. "After a morning of hunting, Rostam lay down in the shade to nap in the heat of the afternoon. He fell into a deep, deep sleep, snoring so loud that the mountains trembled. While he slept, seven knights of Turan spotted Rakhsh and decided to steal him. Rakhsh reared up on his enormous hind legs and trampled two of them; he roared and frothed at the mouth, but finally the remaining thieves captured him. Later on, Rostam awoke. After stretching his arms, scratching his chest, and rubbing his eyes— he realized that his horse was missing. He picked up his *gorz* and followed Rakhsh's hoofprints to the city of Samargand." Grandfather stopped talking and yawned several times, with much drama. He pulled a small, round metal container of *tootoon* (tobacco) out of one of his pockets. He slowly removed the lid, pinched a bit of the aromatic substance, and sniffed it into one of his nostrils. Then he paused to appreciate the sensation.

"Don't stop, Baba Joon, tell the story!"

"Ezat Khanom, Daughter of Chayim, I'd like more tea, and maybe a piece of delicious *gaaz* (pistachio candy)," he said with great affection to my mother. As he nibbled on the chewy confection, his audience waited. After licking his fingers, he continued. "So, Rostam was met on his way by the king of Samargand, who heard of Rostam's loss and invited him to stay in his palace until Rakhsh could be found. That evening the king ordered a feast for Rostam, complete with dancing girls and music. Tahmineh, the king's daughter, secretly spied on the revelers. She couldn't help but notice Rostam, the mighty warrior, and immediately lost her heart to him. I must tell you that Tahmineh was as comely as Rostam was strong. Her beauty was celebrated far and wide by poets and storytellers. Can you comprehend a countenance so breathtaking?" Grandfather raised his eyes to heaven, shaking his head in rapture.

"Tell us more, Baba Joon! Tell us more about Tahmineh, please!"

"Ah, mere words cannot do her justice. The nightingale looked upon her perfect form and ceased his song, dumbfounded. The silver goddess of the night sky was so overcome by Tahmineh's purity that she hid her celestial face behind a cloud in shame, for Tahmineh was much more beautiful than the full moon. Tahmineh had eyes the color of coal, which reflected the light of a thousand stars. Her lips were as red as the seeds of a pomegranate, and when they parted in a smile, the coldest heart would melt away at once. Her limbs were shapely and strong, her skin the color of mountain snow. The black hair cascading down her back was the envy of every raven in the sky. It is said that if you were allowed to be in her presence, you would forget to breathe and fall down in a faint. Many men had died of longing for her." Grandfather reached for a juicy piece of watermelon and began to eat. "I think I've told you enough of the story for tonight, dear family."

"No! No! You must continue. You can't stop now," we all protested.

Grandfather finished his slice of watermelon, then reached for a napkin and carefully dabbed his chin. "That night, when everyone in the palace was asleep, Tahmineh stealthily searched for Rostam's bedroom. When she found his room, she awakened him with a kiss. 'Desire for you makes me insane with longing,' she cried, revealing her love for him. As she settled next to him on his bed, she declared that she intended to bear his child. We will leave Rostam and Tahmineh alone now, to consummate their great hunger for each other."

"What happened next, Baba Joon? Did they get married?"

"A few days came and went: Day turned into night and night into day, as can be expected. The lovers remained in each other's embrace," sighed Grandfather. "On the last morning, Rostam removed his gold, jewel-encrusted armband and handed it to a weeping Tahmineh. 'Take this gift for our child: if you give birth to a girl, she may wear it in her hair; if you bear a son, he should wear it on his arm.' Rostam left the bedroom. He was informed that his horse Rakhsh had been found, so he thanked the king and departed. Nine months later, Tahmineh gave birth to a son. She named him Sohrab. Was baby Sohrab, this offspring of Rostam, an ordinary child?"

"No!" we all chimed in.

"How could he be a normal child, after all? When he was one month old, he looked like a one-year-old. At three years of age he could play polo and by the time he was five he had become skilled in archery and the javelin. One day, when he had reached manhood, he demanded to know who his father was, and Tahmineh told him about Rostam. She warned Sohrab not to tell anyone about his father, for if Afrasiab, king of Turan and Rostam's greatest enemy, were to learn of it, he would have Sohrab killed—and if Rostam found out about his strong son he would summon the young man to join his army. Either alternative would cause Tahmineh to lose her beloved son and suffer enormous grief." Grandfather paused to sip his tea.

"Tell us more about Sohrab! What happened to him?"

"Hmm," said Grandfather, as he set down his glass. "Rostam and Tahmineh's son became a formidable warrior. He was muscular and trim and had great stamina. He could run with the speed of a cheetah and attack with the ferocity of a tiger. Nothing made him afraid. Sohrab was not content to let his name rest in obscurity and so he raised an army of Turks to conquer Persia and dethrone King Kai Kawous, whom Rostam grudgingly served. After capturing the throne of Kai Kawous, Sohrab planned to conquer Turan and, with the help of Rostam, seize the throne from Afrasiab. As you see, Sohrab was full of ambitious plans." Grandfather reached for the plate of *halva* and grabbed a piece.

"Chew quickly! Don't eat so slow," my sister Homa protested.

"Meanwhile, King Afrasiab had learned of Sohrab's plans to invade Persia. By this time, treacherous Afrasiab knew that Sohrab was Rostam's son and the king's intention was to pit father and son against each other. Shrewdly, Afrasiab understood that he would win no matter what the outcome of the battle: If Sohrab were to kill Rostam, Afrasiab would be free to conquer Persia; if Rostam were to kill Sohrab, he would surely die of grief when he realized what he had done. So, Afrasiab sent his messengers Houman and Bahrman to Sohrab, with gifts and a letter pledging his support." Candlelight flickered and danced on Grandfather's face as he prepared for the ending of the ancient tale. He reached for his *tootoon*.

"It's getting very late," my mother announced. "Perhaps Baba Joon should tell us a shorter version of the ending?"

"Very well, Ezat Khanom. Now where was I? Oh, yes, Sohrab met Rostam on the field of battle, and they did not know each other. As they exchanged mighty, super-human blows, Sohrab began to sense that he might be fighting his own father. 'We are evenly matched, Rostam. There is no need to fight each other,' Sohrab declared. But Rostam thought his opponent was trying to trick him, and continued to swing his *gorz*. After many more blows were exchanged, Sohrab gained the advantage; he lifted his massive sword to kill Rostam. 'A true hero never kills at the first opportunity!' Rostam admonished Sohrab, so Sohrab let Rostam go. They continued to fight, but Sohrab feared he was indeed facing his own father in mortal combat. Because of his anxiety and doubt, he lost his concentration and Rostam struck a mortal blow. As Sohrab lay dying on the blood-soaked ground, he told Rostam of his life-long efforts to find his father. As he drew his last breath, he showed Rostam the bracelet on his arm."

"Such a terrible ending," my father whispered.

"Indeed it is terrible," Grandfather agreed. "Rostam was overwhelmed with grief. His screams could be heard for a hundred miles. The mountains shook. He wailed and pulled out the hairs from his beard and his head and tore his clothes, such was his misery. Rostam's ministers brought medicines of secret herbs, to try to revive Sohrab, but *Nushabeh passaz margge Sohrab*— medicine given after Sohrab's death of course did no good. Rostam's lamentations could not be assuaged. 'I am the most cursed man under the heavens,' he cried. 'I breathe, but my heart is dead; I eat, but receive no sustenance. I see, but will never again know beauty.' For all the years that remained to him, there was never an end to his suffering!' Grandfather stopped talking for several moments to let the full impact of the dreadful ending sink into our heads. "Listen children, the story of Rostam and Sohrab teaches you that an apology given *after* evil is committed, is too late. And there are other morals to this story, after all. Do you know what they are?"

"Tell us! We want to know!"

"*A man has responsibilities he must fulfill!* A man must satisfy his duties as a husband and father. You see, if Rostam had not selfishly entered into a relationship and then cast off and abandoned the mother of his child—and if he had not forsaken his son—the terrible outcome would not have occurred. As for Sohrab, he was a traitor to Persia and thus became an enemy of his father and his country. And Tahmineh was punished by the death of her son because of her selfish lust for a man she knew would leave her. All three of them deserved to be punished, and punishment was justified. So it is written, so it is told." Grandfather finished his abridged version of the tale and wished us all sweet dreams.

How could we sleep with visions of Rostam, Tahmineh and Sohrab dancing though our heads?

#24 Koocheh Sharaf
Tehran, Iran
Spring 1955

At my Muslim elementary school, classes ended for the week at noon on Thursdays. On Fridays we had the entire day off. (On Saturdays, I went to classes after I attended synagogue; on Sundays I also attended classes.) I loved to listen to the radio beginning early on Friday morning with a children's exercise program; an instructor would describe the exercises and count out a cadence, while someone in the background beat a *tonbak* (Persian drum).

That program was followed by a children's news hour, during which young people described the day's current events and then entertained us with an installment of a story; those stories were not necessarily Persian—often the tales were from a variety of countries. At 9:00am, the show called "You and Your Radio" came on. The latest, most up-to-date music and the newest singers were introduced during this program. Another feature of the program was audience participation: Questions were asked of the studio audience and correct answers were rewarded with a prize. At noon, *azan*, the call to prayer, was shouted from the mosques, resonating through the streets. The *azan* was also broadcasted over the radio.

Fridays were very special. At lunchtime during nice weather my mother would spread a Persian rug by the flowerbeds, near the pool. Before she served us a light meal of rice soup with bread, *sabzi* and fruit, she turned up the volume on the radio in the living room to its highest volume so that we could enjoy the wonderful afternoon programs. At 12:15pm Mr. Sobhi's story hour commenced. His tales usually had Persian roots and always concluded with a moral, an important lesson of life. I remember one morning in particular Mr. Sobhi told one of my favorite Mullah Nasruddin stories, a well-known Persian folktale:

Once upon a time, Mullah Nasruddin decided to cook something for dinner. He went to his neighbor and asked to borrow a pot and promised to return it the next day. Good to his word, the next day Nasruddin went to his neighbor's house to return the pot. The neighbor took his pot and noticed there was a smaller pot inside of it. "There is a small pot inside the one I loaned you!" exclaimed the neighbor. "Your pot gave birth," Nasruddin told him. The neighbor was very pleased to accept the two pots. The very next morning, Mullah Nasruddin knocked on the neighbor's door to borrow a larger pot than the previous one. The neighbor happily fulfilled his request. A week went by without Mullah Nasruddin returning the pot. Finally the neighbor asked Nasruddin, "Where is my pot?" "It's dead! 'Sareh za raft,' it died while giving birth," answered Nasruddin. "But how can that be?" inquired the neighbor. "If a pot can give birth, then a pot can also die!" Mullah Nasruddin answered.

Mr. Sobhi's program was followed by traditional Persian music, which was a delightful treat. The combination of the warm sun, the fragrance of the flowers, the rhythms and harmonies of the music and the delicious food was heavenly. Once we finished our lunch, we usually took a nap or at least rested while listening to a program of music solos on the radio; every Friday a different instrument was featured—such as *setar, tar, kamancheh, santur,* or piano. The solo performance was followed by an hour-long play, and then there was more *golha,* traditional Persian music.

Because my bedroom was above the kitchen, I smelled the aromas of my mother's cooking. I became very adept at discerning the individual spices and other ingredients that she used. It was on *Shabbat* (Friday night, Saturday morning and evening) that the most delicious food of the week was eaten.

My mother did not know how to cook before her marriage. She and her younger sister grew up on her parents' isolated farm and they rarely, if ever, entertained guests. Her family ate simple, rustic food. During the workweek, their diet was limited to dairy foods for breakfast and dinner, with a simple lunch of eggs or bean soup, but on *Erev Shabbat* (Friday night) they ate plain rice and chicken soup. As with observant Jews the world over, Saturday's meals were always cooked during the day on Friday. In the Persian Jewish tradition, Saturday breakfast always included hard-boiled eggs cooked in soup, deep-fried eggplants, potatoes, carrots, and boiled beets. Her *Shabbat* lunch consisted of a thick soup containing pieces of chicken mixed with rice or barley and occasionally tomatoes. Dinner, usually fish soup or dairy, was served after sunset.

Shortly after my mother married at the age of seventeen, my father brought her from her father's farm in Esfahan to the Jewish ghetto in Tehran. He rented a room in a very large house inhabited by several Jewish families. By observing the other women in the house, she learned to be a great cook. Years later, when my father's parents and four uncles moved into my parents' home, it became my mother's responsibility to feed not only her husband and children, but also an additional six demanding souls. My mother was very athletic, constantly climbing the steps down to the kitchen and back up into the courtyard, living room, or my grandmother's bedroom, all while carrying heavy pots of food. After a meal, she had to lug all the dirty dishes and pots back down to the kitchen, heat water, and wash everything.

We had several kerosene stoves in the kitchen. When my mother needed a very high temperature, especially for boiling a large volume of water for bathing or laundry, she used the *peermouce*—a large burner that produced huge blue flames; it was controlled by a hand pump which increased the pressure of the gas. The *peermouce* was commonly used to boil chicken, turkey, and certain parts of a lamb, such as the feet and stomach. During the boiling of the meat, foam formed on the top of the water that had to be removed and disposed. Once the boiling process was finished, the meat would be transferred to a smaller pot and allowed to simmer on top of a smaller burner. These smaller kerosene burners were used to keep food or tea warm. At all times when the kerosene was being used, the kitchen door was open to the outside air. This was done to ensure that harmful gases would not accumulate in the kitchen.

Throughout my childhood, my mother's saffron rice was in great demand, especially on Friday nights. Large sixty-pound sacks of Basmati rice were kept in our cool, dark basement storage area. She used a special large pot, a *dig*, to boil water, and then she poured the uncooked rice into it and added salt. A few minutes after the rice reached the boiling point, she would empty the pot, pouring the rice and boiling water into a very large strainer, while running cold water from the faucet over the rice to wash it. While the rice was being rinsed with cold water, she would put the pot back on the fire, and pour olive oil in it—enough to cover the bottom about one centimeter deep. Salt, turmeric, and a small amount of boiling water were added to the pot. Occasionally she would add a spoonful of dill seeds or cumin. A minute after the contents of the pot came to a boil she would carefully pour the washed rice back into the pot. She would set a low fire, cover the pot with a clean white cloth, and then place the lid over the towel. On occasions when we had many guests and the rice had to be kept warm but not over-cooked, my mother would put hot charcoals on the lid of the pot. The success of good Persian rice was measured by how fluffy it was: It was supposed to be soft as cotton, with all of the long grains of rice separated from each other. A woman who served a platter of sticky rice was not considered to be a good cook.

While the rice continued to cook, mother would start on her chicken soup, or her various special stews (*khoresh*), such as a heavy mixture made with red beans, dry lemon, pepper, onions, and chunks of meat (*ghormeh sabzi*), or perhaps a pot of fried eggplant, potatoes, tomato paste, fried onions and garlic, turmeric and other spices (*khoresh bademjoon*).

My favorite Friday night meal included mother's chicken soup with *gondi*. To make *gondi*, she would combine ground turkey and ground beef, add powdered chickpeas and lots of grated onions, and finish it off with cumin, salt and pepper and other spices. The meat was formed into balls and added to the chicken soup with some dried lemon and whole chickpeas. On Friday afternoons the delectable smell of *gondi* wafted through the bedroom I shared with my younger brother Hertzel. It was almost impossible for us to concentrate on our homework! As the hours passed, the delicious aromas of her cooking would not only assail my bedroom, but would permeate the entire house. I loved to sneak downstairs to the kitchen before dinner and snatch a *gondi* and some fresh bread and *sabzi* (basil, tarragon, mint, green onions). The *gondi* would usually be served early Friday evening with a drink or two of *aragh*, vodka, or white wine.

My mother's food was always the highlight of our family's day.

Sheihk Hadi Street
Tehran, Iran
Autumn 1955

Bijan and I started the second grade. Our new teacher's name was Mrs. Azar. She was very pretty and tall, with an athletic build. She had short brown hair, and was always very well dressed in an attractive skirt and blouse with a tailored jacket. Bijan, captivated by her dark brown eyes, had an absolute crush on her and decided he would marry her when he grew up. (Coincidently, he did marry a woman named Azar.)

Mrs. Azar was very sensitive and kind to her students. One day she noticed that a student named Abdolah had a very pained expression on his face. "What is troubling you?" she asked him in a gentle voice.

"I am sad because my little brother is very sick," Abdolah replied, as he quickly wiped his eyes with a clenched fist. "I don't understand why this is so."

"There is always a reason, Abdolah," responded Mrs. Azar. She used Abdolah's distress to teach us an important lesson. "Do you know who Mullah Nasruddin was? I see that several of you are nodding your heads! In case you don't know, he was an interesting character who lived long ago in the 13th century. Some of his stories are funny and most of them are very wise. Would you like me to tell you one of his stories?" she asked with a smile.

"*Baleh!* Yes!" shouted the children.

"One hot, sweltering summer day Mullah Nasruddin decided to rest in the shade of a walnut tree. As he rested, he noticed some huge orange pumpkins growing on a vine nearby; he also noticed the small walnuts growing high up on the tall tree he was leaning against. 'Sometimes I just can't understand the ways of God!' he mused. 'I don't understand why little walnuts grow on such a huge tree while gigantic pumpkins grow on delicate vines!' Just then a walnut snapped off and fell smack on Mullah Nasruddin's bald head. He stood up at once and lifted his hands and face to the heavens and shouted, 'Oh, my God! Forgive me for questioning your ways! You are all-wise! Where would I be now, if pumpkins grew on trees?'"

Bijan and I looked at each other and laughed. Some of the other children giggled, too.

"It is all right to laugh, children," Mrs. Azar assured us. "But the meaning of the story is really quite serious. Abdolah, getting back to your problem, Mullah Nasruddin understood that Allah has made things the way they are for a reason. Sometimes a person has to become ill in order to become stronger. Everything is as it should be, according to His design. Do you understand?"

Abdolah nodded "yes" as he self-consciously averted his eyes from Mrs. Azar's gaze.

Once in a while after school Bijan and I chose to leave our raucous group of school chums and walk home together, just the two of us. We had our own routine. First we would stop at Baghali's, the small corner grocery store, to buy chewing gum. The Muslim owner of the store would not allow Jewish children to walk around inside his store, so if we wanted something we knew where we must stand: on the step outside the door.

The grocer held out his hand with a piece of paper on his upturned palm. "Put your money on the paper!" he ordered. We did as we were told. He took the money, placed a piece of gum (which was already wrapped) on the paper, and extended his hand to us. As a Muslim, he wanted absolutely no physical contact between a Jewish individual and himself—or the products in his store. Again we were reminded that Jews were *najes*, unclean—but I devised a way to get even! When the grocer wasn't looking, I touched as many of the pickles in his large clay pickle barrel as I could. I also touched the clay pots in which yogurt was sold. When the grocer happened to see me touching his merchandise, he cursed me shouting, "*Pedar sagg*! Son of a bitch *Johood*!" He chased me and threatened my life because now he had to throw away everything I had touched! Desecrating his food gave me much satisfaction.

Our next stop was our favorite *ghanadi*, a shop that created delectable candy and cakes. Bijan and I stood outside the window, surveying the freshly baked cakes and pies. It was pure bliss to inhale the sweet aromas that escaped whenever someone entered or exited the store. We closed our eyes and inhaled the whiffs of vanilla and rose water that wafted our way. *Shabbat* afternoon was the only time my father allowed us to have delicious cakes with our Darjeeling tea.

Next stop was the establishment owned by old Hakim, the herbal healer. We loved to peer in the window at the multitude of wares displayed in baskets and bins. There were so many different herbs presented in various forms: some fresh, some desiccated, some easily identifiable, others mysterious. Bijan and I inhaled the pungent odors of green leaves, brown wrinkled roots, and complex potions, trying to identify them. I always loved to look at the sign that was posted in the window. The message, "This too shall pass," was hand-written in black ink using the finest calligraphy. During the entire six years of elementary school, I never failed to read that sign and think about it. I asked all my friends, "What do those words mean?" It wasn't until I was in high school that I finally understood the meaning of Hakim's maxim.

As we headed towards my house on a particularly lovely fall afternoon, I broached a subject dear to my heart. "Bijan, my friend,"

I began. "I think you should come with me to evening class at the Hebrew school."

"What would I learn there?"

"The Hebrew alphabet!" I proudly stated.

"I don't know why I should learn the Hebrew alphabet," Bijan stubbornly answered. "I am Iranian and should only learn Farsi! Why should I make myself seem even more different from my fellow Iranians? There is enough trouble without me becoming a bigger target!"

I was determined to convince Bijan. "You have no choice but to be Jewish! You were born of a Jewish mother, Malek Khanom. And since you were born Jewish you should always be a Jew! We need to learn about being a Jew so we can be proud of our heritage. Judaism teaches us to never hate or humiliate others, but rather to respect others."

"So where is this class?"

"At a small Mashhadi synagogue. It's on a long, narrow alley near the Azizkhan neighborhood," I responded. "The teacher is Mr. Dilmani, a very short man from Mashhad. He's an excellent teacher who tells us all about the *Torah* and Jewish prayers. I am in the class with the younger boys. Ruben is in the thirteen- to fifteen-year-old group, which is more advanced. The older students are encouraged to be trained to become a *shokhed*, a kosher butcher. Ruben wants to become a *shokhed*."

"I don't know if I want to go there," said Bijan with uncertainty.

"We have fun at Hebrew school! The teacher gives us treats and also teaches us songs. Some of the older students have heavenly voices and listening to them sing is very enjoyable. And there is another reason why you should attend: Your parents will be very proud of you, as my parents are of me."

"I'll go with you, Isaac, and see if I like it." Bijan agreed.

As we walked down the street, I made faces and gestures to imitate Mr. Dilmani. Bijan laughed at my antics.

#24 Koocheh Sharaf
Tehran, Iran
Summer 1956

Our entire house was in an uproar. My father had decided that he was going to go to Israel and "scope things out" with the idea that if his prospects seemed good, he would move all of us there. On the day he was actually leaving, my mother was very upset.

"I can't believe you are doing this, Agha Joon," she told my father.

"Listen, Mamon Joon, I'm only thinking of my family and what is ultimately the best thing for all of us. I shall not raise my children in this cesspool of fear and humiliation! Our children deserve to feel proud of who they are. Besides, your parents are already living in Eretz Israel," he admonished my mother. "I have made up my mind, and that's it!"

"And who is going to keep the store in business, eh?" she asked, raising her voice.

"My youngest brother Shlomo is more than capable of handling it. And Ruben and Isaac will help their Uncle Shlomo whenever they can," father said with conviction as he looked directly at Ruben and me.

"You are not leaving until I protect you from the Evil Eye!" declared my mother. "I must make sure you have a safe visit to Israel and return safely to us." She hurried off to find the paraphernalia she used for the ritual. Moments later she returned with a metal strainer filled with charcoal. She lit the charcoal and, holding the strainer by its chain, she began to swing it in a circle to make the coals red-hot.

Once the coals were extremely hot, she threw various dried herbs—including the seeds of wild rue—onto the coals creating clouds of aromatic smoke. She continued to swing the brazier as she walked around my father, pronouncing incantations with great fervor.

After receiving my mother's protection, the entire family stood at the front door, holding aloft our *Torah*. My father walked under the *Torah* as he exited the house. He remained in Israel for over two months. When he returned he was no longer very interested in expanding his fabric business in Iran—it seemed as though he had lost interest in his shop. He dreamed about the day he would have enough courage to uproot his family and take them to Israel, where he felt everyone would be better off. It would take him ten more years to accomplish this.

Cinema Mahtab
Tehran, Iran
December 1957

A year after its release in the United States, the movie *The Ten Commandments* arrived in Tehran, dubbed in Farsi. When the Jews of Tehran found out about the movie that told the story of Moshe Ben Amram, Moses the son of Amram, the entire Jewish community was determined to see the four-hour long production. Many families bought tickets for their elderly grandparents and ill members of their family, counting on the blessings of God and Moses to protect and even heal. The movie theatre was very large and ornate, seating almost 1,500 people. Most of the elderly Jews of the Tehran ghetto had never been in a movie theatre and had never watched TV. To them, going to see this movie was a pilgrimage. My Uncle Shlomo decided that he and I should go to see it, too.

We arrived for a matinee along with throngs of other Jewish people. Everyone milled around in the fantastically ornate lobby, standing in line to purchase tickets and talking to each other with great excitement. This was a very special occasion.

As Uncle Shlomo and I entered the theatre and found our seats, I realized that almost all of the ladies were carrying large baskets of food. I figured that people were supposed to bring a picnic to a movie theatre.

The noise and commotion in the audience were incredible! People were shouting to each other across the large room, exchanging greetings and catching up on news and gossip. It was impossible for me, a mere nine-year-old, to raise my voice loud enough to be heard above the din.

Finally the lights began to dim. The Jewish men immediately reached into their pockets, took out their *kippot,* and placed the skullcaps on their heads: They were definitely anticipating a religious experience. Every woman in the theatre stood and emitted a "Shhh!" with all the force she could muster; it sounded like the hiss of a thousand snakes. As the curtains slowly opened a hush came over the audience—as it turns out, this was the only moment of silence for the entire afternoon.

Every time Moses was seen on the screen, the audience cheered, whistled, and begged for a blessing from him. Some of the spectators exclaimed, "Moses, son of Amram, may I be your sacrifice! May I be dirt under your shoes!" Every time the Pharaoh or some other villain entered the scene, the audience booed and shouted its displeasure: "May your name be erased forever!" And so it went, each new scene bringing with it a riotous response from the crowd. No one remained in his or her seat for very long. There was the constant jumping up and waving of fists, or the waving of arms in jubilation when something good happened.

The intermission came in the nick of time. Now the people in the audience could rest and revive themselves. The women unwrapped pots of still-warm food, piles of *sangak,* and bottles of tea. It was time for lunch—after all, how could anyone miss a meal? The intermission lasted one hour, much longer than in America, so that everyone could finish eating and drinking.

The second part of the movie was even more intense for the

spectators, because Moses went to Mount Sinai to receive The Law from God. As God spoke to Moses, several people in the audience fainted, for they were certain that they were hearing the actual voice of God Himself! To the audience, the scene was real. Men rose from their seats, covered their eyes in the presence of God, and began to chant prayers. The women covered their eyes and prayed also.

When Moses came down from Mt. Sinai and saw the golden calf, the audience went wild! I sat wide-eyed and watched the spectacle that was playing out off-screen: Almost everyone rent his or her clothes. The women pulled at their hair and screamed, "Dirt be upon my head!" The wailing was horrible to hear.

By the end of the movie, however, everything was resolved in a positive way: Moses went back up the mountain and obtained two new tablets from the Lord, written by His own finger. The audience became delirious with joy! The ear-splitting noise of the women's ululations rolled in great waves from one side of the theatre to the other. Family members kissed each other, friends hugged, and the theatre was transformed into a synagogue on *Shabbat* when the Torah is removed from the ark: People danced in the aisles and clapped their hands, grateful for God's mercy. I sat wide-eyed, mesmerized by the spectacle unfolding all around me.

Soon it became obvious that watching the movie had caused the audience to become completely exhausted. When the movie was finally over, everyone filed out of the theatre overcome with emotion and fatigue. What more was there to say—after all, hadn't they been in the presence of the Lord, Blessed be His Name?

#24 Koocheh Sharaf
Tehran, Iran
March 1958

Lida, my new baby sister, and my mother came home from the Jewish hospital towards the end of the month. Lida was the first and only child in my immediate family who was born in a hospital. She was extremely small when she was born, and weighed no more than a handful of feathers.

When my parents married they did not know how to conceive a child until my grandfather explained to my father the concept of intercourse and its *mitzvah* (blessing). He stated that it is a man's obligation to be gentle, responsive, and sensitive to his wife, and that intercourse is a joy and commandment that God has blessed for a married couple. However, neither my grandparents nor my parents had any concept of birth control. My grandmother told my mother to breast feed her children as long as possible so that she wouldn't have too many children. My older sister Homa is eighteen months younger than Ruben; I am eighteen months younger than Homa; my younger brother Hertzel is eighteen months younger than I. However, my younger sisters Sara and Shoshi are only one year apart.

After Shoshi was born, my mother no longer wished to have children. However, in the ensuing years, she became pregnant several times. When home remedies didn't work to end the pregnancies, she went to the Jewish clinic operated by Dr. Kamrava Yashar and his wife, Dr. Malihe Yashar, for abortions.

The subject of abortion was a source of major disputes between my parents, but they tried to keep their disagreements a secret. My father felt that abortion was a sin against Jewish laws, but my mother argued that it was better for her to stay alive and take care of her six children and husband, rather than die giving birth to unwanted children. She faced a dilemma: On one hand she had the obligation of keeping her sexuality for her husband, and on the other hand she did not want any more children. In order to keep her husband satisfied and happy, she accepted the responsibility of abortion. "If it is a sin, let it be *my* sin," she declared.

My father could not understand or accept that life began at the time of birth; he was very anxious and upset about the act of removing a fetus from the womb. He agonized over when and if abortion was a sin, or God forbid, murder. He knew that some Jews believe that a fetus has no soul until forty days after conception; and there are those who believe that if a baby dies within thirty days of its birth, the family is not allowed to mourn or perform the traditional ceremonies for mourning because the baby's soul was not fully formed. All of this was very troublesome for my father. To ease his conscience, he decided that abortion was a sin, but it could be erased by praying and giving charity, which he did. He even started to put on *tefillim* (phylacteries) and pray every morning, asking forgiveness for himself and for his wife. (My older brother Ruben was extremely troubled about the subject of abortion. He insisted that no matter what, abortion is wrong.)

Six years after Shoshi was born, my mother again became pregnant. She tried to abort the pregnancy using certain herbs and homemade medicines prescribed by older women in the neighborhood, but she was unsuccessful. Mother went to the doctor, but was told that an abortion could not be performed; her health could not withstand one. When it was time to give birth, mother went to the only Jewish hospital, Kanoune Khir Khah, on Cyrus Street in the Jewish ghetto. My father was jubilant! He was as happy as if his tiny new daughter was his first-born.

Unfortunately, my mother developed a breast infection and was unable to nurse the baby. My grandfather's wife Farha Khanom (whom Baba Joon married after his first wife died) would take Lida to our Jewish Mashhadi neighbor, Shamsi Khanom, who had given birth to her son Moeiz the same week. Shamsi Khanom gave her breast milk to both babies for more than one year. As Lida grew stronger, my siblings and I helped to take care of her. She became the spice of our lives! Her birth was a special blessing for us all, and we were delighted to have sweet, smart, kind Lida with us. (Our entire family loves Lydia—she changed her name to be more American—and she has become the most affectionate member of our family. Moeiz and Lydia stay in touch with each other and are closer than a brother and sister.)

The Robab Family's Farm
Outside Tehran
Summer 1958

My father's fabric store was in the southern part of Tehran, near the Gates of Ghazvin, an area known as *Darvazeh Ghazvin*. He had a number of Muslim customers who owned large farms—and some owned entire villages. The Robab family, long-time customers, not only owned a farm, but their youngest son Hassan was a friend of mine. As a young boy I loved farms, horses, and being outdoors. I begged my father until he finally agreed to send me to live with the Robab family for the summer. Their house, which consisted of one large room, was located in a crowded, lower class area of Tehran about ten miles west of my father's store. Mr. and Mrs. Robab and their sons lived near the outskirts of the city. Each day the father and six boys "commuted" on donkeys to their farm, which was located several miles away in a rural area.

Mr. and Mrs. Robab started their day early in the morning, before the sunrise. They washed themselves outside. Mr. Robab would then go back inside and perform his morning prayers while Mrs. Robab, wrapped in her *chador,* entered the room with a large container of fresh water. She prepared the samovar and spread a long white sheet on the floor to serve as a *sofreh*. With an economy of motion, she hardboiled many eggs, set out homemade cheese, milk and butter and placed bread dough in the oven.

The wonderful aroma of baking bread and fresh-brewed tea filled the room. All of us boys hastily got up, folded the mattresses, pillows and blankets, and went outside to wash our hands and faces. No matter what the season, the water was always cold and the mornings chilly. Hassan had the habit of pouring water over my head to wash my long hair. (Hassan and his brothers all had extremely short, almost shaved, hair.) I hated the feeling of cold water trickling down my neck and back.

Breakfast was always a boisterous and happy time. Mr. Robab told the boys what needed to be accomplished that day, even though they already knew exactly what needed to be done. Often the oldest son, Gholam-Ali ("the Servant of Ali") voiced his opinion about the day's work, which was sometimes at odds with his father's notion. The boys usually agreed with Gholam-Ali. Meanwhile, Mrs. Robab ran around making sure everyone had enough fresh bread to eat. Small glasses of tea and sugar cubes kept coming. I had my own plate and glass and a designated place at the *sofreh*. "*Besmelah*, Isaac Joon! In the name of Allah!" was my signal to start eating. It took at least an hour to eat breakfast.

After the morning meal, the work began. In the large backyard there was a barn in which the cows, goats, and donkeys were kept. There was also a large pool for watering the animals. Milking the cows and goats was first on the agenda for everyone except Mr. Robab. He fed his donkey and set out for the farm, about three miles from the house, to prepare for the day's work. At the farm the Robabs grew a variety of crops including hay, wheat, and fruit—apples, pears, and cherries. He went ahead to check the wheat field to see which rows needed irrigation. At the end of the summer, he would load on his donkey the buckets and ladders needed for picking fruit.

Gholam-Ali was always the first one to finish his chores. He then would call Hassan to feed all the donkeys and prepare them for work. I always rushed to help Hassan. He instructed me in the skills needed to be successful with the donkeys, including how to fill the trough with water and how to make the stubborn animals drink. Hassan and I filled the big cloth feed bags with hay and oats, to take with us. Before we left to go to the farm, we had to clean the barn. We collected the manure from the cows and donkeys and shoveled it out into the yard and spread it out to dry in the sun. Once the manure was dry it was burned in Mrs. Robab's oven to bake the daily bread, or to fuel fires for boiling water, and cooking.

As the sun rose, all the boys except Hassan and me had ridden their donkeys out to different corners of the farm. Meanwhile, Hassan and I waited for Mrs. Robab to call us to help her clean the house before we left for the farm. I loved helping her because she always made sure I had enough to eat and drink. Before we left the house, she filled our pockets with raisins and dates. Hassan and I, sharing a short-legged black donkey that could not walk fast, headed for the chicken coups not far from the house. It was easy work to feed the chickens and gather their eggs—unless they became aggressive and attacked my hands. My screams of pain were met by Hassan's laughter. "You are such a city boy!" he'd giggle.

Before noon Hassan and I would go back to the house. There we would find a smiling Mrs. Robab wrapped in a fresh, light-colored *chador*. She had changed into the clean *chador* for the purpose of saying her prayers. (I recognized the fabric of her *chador* because it came from my father's store. All the family's clothing, even the bedsheets, were sewn from cloth she had bought from my father.)

Mrs. Robab retrieved her prayer rug from a shelf. (For all Muslims the prayer rug was used to separate themselves from the daily world; it symbolized the entering of a heavenly place to communicate with God.) As she unrolled the rug, I noticed a white napkin. The napkin contained her prayer beads and a special stone on which was written the name of Allah, or a very brief prayer. She carefully and reverently unwrapped the stone and placed it on her prayer rug, and then she placed her forehead on the stone while she prayed. (The use of a prayer stone was not uncommon.)

The aroma of cooking filled the room. A large black pot containing our lunch was bubbling. Long pieces of fresh bread were wrapped in a clean white cloth. Fresh green vegetables were wrapped in another white cloth along with several plates, cups and spoons, including my personal plate, glass and spoon. Hassan and I loaded the donkey with the lunch and took it out to the farm where the rest of the family was working. We rode the three miles or so towards a shelter made of tree branches at the far corner of the farm. This was the best part of the day because I would get to ride the donkey— sometimes Hassan would get off and allow me to ride all by myself.

The shack was strategically built near a fresh spring in a heavily wooded area. This clean cold spring was the source of the farm's water supply. Upon our arrival, Mr. Robab and the boys stopped their work and gathered at the spring to wash up. Next each of them rolled out his own little prayer rug and began reciting the noon prayers. While everyone else chanted his prayers, Hassan and

I spread the *sofreh* and set out the lunch. Mr. Robab was the slowest at reciting his prayers and we always had to wait for him to finish.

During lunch, Hassan and I told the older boys about the chickens and eggs. At some point during the meal, the older boys would take the opportunity to advise us that memorizing the Quran was the best way to spend our time—even more enjoyable than riding the black donkey. Mr. Robab would then give Hassan a mild admonishment: "You must remember to study your Quran and your school books, my son," he would say. "And Isaac, you must continue to study your holy books and become a better Jew. We Muslims tolerate the Jews because they are the People of the Book, the Torah. We respect Jews who strictly observe their holy books."

Hassan and I were in charge of the lunch clean-up. We took all the plates and the pot to the spring and covered them with soft dirt. Then with our hands we poured water on them and rubbed the mud on their surfaces to scrub them. I always thanked God that there were no extra bowls or knives and forks to wash, and since the Robab family all shared the same cup, there wasn't too much work. (Of course, because I was a Jew, I had my own cup, dish and spoon.)

While all the men and boys were at the farm for the afternoon, Mrs. Robab and a helper put sheep and cow milk into separate large bags made out of cow skin, and hung the bags from trees on sturdy hooks. They vigorously shook the *mashks* to make butter. The diluted milk product that remained in the bag was subsequently emptied into another container to make yogurt. Sometimes they poured milk into a fabric container with rennet to make cheese. Mrs. Robab also took the eggs that Hassan and I had gathered and stored them in straw baskets, to be sold later. Even though she labored all day, before the men returned home she washed, put on clean clothes and some make-up, and perfumed herself with rosewater.

Meanwhile back at the farm, Hassan and I finally had time to play. We climbed trees, built mud houses, or kicked a ball that I had brought with me. At sunset we returned to the Robab's house, exhausted. We ate a dinner of *deezi,* a stew of lamb, chickpeas, and lots of fat, or lamb on skewers cooked with potatoes, onions, tomatoes and green vegetables. There was always vinegar on the table as a condiment, and of course tea and fruit for dessert. On occasion Mrs. Robab would prepare large omelets with fresh vegetables and onions.

As with lunch, sometimes the dinner conversation turned to the study of the Quran. This confused me, because as far as I could tell, most Muslims only memorized their holy book—they did not study the meaning.

"What does the Quran say that would help me become a better boy?" I asked one evening. "Since you understand Arabic, you must tell me."

"We do not know how to read and write in Arabic. We only know how to recite God's words and think about our problems and our needs," explained Mr. Robab. "Even the Prophet Mohammad did not know how to read and write. Sometimes when we really need His help, we talk to God very quietly in Farsi."

"And what language does Mrs. Robab and the boys use for their prayers?"

"They use Arabic for their prayers, too," Mr. Robab replied.

I remembered that both my father and grandfather did not understand very much Hebrew, and yet they recited all the prayers and blessings in that language. Only the Bible stories (*Torah*) were told in Farsi.

"I believe that God understands all languages, but Arabic is the best language, the sacred language of God. The Prophet Mohammad, the last messenger of the word of God, recited the holy Quran in Arabic," Mrs. Robab quietly stated. "Isaac Joon, if you learned to recite your Jewish prayers in Arabic, instead of Hebrew, God would understand them better," she advised me.

Before I replied, I considered the fact that most Muslims, like the Robab family, learned religion from an *akhoond* or *mullah* who regularly visited their homes. Each *akhoond* had a territory to serve. The Muslim families within his territory were obligated to make appointments with him to come to their home on certain days of the week at specific times to recite the Holy Quran. This form of worship was called *roseh khanie*. The clergyman, sitting on the floor, was made comfortable with many pillows. The family members, including the females, all of whom were wrapped in their *chadors*, sat in front of the *mullah*. Usually the *mullah* would recite several paragraphs of the Quran and then recite the stories of the Prophet Muhammad or his successors, the *Imams*. The most frequently told stories were about the first three *Imams*, Ali and his sons, Hassan and Hussein.

"How do you know that Arabic is the true language of God?" I asked Mrs. Robab.

"The *mullah* told us, of course," she answered.

"So, you get all your knowledge about Islam from this *mullah*? He is your only source for information? He is the only one who gives you an interpretation of your *Shiah* beliefs?" I was incredulous. "You must have many questions for him."

"Our *mullah* is a very wise man," insisted Gholam-Ali. "Who are we to question him?"

"When a learned Jewish man, a *khakham*, tells us the Bible stories, he tries to educate us by asking us many questions—and we are encouraged to ask *him* many questions about the characters in the stories. We are free to question and discuss every aspect of our Bible. For example, we may argue about the holiness of Moses, based on his conduct. We may even question the behavior of God Himself!"

"That is unthinkable!" responded a horrified Mr. Robab. "You dare to question the motives of God? You dare to doubt His perfection? That is blasphemy!"

"You sound very arrogant to us," declared Mrs. Robab. "We are taught that we must submit to Allah. You and your people are incorrect! By not submitting to what is written in your Holy Book, you exhibit a lack of faith! Why do you have to know everything? Why do you have to ask so many questions?"

I thought the Robabs were the arrogant ones because they felt that their way of believing was the "correct" way, and far superior to mine. There was no way I could change their minds. I knew this was an argument I could not win.

After dinner I became Hassan's math teacher for an hour or two. Since there was no electricity, we sat on the floor near a kerosene lamp, bending over our notebooks with tiny pencils in our hands. Before long it was time to sleep.

The summer went by very quickly, as did my experience on the farm. In later years, while helping my father in his store, I looked forward to seeing the Robab family when they came shopping. We always gave them the best fabric at the lowest prices. Since farmers could only pay after the harvest or when their animals were sold, they usually had to make their purchase on credit—but they always brought us lots of fruit, eggs, or homemade cakes. They knew my family kept kosher and would not eat non-kosher meat, so they avoided bringing us beef or prepared food.

When the Robab family came to our house for the *Norouz* (Persian New Year) celebration, we treated them the same way: My mother never prepared a cooked meal for them that contained meat, but instead offered omelets, fruit, nuts, sweets, and tea, served on new, special dishes. Mr. Robab always brought his own knife and would ask my mother to wash his plate and fruit before serving him, even though my mother had thoroughly washed everything beforehand. Then he would carefully peel his fruit and eat it. He never ate fruit that couldn't be peeled. One time my mother offered him a glass of our own homemade wine. "No! Take it away!" he shouted angrily. "Don't you know that wine is *haram*, prohibited?" He would, however, drink the hot tea because the water had been boiled. Mrs. Robab and the children would eat the omelets, *sabzi*, and fresh bread, followed by unpeeled fruit, dried fruit and nuts. The Robab boys constantly asked my mother for more ice cream and cakes.

Our differences aside, my father always offered the best fabric for his favorite customers as a *Norouz* gift. For Mrs. Robab there was colorful, flowered cloth for her *chadors*; Mr. Robab and the boys received material for gray or black suits, and blue fabric for shirts.

Mashhadi Synagogue
Tehran, Iran
December 15, 1958

Many Jewish children studied at the Mashhadi religious school several afternoons each week, after completing their regular school day somewhere else. Once a year, during the weeklong celebration of *Hanukkah,* the older students celebrated their successful completion of religion classes. The seventeen-year-olds, who had begun their studies at elementary school age by learning the Hebrew alphabet, had reached a high level of proficiency in Jewish studies. They could recite the numerous prayers for holidays, *Shabbat,* and special events, and follow along in the Hebrew prayer book. They had also learned to sing or chant a variety of songs and hymns, and could expound on the various books of the Bible. For all intents and purposes, the young people at Mashhadi had also absorbed the essence of Jewish history from their devoted teachers.

The graduation took place in a large, all-purpose room in the Mashhadi Synagogue. The students from all grades filed into the room and found a place on the bleacher-style seating. At one end of the room, behind a long table, sat a committee of learned instructors. A large number of gifts, or rewards, were arranged on the table for all to savor: pens, pencils, albums, transistor radios, and tennis rackets. The teachers sitting at the table each held a list of the students' names, in order of their scholarly proficiency; they took turns calling out the names of the students. One by one, the young scholars were called up to claim the gift of their choice— beginning with the most high-performing graduates, and then proceeding through the ranks of the students in the lower grades.

I waited with great anticipation for my name to be called. Many other names echoed through the high-ceilinged room. My name came near the end of the list. By the time I walked up to the table, there were only pens and pencils left from which to choose. My ten-year-old heart was broken, for I had desired a transistor radio or a tennis racket. I promised myself that from then on I would study my lessons with more devotion and not goof off in class. I vowed that next year I would be higher on the list.

After the ceremony, the children all walked to Kourosh, the Jewish high school, to watch a *Hanukkah* play in Moheban Hall. My sister Homa fried pieces of sweet dough in the shape of donuts in our home after supper. My mother and siblings lit the *hanukiya* (the festival candelabra) and recited the blessing. Jews are encouraged to place their *hanukiya* behind a window that faces the street, but our house had no such window.

As I grew older I came to appreciate *Hanukkah* as a celebration of freedom: freedom of the mind—thoughts and ideas—as well as social, economic and political freedom. The Jewish freedom fighters in 165 BCE were committed to the triumph of the autonomy of the individual.

#24 Koocheh Sharaf
Tehran, Iran
December 28, 1958

I lay in pain, tears running down my cheeks. My mother tried to make me feel more comfortable, tucking me under a big heavy blanket that was thrown over the top of the *korsy*. I was suffering from a reoccurring ear infection, a malady that even repeated penicillin injections had not totally cured. My mother was at her wit's end.

"Here, my darling son, drink some of this," she said soothingly, offering me a glass of hot milk with honey. When I refused to sit up and take the glass from her, she gently lifted my head and held the glass to my mouth. I took a few sips. "There, that's better," she said as she felt my forehead and cheeks. I was burning with fever.

As the day wore on, my mother realized that she needed to call for assistance. She sent for Farha Khanom, the woman my grandfather Elyahu had married shortly after my grandmother died. Farah Khanom was a short fat woman with a face scarred by small pox. She wore extremely thick eyeglasses. Farha Khanom arrived at our house with a look on her face that meant business. She was determined to rid me of the Evil Eye.

She checked me out, nodding her head knowingly as she did so. "Ezat Khanom, give me a raw egg!" she commanded my mother. "I will also need a clean white napkin, a coin, and a black pencil or piece of charcoal."

Farha Khanom wrapped the raw egg and the coin in the napkin. She held the egg over my head and began to move it with a circular motion, as she chanted an incantation. Next she placed her hands, one on each end of the sequestered egg, and gave it a squeeze, pressing her hands towards each other. As she attempted to break the egg, she called out a person's name—someone in the neighborhood who might want to do me harm. The egg did not break. Farha Khanom took the pencil and drew a dark circle on the egg. She repeated the ritual of calling out the names of neighbors or acquaintances who might be jealous or envious of me, all the while squeezing the egg—until the egg finally broke.

"This is good, Farha Khanom!" my mother exclaimed. "Now Isaac will get better."

"*Baleh*, the spell on him is no more," affirmed Farha Khanom.

Soon I was feeling better. Later that day I was able to eat some starchy boiled rice with a little piece of carrot, and a few small bites of chicken. I wondered if I was cured forever, or if the curse of the Evil Eye would come back. Was the act of breaking a raw egg stronger than administering penicillin?

Elsewhere in the world in 1959:
-Fidel Castro's forces are victorious in the Cuban revolution.
-Alaska and Hawaii become the 49th and 50th states.
-St. Lawrence Seaway opens.

Schoolyard at Shahriyar Elementary School
Bazargan Street
Tehran, Iran
March 21, 1959

Whenever I got into trouble with a Muslim boy it was usually during the day, when my father was not home. My mother was put in the uncomfortable position of having to deal with an angry Muslim family, begging them not to beat me for having gotten into a fight with their son. Usually this problem arose with very poor, lower class Muslim families who hated the fact a Jewish boy had nice clothes or a new bicycle—or could afford something as seemingly insignificant as chewing gum! It was not uncommon for me to get severely beaten by some Muslim boy's father or siblings.

It was *Norouz*, the Persian New Year (March 21), which was a national holiday celebrated by all Iranians, no matter their religion. It was the time of year when everyone bought new clothes and wore them with pride. The students at Shahriyar, my elementary school, were no exception. I, too, wore brand new shoes, new pants and a new shirt, as did my playmate, Abdullah. He and I decided to play with a soccer ball during recess in the schoolyard. Unfortunately, my foot caught in one of the cuffs of his new pants, ripping the leg of the pants beyond any hope of repair.

I didn't know what to do. I felt terrible. I rushed home and told my father, who luckily was having his lunch at home that day. He immediately went and brought from his store the most expensive suit fabric and the best English shirt fabric he could find to make clothes for Abdullah. My father knew that Abdullah's entire angry family would soon be knocking on our door. When I returned to school after lunch, the principal was determined to beat me with a stick, but my father came to school to talk him out of it.

Jews were always *very* afraid of getting into some kind of trouble with a Muslim because they would then have to pay the Muslim a bribe. Because of this underlying fear, Jews were very conscious of the need to have some money on hand to pay these bribes. Within the ghetto there were prominent Jewish families who were very trustworthy and would be asked to hold other people's savings until it was needed. The Jews even had their own coins, which were made of gold or silver, with Hebrew letters on them.

The wealthy Jews would accumulate a significant amount of liquid assets, so they could also loan money to people who were celebrating a special occasion (wedding, bar mitzvah, etc.) or wanted to buy some merchandise for their store. These were short-term loans: borrow this week, pay back next week with some interest. These prominent Jews later became bankers in every sense of the word. Even when the ghettos were opened up and Jews were allowed to use banks established by the government, these *saraafi*, Jewish or Muslim-owned "banks," still existed. Going to a *saraafi* was less hassle than using a conventional bank: Business was transacted in these storefront institutions with a handshake, and perhaps most important, the *saraaf* lent or transferred money with absolute secrecy—there was no paper trail. [see glossary]

This was yet another example of Jewish adaptation to a sometimes hostile environment.

Northern Iran, near the Caspian Sea
Summer 1959

Ali Agha and Hajaar Khanom were our favorite family friends. They were devoted Muslims, originally from Esfahan, who lived in a modest house near my father's store. They were also my father's loyal customers.

When summer came, my father, who could not drive a car, closed the store and took our family out of town for a vacation. Ali Agha, who owned a large blue van that he used as a taxicab, became our driver. Hajaar Khanom, who always wore a *chador*, provided jokes and stories that served as our entertainment on the road.

This photo was taken in the summer of 1959, during the family's first trip to northern Iran and the Caspian Sea. Ali, the driver, and his wife Hajaar were Muslims. (Left to right, standing) Ali, Isaac, Ruben, and Isaac's father. (Second row, left to right) Ali's wife, wearing a chador; Isaac's mother; Shahnaz, Isaac's sister; Soriyah, Issac's sister, with hands on hips. (In front) Hertzel, Isaac's brother; Homa, Isaac's sister; and Cousin Mira. This Muslim-Jewish relationship was both enjoyable and complex.

Since my family kept kosher and Ali and Hajaar had to have *halaal* meat, it was always a challenge to meet everyone's requirements. My parents decided we would eat dairy, eggs, and vegetables as much as possible, however, our Friday night meal had to include chicken or beef. Each family brought their own pots, pans, dishes and utensils. We cooked separately but together, and ate on the same *sofreh*. When my mother offered fruit and vegetables to our Muslim friends, Hajaar would first wash the items over and over again. Once I watched Hajaar wash slices of watermelon in murky creek water. When I commented that our freshly sliced watermelon was very clean, she replied, "but your father used his knife to cut it." With no surprise, I accepted her explanation and asked my father to offer only whole watermelons to Ali, so that he could use his own knife to cut it and not feel forced to wash the slices in dirty water.

I also remember that when my father prepared the water pipe, my parents, Ali and Hajaar smoked from the same pipe!

When my family entered the Caspian Sea in their bathing suits, Hajaar wrapped herself in her *chador* and joined us. She learned how to tie her *chador* securely so that her hands were free to splash and play in the water.

In the evening, we all listened to Hajaar's stories and Ali's loud, unrestrained laughter. At night we all slept in the same bungalow.

Once the vacation was over, my family, Ali and Hajaar said goodbye with hugs and kisses.

The Robab Family's House
Southwestern Tehran, Iran
Late Summer Evening 1960

When I was about twelve years old, my father was invited to the wedding celebration of Gholam-Ali, the Robab's oldest son. By that time, the Robab's had sold their farm and moved to a community of very conservative Muslims in the southern part of Tehran. My father convinced my mother to go with him to the wedding, and of course I insisted on going along. My mother put on her make-up, jewelry, and a very beautiful long black dress, and then covered herself in a pretty, flowered *chador*. My father and I wore our white shirts, black suits and black shiny shoes.

The wedding ceremony itself had actually occurred in the afternoon, before most of the guests arrived: A lamb had been slaughtered at the feet of the bride and groom, and then the *akhoond* (clergyman) performed the official religious rites near a special display of the Quran, a mirror, bouquets of flowers, and platters of wedding sweets. The *akhoond* recited the prayers in Arabic, adding some personal comments in Farsi. The religious ceremony, *aghad*, was for immediate family only.

The wedding celebration was held in the evening at the groom's family home. My parents and I entered the Robab's house and exchanged the required polite greetings:

"*Ghorbanat beram!* May I be your sacrifice!" exclaimed Mr. Robab, as he hugged my father.

"*Gholane' shoma!* Here is my son Isaac, your servant," replied my father.

At this point, my father handed a huge box to the mother of the groom. (This was proper etiquette because the groom's family had invited us.) Inside the box was an assortment of fine fabrics: cloth for a suit and shirts for the groom and beautiful textiles for the bride from which she could make nightgowns, dresses, and *chadors*. The box also contained gold jewelry for the bride and a wristwatch for the groom.

"Dear friends, my home is your own house," said a delighted Mrs. Robab as she accepted the box. "May your steps be upon my eyes."

"*Ghaabeli' shoma niest!* It [the gift] is not worthy of you!" declared my mother with a smile.

After etiquette was satisfied, we were led outside to the courtyard where we were met with a spectacle of great beauty. Traditional decorations of colorful lights were hanging from one side of the courtyard to the other, crisscrossed through the trees and flowers. Persian rugs covered the ground of the entire courtyard. Men were sitting on wooden chairs, in a row. I remember that most of the men were freshly shaved and that they all smelled of the same after-shave. They all must have used the same barber!

The tables, covered with white tablecloths, were set with many dishes and bowls of green vegetables, bread, fruit, nuts, and sweets. Bottles of *doogh* (sour yogurt), saltshakers, and dishes of cucumbers were passed to all the men. The pool at the center of the courtyard was covered with sheets of plywood and a layer of Persian rugs; several chairs were placed on the rugs. From this "stage" the musicians and singer entertained the guests.

My father and I were treated like a king and a prince, with great respect. A chair near Mr. Robab was prepared for my father, and my chair was next to Hassan. One after another, Mr. Robab's sons shook my father's hand saying, "Welcome Ebrahim Agha, *chakerim*! We are your servants!" as they bent their heads in a respectful bow. My mother was escorted to the area where the women were gathered. Gholam-Ali, the happy groom, wore a black suit and white shirt, with his long black hair shining like the full moon. The bride was kept in a back room with all the women, but Gholam-Ali kept sneaking a look at her through the window.

Enthusiastic male guests clapped their hands and danced to the traditional Persian music. The plump, half-naked female singer was dressed in traditional, brightly colored Persian clothing. She wore heavily applied cosmetics on her face and much jewelry on her arms and around her neck. She beckoned the guests with sinuous movements of her arms, encouraging her audience to join her in singing the happy melodies. I was sure that all the neighbors had been invited so that no one would dare complain about the loud music! Many of the guests shouted out requests while virtually everyone clapped their hands and danced. From time to time the singer took a swallow from an open bottle of *aragh* that sat on her table. The other guests were more surreptitious about imbibing alcoholic drinks: They drank in secret.

At the peak of the night's excitement, the bride and groom were encouraged to dance with each other; men and women dancing together was normally considered to be *haram*, forbidden, but in this case it was thought to bring good luck. I was happy to see that these religiously observant Muslims loved Persian music, in spite of the clergy's attempts to discourage it.

Dinner was announced at 10:00pm The guests were asked to clear the tables and make room for the long awaited meal. The women of the house carried in large bowls and trays of food: saffron-flavored rice accompanied by *kebabs* (skewers of meat); meat with green vegetables and beans; chicken with eggplant and tomatoes; and a special sauce, *khoresh fesenjoon*, made with pomegranates and nuts. There were also many trays of rice with nuts and sweet orange peel included in the main course, along with huge platters of fresh green vegetables, peeled raw onions, and goat cheese. Soft drinks were served and hot tea was available in great quantities.

While I sampled all the delicious dishes, my mother and father were served fried eggs with fresh bread, yogurt, butter, and green vegetables. Mr. and Mrs. Robab knew that my parents kept kosher and made sure that no meat was served to them.

At midnight a scantily clad belly dancer arrived and the music became even louder. All the men clapped their hands enthusiastically and spiritedly admired the physical attributes of the dancer—to them she was a beautiful object, not worthy of respect. Many of the men joined her in a dance.

Finally, at around 2:00am, my father decided it was time to go home. We wished happiness to the groom and his entire family. Mr. Robab took us to the ladies' area to meet the bride and her family; we gave them our best wishes also. The bride was young and beautiful. Her face was red and wet with perspiration from hours of dancing with the women. Most of the women had removed their *chadors*, showing off their long, luxurious black hair. (I recognized most of the beautiful cloth used to make their dresses and *chadors*—we had sold them the fabrics.) My father and I were considered to be *mahram* (members of the family) and it was acceptable for us to see the women without their *hejab*. The bride and all her female family members hugged us. We were respected by all the wedding guests, even though we were Jewish.

Shahriyar Elementary School
Bazargan Street
Tehran, Iran
Late Autumn 1960

Mr. Abdullah Azimi, our Arabic and Islamic Studies teacher, asked us all to buy a copy of the Holy Quran. Although all non-Muslims could be excused from taking this class, my father insisted that I enroll in it. He purchased a very expensive Quran for me and told me to learn it better than any of my Muslim friends. "Isaac Joon, you must learn how the other side thinks," father advised me.

Our Islamic instruction began with the basics. Mr. Azimi lectured us on what it means to be a Muslim. "These are the most important things to know and understand: Believe in your heart that there is only one God, and His Name is Allah. Believe in Allah's prophets from Adam to Mohammad, peace be upon them. Understand that all prophets came with the same message, which is to believe in Allah and to do good deeds in this world, to be rewarded possibly in this life and certainly in the life hereafter—and that Mohammad was the last true prophet and messenger of Allah. When you believe in those things, you have to make the Declaration, the *Al-Shahada*, in Arabic and by heart. Feridoon, I want you to recite the *Al-Shahada* for the class."

Feridoon squirmed in his seat, not wanting to be the focus of attention.

"What's taking you so long? You must be stupid!" Mr. Azimi shouted at the boy.

By now Feridoon was completely tongue-tied. With great embarrassment, he began to speak in Farsi. "I bear witness that there is no God but Allah and Mohammad is His messenger."

"Not Farsi! Recite in Arabic!" screamed Mr. Azimi, his face red with anger. "Isaac, you recite in Arabic," he commanded.

I stood up and quickly began, *"Ash-hadu Anna La-Ilaha Ella-Ilah Wa Ash-hadu Anna Muhammadan Rasulu-Ilah."*

"Good. That's correct. Now I must tell you that Islam is not only beliefs and words. Actions must support the words. A devout Muslim must practice the Pillars of Islam: He must testify by saying the *Al-Shahada*; he must perform prayers five times each day; he must pay *zakat,* mandatory charity; he must fast during Ramadan; and he must perform a pilgrimage to Mecca, if he is financially and physically able to do so."

Mr. Azimi paced back and forth in front of the class. He was captured by religious fervor and his eyes flashed with intensity as he continued. "Performing daily prayers is the first duty of a Muslim. The prayer is mainly recitations of verses from the Quran, the Most Holy of All Books. Why do we pray in Arabic? To ensure that *all* Muslims in the world perform prayers the same way, giving no room for distortions of translation! There must be no interpretation, only the true and correct words can be recited." He glared at each student, one by one.

I was very proficient in reciting the Quran and performing all the rituals of *namaz,* daily prayer—although I did not understand one word of what I was reciting. Learning the sequence of washing one's feet, hands, back of the ears, face, etc. was not easy to remember.

One day an inspector from the Ministry of Education made a surprise visit to our class. He asked the teacher to call a student to the front of the room to perform *namaz* with all its rituals. Mr. Azimi yelled out my name. As I came forward, he moved his desk to the front of the room and called to a student to bring a container of water, an *aftabeh.*

I removed my shoes and socks, rolled up the sleeves of my shirt, and jumped on top of his desk and performed the entire ritual and recited the prayer. When I concluded, the inspector congratulated me, and I sat down. Mr. Azimi, who was very proud of his class, could not wait any longer. "This boy is the Jew of our class!" he informed the inspector. "Can you imagine how much better our Muslim students are?"

I wondered if the inspector was angry that a Jewish boy was allowed to recite the holy *namaz*. At any rate, I had recited the *Al-Shahada*, performed the daily *namaz*, and had given charity (although to Jews). All I needed to do to become a real Muslim was the fast and the pilgrimage, and since I was underage, I could be excused from fasting and making a pilgrimage. Therefore, technically and practically, as far as most Muslims were concerned, I was a Muslim!

The next Islamic Studies class dealt with the issues of obedience to Allah and the importance of *jihad*. Mr. Azimi reminded us that the obedience of Mohammad is obedience of God, and that disobedience of Mohammad is disobedience of God. "Also, you must understand that the successors of Mohammad are the *Imams*. Obedience of the *Imams* is obedience of Mohammad and God; disobedience of the *Imams* is disobedience of Mohammad and God. You must follow the Quran without question. You must submit totally to the will of God, otherwise you are *mohareb*, an enemy of God. There is a natural hierarchy that must be followed: First is God; the second in importance is Mohammad; next come the *Imams;* followed by the *Ayatollahs;* and finally, the clergymen. Muslims must follow the teaching of the clergy who are in a direct line from God. Obey the clergy! They are our guardians. They will teach us the correct way to worship. They will teach us the path of righteousness, for we are like children and not capable of understanding on our own."

Mr. Azimi stopped lecturing long enough to drink from a glass of water that rested on his desk. "Now for the most important question of the day! What is the highest level of service to which you boys can aspire? Does anyone know the answer?"

Several boys raised their hands. Mr. Azimi called on Akbar who stood and excitedly shouted, "*Jihad!*"

"*Ahsan!* Bravo!" Mr. Azimi's voice boomed. "*Jihad* is the highest level of service to Allah! You must engage in the struggle to spread the words of Mohammad and the Quran to others so that you are assured the reward of eternal life. Who can tell me how the universe is divided into two parts?"

A student named Reza was called on to answer. "The universe is divided into *Daralislam*, the countries and lands under the rule of Muslims, and *Daralharab*, countries and lands not under the rule of Muslims, but under the rule of unbelievers."

"That is correct," affirmed Mr. Azimi. "The *Daralharab* peoples must become obedient to Islam and pay *jazieh*, a tax. Therefore *jihad* is mandatory for all Muslims. The Quran tells us, *"amr bi al-ma'ruf wa nahy 'an al-munkar,"* enjoining good and forbidding evil. Therefore, we are empowered to convey the benefits of Islam to everyone and to convince nonbelievers to abandon all their evil practices. In Sura 2:143 the Quran says, "We have made you a community that is justly balanced so that you might be witnesses for all humanity, and the Messenger Mohammad may be a witness for you."

Mr. Azimi again sipped some water and wiped his face with a handkerchief. He continued, "Sometimes it is necessary to fight for Allah, to commit violence in order to spread His Words. Sura 2:244 tells us, 'And fight in the cause of Allah, and know that Allah is All-Knowing and All-Hearing.' Sura 2:191 and 2:193 teach us, 'And kill them wherever you come upon them and expel them from where they expelled you. But do not fight them at the Sacred Mosque, unless they fight you, then kill them; this is the recompense of the unbelievers. And continue to fight them until there is no more persecution and Allah's religion [Islam] prevails; but if they desist from unbelief [convert to Islam], then there should be no hostility except to the evildoers.'"

"What about the Jews, Mr. Azimi? My father says they will roast in hell. Is that true?" asked a Muslim student.

"Here is what the Holy Quran has to say about Jews," offered Mr. Azimi. "In Sura 3:70-71 we read, 'O people of earlier Scripture! Why do you disbelieve in the revelations of Allah while you see that it is the truth? O people of earlier Scripture! Why do you confound the Truth with falsehood and conceal the truth knowingly?' The Quran goes on to say, in Sura 4: 'And to those who disbelieve and reject

Our Revelations, they shall be the inhabitants of Hell.' And Sura 5:66 in referring to Jews says, 'they are evil in whatever they do.' Does that answer your question?"

The classroom was silent as Mr. Azimi finished quoting the Quran. I looked at Bijan with a confused look and he grimaced at me, as if in pain. Bijan and I felt like Daniel in the lion's den—prey to be devoured for lunch. Jewish students made up only 2-3% of the enrollment in Shahriyar Elementary School, and Azimi's class definitely made us feel more vulnerable than usual.

Mr. Azimi was on a roll. He continued to instruct us about *jihad.* "What is the most glorious act that a Muslim can perform?" he asked rhetorically. Quickly answering his own question, he shouted, "Martyrdom! To die serving Allah is truly divine and brings great honor and prestige to the martyr's family and the entire community."

Again Bijan and I glanced at each other. We were stunned by the words we had just heard. Now we understood that we were not only *najes,* we were also enemies of Allah.

My Father's Store
Malek Street, Near The Gates of Ghazvin
Tehran, Iran
Summer 1961

When my father moved to Tehran from Esfahan, he sold fabric that he carried on his shoulders. Later on he purchased a bicycle and divided his territory into four parts—north, south, east, and west— visiting each in turn. As business improved, he decided to open a store and have customers come to him.

His store was located in the southwestern area of the city, a prominent place for commerce in those days. There was a huge population coming and going on Ghazvin Street because it was the terminus of the bus line. His store, named "The Store of the King," was positioned on the main intersection. A large population of drug dealers, opium users, prostitutes, pimps, and gamblers lived in the vicinity. There was always lots of hustle and bustle and heavy traffic, in fact, the odor of diesel exhaust constantly hung in the air. My father had to pay bribes of fabric and protection money to the local hoodlums in order to conduct business there.

Inside Malek Fabric Store, Isaac's father's shop, located near Dharvazeh Ghazvin, off Malek intersection, early 1950's. (Left to right) Mansour Yomtoubian, Isaac's father's cousin; Shokri; Elias Shamash, Isaac's violin teacher; Uncle Aharon; and Isaac's father, behind the counter.

Before the reign of Reza Shah, a man could have three or four permanent, legal wives, and several temporary wives (*sigheh*). It was a very common practice. Reza Shah said, "No more!" Instead, the government set up a district for prostitution called Shahreh Nou, The New City. This New City, with its high brick walls and huge gate, was very near my father's store. The prostitutes had to have the most beautiful fabric to make the most beautiful dresses, and they usually had lots of cash. They became the best customers of my father! I was the store's wrapper, so I packaged the fabric for the prostitutes. Fortunately for me, they were very big tippers.

The New City allowed for government control of prostitution: licensing was required, health care was provided, and every prostitute was regularly checked for disease. Many prominent men visited the prostitutes. It was not uncommon to see a *mullah* walking down the street with his wife, who was wearing a *chador*, and a prostitute walking down the same street, near the clergyman, and they did not interfere with each other. My father became very prosperous as a result of the store's proximity to the New City.

I always loved working for my father in his store. At the age of eleven I learned to ride a bicycle and became responsible for picking up lunch from home and delivering it to the store. Since a number of people worked for my father, my mother needed to cook for over twelve people daily, nine of our own family and three or more of the store workers. My father's employees were all young Jewish men who had come from the Esfahan ghetto.

At the age of thirteen I decided to assist my father in collecting the weekly payments from our customers. I was able to help him on Fridays because I had no school that day. Grandfather Eliyahu, who worked for my father, showed me my route and introduced me to the customers from whom I would be collecting. Each street and narrow alley was identified by its landmarks, such as corner shops, homes, even trees. A customer's name was marked in pencil in small Hebrew writing at the top left side of the doorframe, not clearly visible. The route was limited to a distance that my grandfather could cover from 8:00am-4:00pm. on foot. Soon after I took over his route, I cut the time by two hours because I rode a bicycle.

All of our customers were conservative Muslims with moderate to poor economic conditions. Over 60% of them would make their weekly payments from their home, and the wife of the house was usually the one who handed it over. The remaining customers

Isaac's license to ride a bicycle. It states his name, Es,hagh Yomtoubian, son of Ebrahim Kalimi (the Jew); birthdate; ID# 314; date issued; and the name of the chief of police. Isaac needed a bicycle to collect money owed to his father's fabric store.

would pay at their place of employment, such as a bakery, public bath, slaughterhouse, restaurant, grocery store, shoemaker's shop, small repair shop—or house of prostitution.

When I arrived at a client's place of business I had to park my bicycle a suitable distance away from the door, remove my hat and enter saying, "*Salam*." Whoever met me at the door would turn and yell without hesitation, "The son of Ebrahim the *Johood* is here!" Then I would wait patiently at the door until the client appeared with the weekly installment of money. It was not customary for me to engage in chitchat or ask questions.

That said, I must mention that not every transaction was brusque and impersonal. My favorite destination on the route was the slaughterhouse, where many butchers were our customers. I always planned to arrive around noon, when the butchers would invite me to join them to enjoy a BBQ feast. They would give me the most delicious pieces of meat—liver, heart and kidney—wrapped in a large piece of warm *sangak*. To quench my thirst, they offered me a cold bottle of beer. While I was eating and drinking, the butchers handed me their weekly payments. They always treated me with respect.

My second favorite stops were the houses of prostitution, all located within Shahreh Nou, a gated area guarded by police and private security. Each dwelling in this district housed at least three prostitutes. I would lock my bicycle at the gate and walk inside the compound. It was common practice to have an old woman sit outside by the door of each house. Once I greeted the old doorkeeper, she would walk into the house and shout, "The son of Ebrahim the *Johood* is here!" She would then offer me a glass of tea while I waited.

Since Fridays were the prostitutes' busiest day, I would plan to arrive early in the morning, before their customers arrived. Often I was too early and my customers were not yet awake. In that case, I would continue on to another house and return later. Occasionally one of our customers was not working due to an illness (or her monthly menstrual period); in this case, I would leave a note to remind her that next week she was expected to pay double.

In Shahreh Nou there were many bars and they were open long hours. Drunken men often got into fights, and the local police and security guards had to become involved. Sometimes fights broke out between an older prostitute and an enticing newcomer who was attracting all the men, though usually the veterans mentored and protected the younger girls. In fact, it was the more established prostitutes who brought the new girls to our store to shop, helping them to obtain credit for their purchases. All of the ladies honored their credit obligations and paid on time.

When the prostitutes went outside of Shahreh Nou, they covered themselves with a *chador* and conducted themselves with great dignity. They were also very pleasant and kind, and although they called me "the son of Ebrahim *Johood*," they treated me with respect. Many times they would ask me how I was doing in school and advise me to become a professional, such as a *mohandes*, which is Farsi for "engineer."

The toughest, most difficult portion of my route was South Tehran, the district in which the poor, new immigrants from Tabriz, Ghazvin, Qum, and Mashhad lived. They hardly knew Farsi and their credit was always bad. I constantly reminded my father about the terrible time I had collecting from those customers, but it was hard for my father to reject them. One time, when I asked one of our Tabrizi customers why he hadn't paid his bill for over six months, he screamed at me, "How dare a *Johood* harass me!" He ran to find a stick with which to beat me. Fortunately, I jumped on my bicycle and he couldn't catch me. Many other times I was not so lucky and I returned to our store with black and blue marks. Finally, my father stopped selling to the "difficult" customers on credit. He learned to pay off the *Akhoonds*, in order to partially collect payment on the bills; the leftover balance had to be forgiven, and so he lost money on those transactions.

Collecting money at a customer's home went something like this: I knocked at the door using the "men's knocker" (which made a different sound than the "women's knocker"), and then stepped aside. Usually a child, hidden behind the locked door, would ask, "Who is there?" I would respond, "*Bazazi*! The fabric man!" At that point I would hear the child shout, "The son of Ebrahim the *Johood* is here!" I would stand away from the door with my head down, waiting for the wife to arrive. Eventually, I heard the click of the lock and the door would open a crack. I would greet the woman who hid behind the door, wrapped in a *chador*. She extended her hand with the money tucked into a payment booklet that my father had given her at his store. I took her booklet and entered the amount she had paid in it, calculated the new balance, and then handed it back to her. End of transaction.

As my father's business grew, he added Sunday, Wednesday afternoon, and Friday night to his collection schedule. Sunday and Wednesday were given to my older brother Ruben, and he covered the wealthiest areas of town. I took the Friday night route, covering the nightclubs and restaurants near Shahreh Nou.

Of course, Friday nights were *Erev* (evening of) *Shabbat*. On that holy occasion the entire family gathered for a special dinner, prayers and songs. Once dinner was over, however, I received my father's permission, even though it was *Shabbat*, to ride my bike to the nightclubs and restaurants in and around Shahreh Nou. I began my collections at the restaurants that closed at midnight, then progressed to Shokoufe Nou, the largest nightclub.

The last stop on my route was a small club in which the owner was the most friendly. I would lock my bike and walk upstairs to the main entertainment hall, where the cashier was located. The cashier would pay me my weekly payment. Soon the owner would spot me and yell, "Hello, son of Ebrahim *Johood*! Come on in!" He always invited me to sit in the back of the room with him and eat. When I first began the Friday night route, I refused to go in, but as time went by, I decided to accept his generous offer. I was treated to a dinner of white rice with saffron, served with skewers of *kabab* of ground BBQ beef or chicken. I was also served yogurt mixed with cucumber, *sabzi*, and plates of pistachios and almonds. The drink offerings included vodka, arrack and beer. None of this was kosher, but that didn't matter to me. I did not observe the Jewish dietary laws when I ate food away from home.

The clientele in this establishment was solely male, and the hostesses were young and friendly prostitutes and performers. At one end of the room stood a stage on which a group of musicians played Persian songs accompanied by a woman who danced as she sang. Word soon got out that I was a bill collector with a pocket full of cash. Even though I sat in the back protected by the owner, the young ladies seductively tried to get their hands on the *toman* that filled my pockets. Unlike American nightclubs, the Tehran clubs were well lit, with no dark mysterious corners.

When I wasn't out collecting money or wrapping fabric in the store, I had other chores to perform, such as decorating the store on Persian holidays so that it would look festive. Though we did not participate in Muslim holidays, we often experienced pressure to hide our non-Muslim behavior. For example, during the daytime fast during the month of *Ramadan,* we were told that we could not eat our lunch or a snack in front of Muslims—we had to go somewhere that was not visible to customers or people who were walking by—out of respect for their holiday.

During the month of *Moharan,* the entire *Shiah* population of Iran would mourn the murder of Imam Ali's sons, Hassan and Hussein. My father and I and all our employees wore dark shirts and pants out of respect for *Moharan.* My father also did not shave during that month. It was a tradition that the poor, conservative Muslims would parade down the streets wearing all black, chanting prayers, while beating themselves with sticks and chains. Often these religious parades would come down the street by our store. In an attempt to be good citizens, we would put a barrel of ice water, with a glass cup chained to it, on the sidewalk near the curb. The Muslims marching down the street seemed to know we were Jewish, because they avoided the glass cup and chose instead to drink from their dirty hands.

Life was never boring at my father's store, or out on the collection route. I learned many life lessons about human nature and the world of business from that experience. For instance, I learned that it is much better to ascertain whether a person has a means to repay, *before* extending them credit; I learned to be kind and respectful to customers; and I realized that a businessman must always be prepared for setbacks. Experience also taught me that being the proprietor of one's own business is a tremendous amount of hard work.

> **Elsewhere in the world in 1961:**
> -President John F. Kennedy establishes the Peace Corps.
> -Soviets build wall dividing East and West Berlin.
> -Soviet Cosmonaut Yuri Gogarin becomes the first human in space.

Kourosh High School
Koocheh Hateff
Tehran, Iran
Autumn 1961

When I was thirteen years old and about to enter the seventh grade, my father enrolled me in Kourosh, a private Jewish high school located on Koocheh Hateff, east of Sheikh Hadi. Ruben and Homa and Hertzel had been enrolled in Kourosh from the first grade on.

The word "Kourosh" means "Cyrus," and it refers to Cyrus the Great (600-529 BCE), the creator of the Persian Empire. Cyrus was the first king that we know of who established a Bill of Rights to ensure the religious freedom of his citizens. He defeated the Babylonians and liberated the Jews, who had been held captive since the destruction of the Temple in Jerusalem. Many Jews chose to accompany Cyrus to Persia, where they flourished under his enlightened rule.

Usually, I rode my bike to school and locked it near the main entrance. The Kourosh building was tremendous: It was an L-shaped, multi-level edifice built around a courtyard. The structure itself was made of bricks and the massive front doors were steel. Upon entering, you would find yourself in the foyer; down several steps on the right were rooms for the caretaker and his family. A long hallway, lined with administrative offices, led to a small chapel. Classrooms were on the second and third floors; they accommodated grades one through twelve.

One huge hall was dedicated as the main synagogue, though some of the classrooms were converted into smaller places of worship, as needed; sometimes there were as many as eight, nine, or ten of these smaller "synagogues" or chapels. Why so many? The Jews of each city in Iran needed their own place of worship! Each town had its own dialect—even the melodies of the hymns and the rhythm of the chants were different from place to place. I remember that the poorest Jews attended services early in the morning, at 6:00am or so, and then they would go to work. The more affluent Jews attended services at 8:30am, and then they would go open their shops.

On the top floor of the school there was a large auditorium with a stage, Moheban Hall, which was used for plays and theatre productions and concerts; such cultural events rarely occurred in the Muslim schools. Kourosh was the center of Jewish life, hosting all major celebrations—weddings, *bar mitzvahs*, Israeli Independence Day—as well as religious holidays, such as *Yom Kippur* and *Rosh Hashanah* (known as the High Holidays), and Friday night *Shabbat* services.

It felt so good to be among so many Jewish students! Boys and girls did not attend classes together, but they ate lunch together in the same room and could even sit at the same table. During the breaks for recess, the boys and girls were allowed to talk to each other over the low wall that divided the schoolyard.

Suddenly, major social and religious barriers disappeared and all my friends were like me, from the same tribe. Kourosh was very different than my Muslim school, because Kourosh encouraged teamwork! In every phase of school activities there was cooperation between students.

Kourosh became the center for my empowerment. We were taught that we could achieve anything, as long as we studied hard and dreamed big. The Jewish children had a personal drive to succeed; none of them had to be forced to study. Most of my classmates majored in math. [Ultimately, all of my friends, except for one who became a medical doctor and another who became a geologist, received degrees in engineering or architecture. The majority of them served in the Iranian army and remained in Iran through the Islamic Revolution; they left Iran after the revolution. –Author's note.]

Even my teachers were Jewish and they were much more flexible and democratic than the instructors at Shahriyar Elementary

School. For example, if you didn't do your homework you had to stay after school to finish it—you didn't get beaten. I remembered seeing corporal punishment dished out quite often in the Muslim school, but there was a warm feeling of kindness and a nurturing spirit at Kourosh.

Surprisingly, there were some Muslim teachers at Kourosh. Many Muslim teachers tried to obtain jobs in Jewish schools because the students were more disciplined and generally polite. Also, there were many days off for Jewish holidays, in addition to the mandatory days off on the Muslim calendar.

The government required that Islamic studies be taught; consequently certain Muslim teachers were forced on the Jewish schools. As might be expected, those teachers displayed intense anti-Jewish behavior. Mr. Azimi, the anti-Semitic Islamic studies instructor from Shahryar Elementary School, obtained a teaching position at Kourosh. When I arrived at Kourosh, he was already there! He would put a piece of paper on a chair before he would sit on it, not wanting to contaminate himself by sitting on a chair on which a Jew had sat. Also, he would hold a napkin as he grabbed one of our ears to punish us. Mr. Azimi obviously thought that Jews were *najes,* yet he always had a grimy face, unpolished shoes, and food-stained clothing.

Mr. Azimi lectured us on a variety of topics. One topic was *Shariah*, Islamic law. We learned that *Shariah Law* categorizes offenses by the types of punishments they engender; offenses are assigned a specific *hadd,* or punishment: Those for which the punishment is at the judge's discretion (*ta'zir*); those offenses in which a form of retaliatory action or blood money is inflicted against the perpetrator or his kinsmen by the victim's kinsmen (*jinayat*); offenses against the public policy of the state, involving administrative penalties (*siyasa*); and offenses that are corrected by acts of personal penance *(kaffara)*.

After Mr. Azimi listed the categories of offenses, he took great pleasure in telling us some of the punishments. "The punishment for drinking alcohol is forty to eighty lashes in public. The punishment for masturbation is death. The punishment for robbery is cutting off the right hand; for the second offense, the left leg is cut off; for the third offense, the left hand is cut off." He glared at us for several moments, to make sure we understood the severity of his words. I was convinced that Azimi thought of himself as an avenging angel of Allah.

"When a Muslim man murders another Muslim man, the killer may offer money *(deyeh)* to the family of the murdered one," Mr. Azimi continued. "If the family of the murdered one accepts the money, then the killer goes free and the government has no right of punishment over the murderer. If the family does not accept the money, they may choose to murder the killer the same way, or faster than the manner in which the victim was killed. The judge and executioners are the family of the victim. If a Jew kills a Muslim by accident, he must pay a hefty penalty ("blood money"), but if a Muslim kills a Jew by accident, he pays a nominal fee. If a Muslim woman is murdered, the amount of money given to her family is one-half that of a Muslim man. A comprehensive study of *Shariah* Law will reveal that it is superior to the civil law of the Western nations."

Azimi paced back and forth in front of the classroom. "Speaking of women," Azimi continued, with disdain, "a man may have four legal wives at one time, but he may have as many *seigheh*, temporary wives, as he wants."

I already knew about "temporary wives"; this practice was a way for lovers to have legal sex, though as a consequence, the woman or girl would lose her honor and possibly her worthiness for marriage. I also knew that in all issues dealing with women, the reputation of the family was paramount. For example, if a woman is raped, she must have four male witnesses to attest that she is a victim, otherwise she will be found guilty of fornication. I had also heard stories about young female rape victims being murdered by their own male relatives, in order to cleanse the family name. As a Jew, I did not share the Islamic view of women being unworthy of the same rights as men.

Another of Mr. Azimi's lectures described how a Muslim family is required to pay a donation to the clergy for a deceased Muslim man. How does the family figure out the amount of money to donate? Here is a formula: A Muslim man is expected to pray five times a day, and more on Fridays and some holidays; he is also required to fast thirty days in the month of Ramadan, and other days during the year. If the man dies at the age of twenty and his life expectancy was sixty-five years, then he owes God forty-five years of prayers and fasts! The number of "missed" prayers is over 82,000 and the number of "missed" fasts is over 1,300. It is a custom for the family of the deceased to purchase the missed prayers and fasts. Using U. S. dollars, at one dollar per prayer and five dollars per fast, the total bill comes out to about $88,500! If a clergyman had only ten households per year that paid for missed prayers, he would earn $885,000! I began to understand that Muslim clergymen enjoyed a lucrative profession.

For me, attending Kourosh was like being in heaven! In addition to the excellent educational opportunities, there were many clubs and extra-curricular activities. For example, there was a bike club sponsored by the school, as well as a variety of other clubs. We were encouraged to play volleyball, soccer, and basketball in school. We realized that a good athlete was admired by his peers and enjoyed the rooting of the spectators. The girls also were encouraged to play a variety of sports on their side of the schoolyard.

Students could also participate in a choir or one of several musical groups that performed for the school. As a matter of fact, I played violin, Ruben played the accordion, and Hertzl, my younger brother, played the drums in one of the informal performance groups. Creative writing also found eager participants; my sister Homa recited poetry and wrote plays. There were also drawing and painting classes.

I remember that there was even a class that taught us how to build bridges and other architectural structures, using tiny saws, balsa wood and glue; I diligently built a model of the Eiffel Tower. In addition, we attended Hebrew classes. At Kourosh there was an abundance of things to do and learn. We enjoyed a very rich curriculum.

There was one outstanding Muslim teacher, Mr. Zamani, who eventually became the principal at Kourosh. He was a scholar of many intellectual disciplines and a man who wanted to bring the world into his classroom. One day he asked us, "Do you know what the Holocaust was?" He was amazed that we did not know and decided to teach us about it. "You have two weeks to research the Holocaust and plan a program about it."

Mr. Zamani gave each of the forty students in the class an assignment. I was given the task of reciting the names of the concentration camps and the number of Jews killed in each camp. I had never heard of any of this. I went to my father, and he didn't know anything about it either.

Someone told me that there were some books about the Holocaust in the synagogue, so I went there. I was told I could find more information at the Zionist office in Tehran, so I gathered my classmates and we all went there to speak to the man in charge. He promised to get us posters and other material for our project, and he did.

On the day of the presentation we taped posters to the walls that were copied from those which hung at *Yad Va'Shem* in Jerusalem. Mr. Zamani invited every class in the school to our program. I was shaking with great anxiety because I had never spoken in front of so many people. As I stood there reciting the numbers of the dead, I began to understand what the Holocaust was. The program was supposed to take two hours, but we students presented all our material in only thirty minutes. Mr. Zamani then stood up and lectured to the entire audience on the Holocaust for more than an hour, educating the students and all the teachers. He spoke about how the Jews of Europe lost their civil rights, their jobs, and then their lives. He described the concentration camps. He talked about the mindset of the people who blindly followed Hitler, foregoing rational thought.

"We must learn our lessons by studying the Holocaust," Zamani said with conviction. "We must educate ourselves and thus prevent such a phenomenon from happening in Iran. Fascism is not confined to Hitler's Germany! Our own country could easily fall victim to fascism in the form of a theocracy—a mishap that would take us backward, rather than forward to modernity. We must think for ourselves, and carefully weigh the words of those we decide to follow, for if we make a mistake in judgment it will prove to be disastrous for us, and possibly the world."

When I spoke to people in the street about the Holocaust, they had no idea what it was; only Iranian intellectuals seemed to know what was going on in the world.

It became a habit for most students to study free of distractions—out of their homes and away from Kourosh—in the beautiful city parks and along the tree-lined streets of Tehran. A study hall in the streets!

I would pack my history, biology, and chemistry books in a book bag and head north on Sheikh Hadi Street to Jami Street, and then west towards Pahlavi Street and Kakh Street. At the intersection of Pahlavi, on the south corner, was the Central Police Station (Kalantarye Markazi). Across Pahlavi to the west, Jami Street continued and became Kakh Street, one of the most beautiful and majestic streets of Tehran.

The tall maple trees that lined both sides of Kakh Street formed an arch over the road. This dense canopy of leaves allowed only a few flashes of sunlight to shine through. Rain could penetrate through the trees only in late autumn, when most of the leaves had fallen to the ground. In summer, the breezes always felt cooler when they melded with the melody of rustling leaves dancing above my head. During the winter, snow could not cover the sidewalks and streets completely because the massive branches protected pedestrians and pavement alike.

Throughout the seasons, the trees on Kakh Street were home to many kinds of birds. In the spring, their songs were uplifting and hopeful. In the summer and autumn, people would stop along their way, tilting their heads towards heaven, to be bathed in sunlight and birdsong. In winter, the raucous shrieks of large black crows caused passersby to gather their coats more tightly around themselves.

At the important intersection of Pahlavi and Jami Streets was a major bus stop. One bus stopped to take passengers north to the Moulin Rouge Movie Theatre, Nahré Karaj Boulevard (now called Elizabeth Boulevard), Vanak, and ultimately to Shemiran. A second bus took passengers south to Amirie'h, near my father's store, and further south to Tehran's central rail station. Other busses were available to travel southeast to Tehran's main bazaar.

This is how I'd study: At the beginning of Kakh Street, I would take my first book out and start reading while walking on the north sidewalk, heading west. As I completed the first chapter, I arrived at the intersection of The Four Palaces (I never learned the name of that intersection; all I knew was that on each corner there was a different palace of the Shah.) On the southeast corner was the Marble Palace, the one we could see clearly from the rooftop of our house. This palace was where all of the ministers and administrators met and held office. On the northwest corner was the actual residence of the Shah and his family. At this corner I would close my book and cross the street, marveling at the guards and the beauty of the entry gates.

Once I crossed, I took out my second book and slowly walked further west. Every so often I would stop under a tree and finish reading several pages. Looking up from my book, I gazed at the clear clean water flowing in a canal near the sidewalk; this was the cleanest water in the city, originating in a spring not very far away.

A long line of black Mercedes, black Cadillacs, and many black Rolls-Royces were parked on the north side of the street. The drivers for government ministers and officials stood alongside, proudly shining the cars with white handkerchiefs, waiting for their VIP passengers.

When I arrived at the Pasteur Institute I knew I had reached the halfway point of my enjoyable walk. The Kakh neighborhood, where the Pasteur Institute stood, was always calm and quiet with very little traffic. The pedestrians were mostly students. Occasionally a group of two or three students sat down under the trees, took off their shoes and socks, and dipped their feet into the clear spring water as they discussed their studies. Rarely, a group of female students could be observed studying together near the Institute. Once word spread that there were females studying together, this stretch of Kakh Street became "prime real estate," as many males came to check the girls out. During exam time the parks were filled with students.

It was a pleasure for me to return home having completed all of my reading in a most joyful way!

At night these streets were very quiet and dark and Kakh Street became a romantic walkway for lovers. Boys and girls found the courage to hold hands and walk together. I observed lovers in the heat of their intimate communications—exchanging tender compliments, whispering raw feelings and simple words—trying to keep their meeting a secret from the rest of the world. I saw tears at the corners of their eyes while they happily caressed each other. When it rained, they shared a raincoat. In the winter, the steam from their mouths could not be separated.

End of the Bus Line
Vanak, Iran
Spring 1962

Besides our scholarship, another great joy associated with attending Kourosh were the young people I came to know. For example, I became acquainted with Enayat M.—Eddia was his nickname—our student body leader. He was handsome and very well dressed and everyone was in awe of his academic and athletic prowess. During literature class every student listened with rapt attention as Eddia recited poetry in a clear, impassioned voice. He was the *mobser*, the class disciplinarian, who kept everyone in line—neither profanity nor improper behavior was allowed in his classroom!

As soon as I felt comfortable and adjusted to my new situation, I formed a small circle of friends that included Bijan M., David S., and my cousin Mousa. At age thirteen, we became the academic and social leaders of our class. To strengthen the bond between us, we planned group picnics and excursions. Our organizational meetings had detailed agendas, which enabled us to plan all of the meals we would eat and all of the group activities we would engage in. Those planning sessions sowed the seeds of leadership and management skills within each of us.

Our very first outing was a Friday day-trip to Vanak, a village about fifteen miles north of Tehran. The core group—Bijan, David, Mousa and I—met at my home, in my small bedroom. First we selected the destination and the date; then we agreed upon the games we would play and the food we would eat for breakfast, lunch and dinner. We were very serious about planning all aspects of the trip. Each person was assigned to bring a portion of the supplies on the list: a soccer ball, a volleyball net, blankets, food, utensils and plates, camera, radio, soap, etc. Each of us had his own list and one of us was chosen to keep track of the master list. Finally, we computed how much money each classmate would need to bring, and made the decision to meet early Friday morning at the bus station, where we would board the bus to Vanak.

Several days later we happily carried our provisions onto the appropriate bus and excitedly bounced along the road to Vanak.

When we arrived at the end of the line, we began to search for the perfect place to have our picnic. We found a shady, grassy spot near a clear, gently flowing stream.

After a lively game of soccer, we collapsed in the shade to rest. For a few minutes, no one spoke. We were happy just to be young and healthy, gazing at the green leaves and pristine blue sky above us.

Finally, the silence was broken. "What do you think you will be doing in a few years, when you've grown up?" Mousa asked no one in particular.

"Whatever I'm doing, I intend to have a lot of money and a big house!" I admitted.

"Me, too! I definitely see myself as a rich man in the future. Money provides both status and the comforts of life," agreed Mousa, in a serious tone of voice.

"I definitely want to go to college," said David.

"Me, too!" Bijan and I chimed in together.

"So, what will you study?" Mousa inquired, lying on his back with his hands behind his head.

"I want to study engineering," I offered. "I hope I can attend the University of Tehran."

"I'm thinking of engineering also," added Bijan. "Maybe we'll be lucky and qualify for scholarships."

"I don't know yet what I want to study at university. Maybe

engineering, maybe medicine—but I may end up a tailor like my father and make men's suits," David laughed.

"There are worse things than following in your father's foot steps," I interjected. "I enjoy working with my father at his fabric store."

"I spend lots of time at my father's fabric store, too," said Mousa. "It's down the street from Uncle Ebrahim's store, a great location for a business."

"And I like to work with *my* father at his store. I love to sell perfume, purses, and fancy sunglasses to the ladies who come in," admitted Bijan.

"Ah! The women!" I exclaimed, kissing the tips of my fingers in a gesture of appreciation. "The other day a beautiful woman came into father's store to buy fabric. I think she was a prostitute from the nearby New City district. Her perfume smelled like heaven! And her smile made my heart beat so hard it almost came out of my chest!"

"Speaking of attractive women, how about Esther, the ninth grade beauty at Kourosh? I would like to write her a poem and tell her how much I admire her beauty," sighed Bijan.

"You are such a romantic! You are going to write poetry? Esther's nice-looking, but she's still only a girl," I countered. "Myself, I prefer grown-up women."

"Oh, sure. Dream on!" teased David. "I don't think you have a chance with a grown woman. As for me, I prefer girls who are on the plump side, with large breasts and white skin."

"I like slim, athletic women, " added Mousa, with a dreamy look on his face.

"Mousa, I feel in my heart that you will date a world famous fashion model in the near future," I said with certainty.

"Really? You think so?" asked Mousa in a serious tone of voice. "I know I'm handsome but—oh, I get it! You're making fun of me."

"Ha! I got you! Like the old Persian adage says, '*You have a watermelon under both of your arms!*' That means you are pumped up with pride, my friend. Where do you think *you* will meet a model?" I laughed.

The conversation quickly degenerated into a raucous, sexually charged discussion of the various attributes of several girls that we knew. When we ran out of things to say, we realized we were hungry. We ate a lunch of eggs and dates, with *sabzi* and lots of fruit. Then we set up the net we brought and played volleyball for hours.

We happily ended our day sitting in the dark, eating bread and yogurt mixed with raisins. We packed up our sports equipment, utensils, and other paraphernalia and returned home by bus, the last one of the evening.

Our first picnic expedition was a success! The news of our trip became the topic of conversation in our class at school for several days. Many of our classmates came to us and asked to become a member of our group. Feridoon, Yousef, Habib and Houshang, Farhang, Shaheen, Saleem and Behrooz were especially eager to join us. We allowed them to become participants in our outings from time to time, but they were only "peripheral members" and had no desire to assist in the planning and organization.

We forged strong bonds with each other that lasted throughout high school and, in many instances, endured to the present day. [In 2006, after almost forty-five years, we organized a reunion in Los Angeles, California; over eighteen former classmates attended with their wives. Friends arrived from Manchester, England; New York City; West Orange, New Jersey; Great Neck, New York; Cleveland, Ohio; the state of Washington, and many cities in California. Every one has at least a Bachelor of Science degree, with many having multiple advanced degrees. Today all my high school friends are entrepreneurs engaged in a variety of businesses, or professions. – Author's note]

Karaj, Iran
Early Summer 1962

Summer was just beginning and the weather in Tehran was already very hot. Our group of four friends decided that it was time to embark on another adventure. This time the group decided to go on an excursion to Karaj, a city about 40km west of Tehran, at the southern foot of the Elburz Mountains. Karaj is famous for its nice weather and many people escape from Tehran's summer heat by spending weekends or vacations there.

David and I volunteered to be in charge of bringing the food for the picnic because the two of us had already formulated a plan: We would buy a lamb, butcher it, and bring the meat to Karaj for a BBQ. Some of the herdsmen who took care of flocks of sheep near the Muslim slaughterhouses were customers of my father, and so I knew them very well. I approached one of the herdsmen and told him we wanted to buy a lamb.

"I have many tender lambs," he informed us, extending his arms wide as if to encompass his entire flock. "How much money do you have?"

"I have twenty *toman*," I replied.

"Twenty *toman*! That is not nearly enough for a lamb. Hey, Ahmad!" he shouted to a fellow herdsman, "this young man wants to buy a lamb for twenty *toman*!"

"That's a joke, right?" Ahmad laughed sarcastically.

"Tell me what can I buy for the money I have," I insisted.

"A goat! You have enough money for a goat. I just happen to have some goats for sale," the first herder informed me.

"Be careful, Isaac, that herdsman is trying to put a hat on your head," David warned me, using a Persian expression that meant, "pulling a fast one."

I had no choice but to buy a goat. "Give me the smallest one you have!" I ordered. I had no idea that there was any difference between lamb and goat meat. Never before had I eaten a goat.

David sat behind me on my motorcycle, the live goat cradled on his lap. During the entire hour-long trip back to my house, the goat licked David's face as he spoke to it. By the time we arrived at my house, David was quite fond of the goat and not sure that he wanted to eat the animal.

I went to find the *shochet*, a religious Jew who is trained and duly licensed to slaughter animals in the kosher manner. Meanwhile, David remained with the goat, talking to it and giving it water. When I returned with the *shochet*, David left the courtyard and ran inside to hide. He didn't want to watch the slaughter of the goat.

Next on the agenda was the skinning of the animal. I had learned how to do this by assisting my father many times: I cut a slit at the ankle of one leg and inserted a metal skewer and worked it around, trying to separate the skin from the meat. I blew into the space between the skin and the flesh, inflating the skin like a balloon. After several minutes of intense blowing, the skin was easily removed— all in one piece. It was a relatively easy process.

I hung the carcass upside down from a tree and slit it open, emptying the contents of the chest and abdominal cavities, throwing everything into a large pot. I removed all the organs and washed the inside of the carcass thoroughly, several times. While I proceeded to butcher the animal into manageable pieces, David added the head and legs to the large pot, which already contained the stomach, intestines, and internal organs. We had decided that he would take the pot home to his mother so that she could make a stew called *sirabi*. What an unpleasant mess was in that pot!

Very early the next morning—I remember it was a Friday—David, Mousa, Bijan and I met at the bus station. Bijan lugged his accordion, on which he could only play one song. I carried the pieces of goat meat, wrapped in a cloth. David arrived with the large pot, wrapped in fabric because it was very hot. A horrible smell emanated from the pot. None of us could believe that David's mother had cooked the concoction. We figured that David had boiled the nasty mess all by himself.

"What is that horrible stink?" Mousa asked, holding his nose.

"That's our breakfast!" Bijan choked.

An hour and a half later we arrived in the outskirts of Karaj. We hiked for twenty minutes down a dirt road, through orchards of apple, pear, walnut, and mulberry trees. We could hear the sound of rushing water long before we could see it. Finally, we found a beautiful spot near the river and set up our picnic site. We spread a *sofreh* on the ground and set out the food and utensils. The pot of stewed meat was still hot. We were all very hungry and determined to eat the contents of that cauldron. In unison, each of us grabbed a large piece of *sangak* and dipped it into the pot.

"I can't eat this!" gagged Mousa.

"Me either!" I said, retching.

"There's even hair in it!" Bijan wailed as he spit the food out of his mouth.

"*It died giving birth*!" exclaimed David, using a well-known Persian saying. "Let's throw this foul stuff away! I think we should just eat the bread," David suggested.

After consuming all the *sangak* we had brought, we put on our swimsuits and went swimming in the river. The Karaj River ran swiftly and with great turbulence. The sun was high in the sky and the air was warm, but the water was icy. The strong current could have swept us away at any moment, so we tried to stay close together as we swam out to a huge boulder in the middle of the river. The danger and the cold water were thrilling and exhausting. After a while, our hungry stomachs needed to be fed.

We built a large fire with wood we gathered in a forested area nearby. Our hopes for a decent meal hinged on the BBQ. I opened the large package of meat that I had brought. It smelled "different," but we skewered chunks of meat anyway.

"It will taste good once it's cooked," I said hopefully, as I held a skewer in the fire.

"We paid for it, we'll eat it," declared a determined Mousa.

"It needs more salt," complained Bijan.

"It just needs to cook more," I assured everyone, thrusting my skewer deeper into the flames.

We choked down the meat because we were famished, but it was very unpleasant; it smelled bad and had a slimy, gelatinous consistency. Later that afternoon we purchased fresh dates and bread at the bus station.

Two or three weeks later, we were ready to try another excursion to Karaj—without goat meat. Our good friend Yousef Tishbi wanted to accompany us. He pleaded with his mother and father for permission, but they would not allow their only son to join our band of adventurers. They always kept Yousef close to home, under their watchful eyes. In desperation, Yousef convinced Bijan and me to talk to his mother, Gilan Khanom, on his behalf.

"Gilan Khanom, we will protect Yousef from harm. We are all classmates of his and we are very good boys," I assured her. "We have gone on picnics many times and many of our classmates have accompanied us in the past."

"I don't think this is a good thing for my Yousef, this picnic," she stubbornly persisted. She was a petite woman, but very strong willed.

"Please, let him go," Bijan begged. "He will be very disappointed if he cannot go with us."

"You promise not to let him swim in the river?" Gilan Khanom sighed.

"I guarantee his safety," I promised her.

"Very well, will you agree to come here tomorrow morning and walk him to the bus station? I don't want him to walk there unattended."

Bijan and I returned to Yousef's house the next morning and walked with him to the bus station. There we met the other boys and boarded the bus to Karaj. We all happily joked with each other as the bus bumped along its route.

Suddenly we realized that the bus was slowing down. "We can't make it over this hill!" observed Mousa, stretching his head out of the window. The bus rolled to a stop in a cloud of diesel exhaust.

"We are experiencing mechanical problems!" the driver shouted over his shoulder. "Please, everyone must send a *salavat,* so that God will help the bus overcome this difficulty and climb the hill."

As the passengers began to pray in unison, "*Allah hom saleh Allah Mohamad va'alleh Mohamad!*" David leaned over to me and quietly said, "Isaac, they would be better off if they just got off the bus!" As it turned out, David was right: The *salavat* did not magically enable the bus to climb the hill. The driver told everyone to disembark and walk up the hill on foot. Once the bus had crested the hill, we were allowed to reboard for the downhill run.

"Yes! Wonderful! *Marhaba!*" exclaimed the driver. "Let us all send a *salavat,* to thank God for helping us along our way."

Bijan, Mousa, David and I exchanged glances and rolled our eyes in disbelief. "As if God had anything to do with it!" Bijan whispered. Not wanting to draw attention to ourselves, we five Jewish boys recited the prayer with the other passengers: "*Allah hom saleh Allah Mohamad va'alleh Mohamad!* Almighty Allah! Please send my geetings of peace to Mohammad and to his descendents!"

Once we arrived in Karaj, we walked until we found a suitable place for our picnic. We opened our bundles of provisions and ate breakfast. After the meal we played soccer until we were exhausted. Later in the morning we met a man who offered to rent us his donkey, so we agreed on a price and took turns taking rides. In the afternoon we decided to go berry picking for the huge white berries that were ripening high in the mulberry trees.

"We will climb the trees and collect the berries, and we'll give you some," I told Yousef. "I don't want you to climb any trees. I promised your mother that you would not participate in any risky behavior."

While Mousa, David and I picked berries up in the trees, Yousef grew impatient. Finally he picked up a large rock and threw it straight up, trying to knock down some fruit for himself. The rock fell back to earth, striking him in the forehead on its way down. He fell backwards, blood spurting from a long cut on his forehead, above one eye. Despite all our efforts—wrapping his head in a wet undershirt and applying pressure—we couldn't stop the flow of blood. I sent David to find a pharmacy to buy bandages and mercurochrome.

Meanwhile, the owner of the orchard came to help us. He took out a long knife and cut another undershirt into bandages and wrapped them tightly around Yousef's head. Yousef remained calm. What was taking David so long? It turns out our friend had stopped to listen to a *morshed*, a storyteller, on a street corner in the town!

Carefully we unwrapped Yousef's head, washed the wound and applied mercurochrome. We wrapped his head with the gauze bandages David had bought, and walked Yousef slowly to the bus station. Once we arrived in Tehran, Bijan and I had to walk Yousef to his house. "Why did this happen to him?" I lamented. "I wish *I* were the injured one!" I felt very guilty and ashamed—and afraid of what Gilan Khanom would say and do.

Bijan and I were cowards. We delivered Yousef to his doorstep, rang the bell, and ran away. His mother opened the door and saw her son with yards and yards of bandages wrapped around his head. We heard her scream, "May God kill me! Dirt be upon my head! Look what has happened to my son!" as we turned the corner and continued running.

Later that evening, Gilan Khanom came to my house. She spoke to my mother while I remained hidden in my room: "Tell your son that Yousef is fine. I took him to Dr. Refuah for some stitches. I know your son feels very bad about what happened."

[I did not face Gilan Khanom until 2009, when I attended a Passover *Seder* at Yousef's house in Manchester, England. Yousef is now a successful architect and developer. He's a very elegant man who speaks English with a British accent. I apologized to his mother and she gave me a hug and assured me that all was forgiven. – Author's note]

Our picnics became so popular that many Muslim friends—Fazlolah, Hassan and others—joined us on our next trips. Jewish and Muslim boys got along very well most of the time.

Picnic at Karaj River, (left to right) Isaac, Bijan, David (Mousa took the picture), "The Gang of Four."

Playing in the Karaj River. Isaac (in front), Bijan with accordion, Mousa and David (in back), "The Gang of Four."

Isaac (squatting, right) and his Muslim friends on an excursion at Damavand. Fazlolah (wearing glasses) and Hassan (standing behind Fazlolah) were two of Isaac's close Muslim friends. There are several other Muslim friends in the photo.

An excursion to Niavaran. The friends, (left to right) David R., Bijan, Isaac, Salim Y., and David S. pose on a rock next to the Karaj River. Mousa took the photo.

The "Gang of Four": (left to right) David, Bijan, and Isaac; Mousa kneels in front. Bijan is happily playing the only song he knew how to play on the accordion. Karaj, 1963.

An early spring excursion to Niavaran, 1962. (Left to right) Salim, Mousa, Isaac, and Bijan; David R. is kneeling.

Hiking in the Niavaran Mountains, circa 1965. (Left to right) David S., Bijan, and Isaac.

An excursion to Damavand Resort, our only overnight trip, 1965. (Left to right) Isaac, on donkey; David S.; Bijan, on donkey; Fazlolah; and Hassan, on donkey. The three younger boys are villagers from the area.

The four best friends (left to right) Isaac, David, Mousa, Bijan, "The Gang of Four" to their peers, at Shi She' Zari Nightclub, in Lalezar, Tehran (the entertainment area of the city). This was the first time they went to a club and drank alcohol.

#24 Koocheh Sharaf
Tehran, Iran
Mid-Summer 1962

The heat was intense in the summer months. When the temperature in the interior of our home became oppressive, it was the custom to spread Persian rugs on the floor of the balcony and eat our dinner there. Several hours later, we all slept in the open air. It was pleasant to feel the night breezes and gaze up at the stars.

One day during my fourteenth summer, my father brought home our first television, a large RCA that delivered programs in black and white. Watching TV became a family pastime during the evenings, the only time of day when the limited schedule was broadcast. The choice of programs was also very limited, and consisted mostly of American shows such as *I Love Lucy*, *Lassie*, and *Gunsmoke*. Sometimes a movie from India or Egypt would be shown. We placed the television up in Ruben's room, then we opened wide the large doors which faced the balcony. Our Saturday nights were often spent relaxing in the front of the television set, in Persian style: Rugs were spread on the balcony floor and piles of pillows were scattered around to ensure everyone's comfort. My mother provided special desserts accompanied by plates of fruit, nuts, pumpkin seeds and glasses of tea.

#24 Koocheh Sharaf
Tehran, Iran
February 1963

It was a school day in the month of Esfand, late February. My siblings and I returned home for lunch to find that my father had hired a crew to renovate our rooms. As part of this project, layers of tar had to be placed against the lower parts of the walls. Barrels of tar had to be kept on a very hot fire to ensure that the tar remained in liquid form.

After we ate, my brother Ruben and I decided to play racquetball against the wall of our courtyard. The mid-winter sun was warm enough at midday to inspire a competitive game. We put on wool sweaters that had been lovingly knitted for us by our mother and began to play. Half an hour into our game, Ruben hit the ball high and hard against the wall. I tried to run backward to intercept it, but ran into the barrel of boiling tar and lost my balance. I tried to stop myself from falling and reached out reflexively with my left hand—it disappeared into the bubbling barrel. My scream was heard throughout the entire neighborhood.

Immediately, my mother shouted from our basement kitchen, "Drop him into the water! Drop him into the water!" My brother grabbed me and threw me into the ice-cold pool. It took several minutes for my left hand to stop burning. When I finally scrambled out of the pool I realized that my hand was encased in a ball of tar at least four or five inches thick. It was solid as a rock.

I went into the living room and tried to change my wet clothes, but the left sleeve of my beautiful sweater was completely covered in tar. I was in tears. My worried mother cried, "May death be upon me! May dirt be upon my head!" as she used a large scissors to cut the sleeve of the cherished sweater. It was difficult for me to finish dressing myself. Meanwhile, my siblings returned to school, abandoning me to my fate.

I was faced with the daunting challenge of figuring out how to extricate my hand from the ball of tar. At first I tried kerosene and paint thinner, but they were totally useless. The members of the construction crew decided to use a hammer, chisel and knife—to no avail. Finally one of the laborers had an idea: He put a large knife in the fire until it became red-hot and then used it to scrape off a thin layer of the tar. Although the process was slow, it was successful. A few hours later, the remaining layer of tar was so thin that I could feel the heat of the knife. "What should we do next?" I asked the sweaty, heavyset worker whose grip on my arm was as strong as steel.

"Now we'll use kerosene!" exclaimed the laborer, using a heavy fabric soaked in kerosene. As he made progress, my left upper arm became numb, but the burning sensation in my hand from the damaged skin was excruciatingly painful. He had to stop.

"That's enough!" my mother proclaimed when she checked on our progress. It was obvious that my skin was severely burned as pieces of it were now sloughing off with the tar. "Now it is a job for a doctor." My mother grabbed me and took me to the medical clinic located a few blocks away.

As soon as we arrived, the nurses took one look at my arm and gave me an injection to alleviate the pain. Next they gave me a pill that put me to sleep. I awoke in the evening and found my left arm encased in a soft white cover and my parents sitting next to my bed.

"The good news is that your right hand is perfectly alright and you can still go to school and do your homework," my father said with relief. "The bad news is that you will have to take excellent care of your left arm until new skin grows. It must be kept clean to prevent infection."

It took a month of special oil therapy before I finally began to see any new skin. I remembered the other near tragedies in my life: the morning I fell into the water-storage well, and the day I accidentally broke a bottle of acid over my head. I was convinced that an Unknown Being we call God had been protecting me. Even with a severely burned arm, it could have been much worse—I could have fallen into the boiling cauldron and been killed. My brothers and sisters often called me a cat, because I had so many lives!

Mr. Notash's Pharmaceutical Store
Naser-Khosro Street
Tehran, Iran
June 1963

I was working for Mr. Notash in his pharmaceutical distribution store on Naser-Khosro Street when the first pro-Khomeini riots broke out. Large numbers of protesters began running from Tehran's Bazaar, breaking into stores and banks, setting many on fire. As the frightening chaos approached Notash's store, I decided to try and find a safe place to hide. I ran as fast as I could towards my neighborhood, down Hassan Abad Street to Sepah Street, and then onto Sheikh Hadi Street.

The first "safe house" I could find was on the west side of Sheikh Hadi, the home of Akbar Shikholislami, one of my Muslim friends from elementary school. Akbar had been known as the school bully. He was an average student and a devoted Muslim who would stop in the middle of our games to wash himself and quickly pray. It was always difficult to study with him because he could never accept the fact that I understood the lessons that he had trouble learning. Sometimes he begged me for help and sometimes he demanded my assistance. If I refused to assist him or do his homework, we would get in a fight—and he hated to be beaten. The best place to fight was in the back corner of the schoolyard where none of his friends could help him. I kept a strong stick behind my favorite tree; it came in handy when I needed a weapon.

I knocked at the door as hard as I could. Akbar's mother, totally covered in her *chador*, opened the door and recognized me. "My son, why are you breathing so hard? Why are you so frightened?" she asked me in a sweet, calm voice. She called to Akbar to come and escort me into their courtyard. They lived in a very large house that included many rooms for servants and caretakers.

I spent the entire afternoon and evening arguing with Akbar about the rights of citizens and the role of the clergy. He believed that our country and its people were becoming too dependent on foreigners and that we were straying too far from conservative Islam.

"You know very well that many of our women and girls are walking in the streets like Westerners, without being properly covered," he stated emphatically. "This results in our men having impure thoughts."

"The fault is with *you*—*your* eyes, *your* mind—not the women!" I countered. "It is none of your business to force anyone to wear what you think is correct for them. Your mother chooses to cover herself; it is her choice. But if my mother wants to wear a nice dress with no sleeves, and no head cover, it is *her* choice. Women should have equal rights! Who said that only Islamic beliefs are the right ones?"

"Our Prophet Mohammad has decreed it! It is written in the Quran!" Akbar insisted.

"There are other holy books and other prophets, my friend. You do not have a monopoly on the Truth. In Judaism, we are encouraged to question our beliefs; we are allowed to adapt our religious laws when it is necessary to do so. Islam does not allow you to question anything. In Islam there is no discussion or debate—a person's beliefs are either right or wrong. There is no process by which you can bring Islam into the twentieth century! If indeed Islam is such a good religion, which fosters such an admirable way of life, allow people to choose it. Don't force it on others!"

"You Jews are so arrogant. How dare you think you can argue with a Persian Muslim," Akbar shouted.

"As a Persian Jew, I have a much longer, proven history of being in this country than you! My people were here long before Islam arrived! Your family came to Tehran from Tabriz, in Azarbaijan. You do not even speak fluent Farsi. It is unbelievable that you think you are more Iranian than I am!" I shouted back at him. "My people have been here for 2,500 years—since Cyrus the Great brought us here from Babylonia—but I have no equal rights with Muslims in the courts. I can't even go into a restaurant that decides to only serve Muslims! How do you think I feel when I see the sign: VIJEH MOSALMANAN (ONLY MUSLIMS) in an establishment? Muslim restaurants in the bazaar are the most likely to have those signs."

"That is as it should be, because you are a nonbeliever and *najes!*" screamed Akbar, as he waved his fist in the air. "You don't believe in the Holy Quran and the Prophet Mohammad. You don't believe in the coming of the 12th Imam. How do you expect to live in a Muslim country and not be Muslim?"

This was a very familiar "logic" that I had heard many times. Of course, I was as clean, if not cleaner, than Akbar—but since I was not a Muslim he had to avoid any close communication or relationship with me, even though we were supposedly "friends." (I realized it was my choice to reject him as a friend.) I had been told while attending the Muslim elementary school that I recited the Quran better than my Muslim classmates, including Akbar. So *knowing* the Quran is not really the issue, but *believing* and *submitting* to Islamic beliefs—that is the underlying bone of contention.

Since I have a free will, even according to the Quran, I should be able to choose *if* and *to whom* I want to submit myself. I was born to a Jewish mother, so I am a Jew. A child born to a Muslim father is a Muslim. Therefore, neither Akbar nor I had any say in choosing our religion and beliefs; therefore, he and I cannot blame each other and must not do so. Isn't it best to accept each other as we are and remain friends?

"This country should be a place where *all* people have a say in the government. We should be a republic, with civil laws and guaranteed human rights—and religion must be separated from government,"

I insisted.

"When the dictatorship of the Shah is vanquished, the Ayatollah Khomeini will establish a democratic government," Akbar assured me.

"But shouldn't the hoodlums who are rioting and burning other people's property use legal means to change what they do not like?" I retorted.

"There is no legal channel open to us now! There is no way to express dissatisfaction and change unjust laws except protesting in the streets," said Akbar. His eyes were aflame with the true believer's zeal. Akbar's passion bordered on fanaticism.

I thought of another of my Muslim friends, Fazlolah Hajj Ashi, who had also attended the Muslim elementary school with me: Fazlolah was the son of Hajj Ashi, who owned a large soup restaurant south of my father's store, near Shareh Nou. Fazlolah was tall and handsome, and an excellent student favored by all the teachers. It was a joy to study or play with him. He was open-minded and liberal in his thinking about Islam. I wondered what he thought about the riots in the streets. I wondered what decisions he would make to ensure a good future for himself.

As I walked home that evening in the deepening twilight, I listened to the distant sounds of the protestors shouting, "Down with the Shah! Long live democracy! Long live Khomeini!" I hoped that Akbar was right, that Khomeini would bring something better, not worse.

My Father's Store
Malek Street, Near The Gates of Ghazvin
Tehran, Iran
July 1963

Abbas Agha had been a friend of my father from the time Father arrived in Tehran at age seventeen. Abbas was a tall, heavy man, powerfully built with a robust, muscular chest. He grew an imposing mustache that served to make his large facial features all the more impressive. Abbas Agha was a very wealthy man who managed to become wealthier every year. He owned orchards and other income-producing properties, including a major interest in the largest slaughterhouse in Tehran.

For all his wealth and influence, it must be understood that Abbas was a hoodlum, a thug, a *jaahel*—a man of few scruples, devoid of ethics or sense of righteousness. He was involved in the opium trade and conducted various strong-arm activities that included physical intimidation and putting the squeeze on people whether they deserved it or not. Abbas always wore a white shirt and a solid black suit, sporting the jacket over his shoulders in some sort of lazy fashion statement. His black hat was always perched haphazardly on his head, and he wore his large black shoes like slippers, breaking down their heels with an air of nonchalant indolence. He spoke only "street Farsi" and was unschooled, unrefined and boorish.

Now, at the age of forty, with a wife and children and a mother-in-law under his roof, Abbas decided that he should become a devout Muslim and make *hajj*, a pilgrimage to Mecca. (It is my understanding that any Muslim who decides to make a pilgrimage must have no personal assets and must divest himself of all he owns. It is customary that he transfer his worldly possessions to someone he trusts and proceed empty-handed, wearing only simple, white kaftans.)

Abbas decided that my father was to be the trusted individual who would look after all his possessions and items of value. I was in my father's store when Abbas Agha spoke to my father about that arrangement.

"Ebrahim Agha, good morning! *Chakeram!* I am your servant, my friend," Abbas Agha's loud voice boomed like a cannon.

"Welcome! May your steps be upon my eyes! Why am I so honored this morning?" my father asked.

"It's like this: I need to ask you a little favor, Ebrahim."

"A *little* favor?" my father warily replied. My father, remaining calm and composed, knew that Abbas Agha was a troublemaker, and not the most honest person. "I am *mokhlesam*, your flawless, humble servant."

"Yes, you see I am about to make *hajj* and I choose to transfer all my assets to *you* while I am gone. When I come back, of course you will return everything to me."

"You are joking! Ha! That's a good one!" my father laughed.

"No, I am very serious."

"Abbas, the practice of temporarily transferring your belongings to another person reminds me of one of our Jewish traditions. Before the holiday of Passover, we store away all foodstuff and dishes that are not kosher for *Pesach,* and divest ourselves of those items by selling them to the synagogue for a nominal amount of money, a *toman.* Then, when the eight days of celebration are over, the belongings are "sold" back to us."

"That's an interesting similarity, my friend," Abbas conceded. "But let us now discuss *my* situation. Now it is time for me to become a devout Muslim. I must be concerned with the purity of my soul, after all. Also, I want to elevate myself in society, Ebrahim Agha. I want to be respected by the clergy and earn a better place in the mosque. I will return with a new name. *Hajj* Abbas is a name that people will say with reverence. And it won't hurt if I donate money to Islamic causes when I return, eh?

"So, you want to elevate yourself in society? That is certainly a lofty goal."

"It is time for me to change my life for the better, Ebrahim. And it's time for us to conduct business," Abbas Agha loudly stated, as he thrust into my father's hands a piece of paper containing the agreement, along with a leather pouch and a locked box that held jewelry and important deeds and documents. "Oh, there is something more I must ask of you," Abbas Agha quickly added. "I may be away from home for a week, two weeks, maybe more. You

Hajj Abbas greeted my father, *"Al salam alikam!"* with a demeanor that was very subdued and calm, not like he had been before his journey to Mecca. He asked my father to retrieve the pouch and the locked box and return his property. My father immediately brought back the items. Hajj Abbas checked the contents, and seeing that everything was there, he nodded a cursory "thank you." There was tension in the air and the uneasiness between the men was palpable.

"Well, Ebrahim-the-Jew," he said, finally breaking the silence with a disrespectful epithet. "I have heard some disturbing news." His face became red with anger as he continued. "My neighbors are all very upset with me because of something *you* did. You bastard! You took my wife to a hospital! How dare you go into my bedroom and carry my wife out of the house, without a Muslim helping! The neighbors were upset at the sight of all that blood, and, to make matters worse, you took her to a *Jewish* doctor!" By now Hajj Abbas was shouting.

"Before you say another word, you need to go home and get the true story from Khanom Bozorg. Forget about the neighbors and what they saw!" my father shouted back.

Hajj Abbas stood up, banging his fist on the table. "I won't allow a Jew to touch my wife and get away with it!" he thundered.

My father picked up a metal measuring stick. "Before I smash your stupid skull, I want you to know one thing. I want you to know I took good care of your family and your property while you were gone. You have come back a far worse human being than before you left! I'd rather see you like you were before you left—the hoodlum, *Jaahel* Abaas, instead of the new *Hajj* Abbas. Go home and talk to your wife and mother-in-law, and then come back here to apologize!" my father roared. He was furious—and fearless.

The next morning, when we went to open the store, Hajj Abbas and his mother-in-law were waiting at the door. Hajj Abbas carried an enormous bouquet of white flowers that almost obscured his huge body. Next to him stood his tiny, stooped mother-in-law wrapped in her black *chador*, holding a box of candy.

"Good morning, Ebrahim," she said. "I want to offer my apology to you." She spoke with a firm and steady voice. "A great injustice has been done to you, and I am very sorry," she added respectfully. Then she turned to her enormous son-in-law, who stood silently beside her. "Apologize to Ebrahim, you fool!" she shouted at Hajj Abbas with unrelenting fury.

"I beg your forgiveness," Hajj Abbas muttered to my father, with his head bowed in contrition.

"Tell Ebrahim Agha for what you are apologizing!" the woman goaded her son-in-law. There was unbridled loathing and disgust in her voice.

"I apologize for my big mistake, for doubting your friendship and honesty," Hajj Abbas offered. He took my father's hand and kissed it as a sign of respect. "I am very sorry, Ebrahim Agha. *Man chaker va mokhleseh shoma am!* I am your humble servant! May your shadow always be upon me and my family!"

"Please forgive my son-in-law," the woman entreated. "He acted like a stupid child. Instead of kissing you in gratitude when he arrived home, he made unfounded accusations. Instead of gaining wisdom on his *hajj,* he lost what little wisdom he had!"

"I'm glad you put some brains in his head," my father said to her. "Hajj Abbas is lucky to have such a wise and dignified woman as you in his house."

Hajj Habib's Store
Malek Street
Tehran, Iran
Early August 1963

Hajj Habib had a large store on the southeast corner of Ghazvin and Malek Streets, about sixty yards west of my father's store, on the same street. Hajj Habib sold rice, salt, barley, beans, spices, and other sundry items needed for daily life. All of his merchandise was neatly organized in the front of the store; a heavy curtain separated the front and back of the premises. Hajj Habib was a devoted Muslim and he made sure that all of his neighbors saw him going to the mosque across the street several times every day. He was a big heavy man with a loud voice. My father and Hajj Habib did not get along and generally would avoid each other.

On many occasions when I walked by Hajj Habib's store, I did not see him. Since the store was large, I assumed he was in the back, hidden from view by the curtain. I also noticed that at midday many clergymen visited his store. It was interesting to me that Hajj Habib was very wealthy, yet he never had any customers!

On Fridays, Hajj Habib's son sat behind the cash register and read books. He was three or four years older than me, and very friendly and kind. Unlike his father, he often visited our store and examined our men's fabric. Over time, he and I became friends. We often met to discuss books: I loved to read romance novels and short works of fiction, while he only read serious books about history and religion.

"What are all those clergymen doing in your store every day?" I finally asked him.

"My father has formed a committee of learned Muslim clergy, *olama*, who meet every day to find ways to help the poor and needy, especially the widows, orphans, and the sick," he explained.

"That is a very noble task," I conceded, "but how do people know about your father's group?"

"Muslim families who attend the neighborhood mosques go to their assigned clergy and request help. The *olama* lists the names of those who are in need and brings the list to my father."

"How many families do you support?" I inquired.

"You see, each clergyman chooses approximately one hundred families," said my new friend.

"That must be very expensive! How can your father afford such a large amount of charity when there are never any customers in your father's store?"

"We have many friends who donate money. We fill the orders with the needed items and deliver the orders in a truck," he explained. "We also make sure these poor families are protected, and we see to it that their children attend Muslim schools."

When I grew older, I better understood the organization that is called the Muslim Brotherhood: their planning, management, and administration—all based on the Islamic rules of business and charity. I realized that this Islamic Brotherhood operated from the back of Hajj Habib's store.

Hajj Habib had significant influence and control over our neighborhood. Almost all the policemen, shopkeepers, merchants, teachers, and even taxi drivers had a profound respect for Hajj Habib and his clergy. Eventually his operation grew so large that he had to hold his meetings in the mosque across the street. Many men and women went there to pay him respect and ask for help. Even some opium traffickers started to consider Hajj Habib their mentor and leader.

In the summer of 1963, when the anti-Shah riots started in Tehran, a large number of young men were captured and jailed. I remember that during the weeks that followed, Hajj Habib's store was packed with crying women wearing black *chadors*. They had gathered at Hajj Habib's store to beg him to get their husbands, brothers, and sons out of jail. Many of these women had to wait in the hot sun outside of Hajj Habib's place of business. My father kept a large metal tank of cold drinking water outside his store so that pedestrians could stop and take a cooling drink when the summer heat became unbearable. My job was to keep the tank full of water and to keep adding ice to it. The Muslim pedestrians who knew we were Jewish poured water into their hands, rather than drink from the cup that we provided.

One particularly hot day, my father saw a long line of women in heavy black *chadors* trying to drink from their hands. He took pity on them and told me to go to Hajj Habib and ask him for some cups so that the women could drink. I asked his son and was given two tall glasses. We gave water to everyone. Later, Hajj Habib stopped by to make sure that I had not put my fingers inside the glasses and that no one had received "unclean" water. Hajj Habib revealed to my father that he was working on freeing all the Muslim boys who were jailed for rioting. He asked my father to keep an eye on his son and his store while he busily negotiated the protestors' release.

Sheihk Hadi Neighborhood
Tehran, Iran
Late summer 1963

By the end of the summer I was asking myself, how can I make money without working for my father? I tried to think of something that would be both lucrative and enjoyable. My friends and I loved going to the movie houses to watch American films. The movie theatres in Tehran were very large and could accommodate 1,500 to 3,000 people. Tickets for seats in the front row sold for the equivalent of sixty cents U.S.; middle rows sold for the equivalent of about one dollar U.S.; and loge seating cost a dollar and a half. Young children, students, large families, and the poorer population could only afford the cheapest tickets, and the rest of the seats would remain almost empty.

Here was my opportunity! If I could convince a theatre owner to open on a Friday morning at 10:00am, I could show a movie from 10:00 till 12:00 noon, then show the same movie again at noon. This way I could sell 3,000 seats at an average price of sixty *rial* (75 cents U.S.), and generate 1,800 *toman* ($225 U.S.). My costs would be minimal; I would have to pay the theatre owner for the cost of lights, cleaning, etc., plus his profit.

Within one month I had made an agreement with a theatre owner to lease his theatre for 500 *toman* ($62.50 U.S.), plus expenses. Then I printed 6,000 tickets: 3,000 for the first showing and 3,000 for the second. I priced the best seats at seventy-five *rial* (95 cents U.S.) and the cheap seats at forty-five *rial* (56 cents U.S.)—significantly lower than the market prices. I also calculated a 50% no-sale, which required me to print twice as many tickets as the available seats.

To start off, I took the freshly printed tickets to my school and offered them to all students at a 10% discount, with two loge seats selling for 10.8 *toman* ($1.35 U.S.) and two cheaper seats for the equivalent of 80 cents a pair. Some of the students bought ten, twenty, or thirty tickets with the hope of reselling them at higher prices to other students and neighbors. Next I gave one free ticket to each storeowner in the neighborhood; soon they purchased twenty or thirty tickets for their customers and family. I left stacks of tickets in the local beauty shops, butcher shops, grocery stores and bakeries, on consignment.

Soon I had no tickets left—but I had only *sold* 700 of them! I decided to print another 3,000 tickets. By now I had dispersed 9,000 tickets for 3,000 available seats, for both showings of the movie! I started to sell tickets on consignment to shop keepers. My best customers turned out to be schoolteachers. They received free tickets for themselves and their families, if they would agree to sell tickets to their students.

The Friday of the first show finally arrived. I went to the theatre at 9:00am to make sure the building was ready. There were no assigned seats, so it would be "first come, first sit" for seats in the front and the rear of the theatre. I was worried that all the tickets had been sold and 4,500 people would show up. At 10:00am there were 1,000 people. By 10:15 the number reached 1,200. The noon showing was better, with a total of 1,300 in attendance. Everything went fine—there were no fights or disturbances among the attendees. Afterwards, the theatre was cleaned.

The next day I counted all of my cash and paid all my expenses. I netted only a 125-*toman* profit, which was not entirely disappointing, but far less than I expected. When I shared the news of the financial outcome with my friends, they concluded that since none of us could earn 125 *toman* in a month, working forty hours per week, I should consider the operation a success.

I continued the movie ticket business for four more weeks, and each time I earned a little more. During the final week, I discovered that a number of young Muslim men had found out about my enterprise. They decided that such a clever business should belong to them, not to a Jew. Three of them came to my home and asked me to come outside to talk to them. I walked a short distance with them and listened to their threats. I agreed to pay them all my profit from the last week of business and discontinue the operation altogether. Luckily, I had already used 500 *toman* of my profits to buy a beautiful Persian rug, made in Esfahan. (That rug always reminds me of my first attempt at entrepreneurship—and my unfortunate dealings with Mafia-style hoodlums.)

My Father's Store
Malek Street, Near the Gates of Ghazvin
Tehran, Iran
Late Spring 1964

I was assisting my father late one Thursday afternoon when a group of officials and one policeman entered our store. They showed an official-looking form letter to my father that stated he had not paid a large bill that he owed. It was their intent to collect the money.

My father looked at the signature on a bill that the men claimed was his. "This is not my signature!" he screamed. "This is a fraud!" However, nothing my father said changed their minds. The officials and the policeman were determined to pack up part of our inventory and take it away.

My father convinced the men to give him thirty minutes to gather enough money to post bond. Posting bond would buy time to hire an attorney and fight this fraudulent claim. Meanwhile, I was shaking with fright. I ordered tea and sweets for the visitors and asked them to sit and wait.

My father went to his neighbors, both Jewish and Muslim, asking them to lend him enough money to post the bond. In fifteen minutes he returned with the money, paid the officials, got a receipt, and escorted them to the door.

We had never before had a legal issue requiring a lawyer. We did not know where to start. My father talked to some of his friends on Saturday morning in the synagogue, before services. It was common for the men to arrive at the synagogue early and talk about business, interest rates, the price of gold and real estate. They stood in groups and exchanged ideas and information. Many of the members were also fabric salesmen and the best and most reliable information on pricing, availability, and quality of fabric was shared in these informal gatherings.

One of the fabric wholesalers who worshipped at the synagogue owned a shop in the bazaar. This fabric wholesaler recognized the names of the people who claimed that my father owed them a large sum of money. Apparently these hoodlums began the scam by seeking out and bribing a Jewish person, and asking him to write the name of a Jewish storeowner, such as "Ebrahim Yomtoubian," in Hebrew. Then they would create many fraudulent invoices, each signed in Hebrew by the storeowner they were scamming—and of course, these signatures were forged. The fake invoices in my father's case were for a large order of blankets and fabric we never bought. The Jewish fabric wholesaler my father had consulted recommended the name of a Muslim attorney who was also a member of the clergy.

On Sunday my father went to the courthouse and obtained the address of the attorney and rushed over to see him. The attorney could clearly see that the signature was not my father's. However, how could a Jew win in a Muslim court? The attorney recommended that my father should agree to a settlement. (After talking to many of his friends in the synagogue, my father became convinced that there was no assurance of legal justice for Jews in Iran and it was in his best interest to pay a settlement price.) My father was outraged at the injustice and it hurt him deeply. As a result of this incident, father became more convinced than ever to leave Iran.

This incident was a turning point in my life. After it occurred, I decided to quit the wonderful, beloved Kourosh High School and work with my father in his store during the day—to be with him in case there was further harassment—and attend night school, with much older men. I selected the prestigious and famous Kharazmi Night School, which was known for its excellent instructors. This is how my 11th grade experience went: Night school began at 7:00pm and concluded at 11:00pm. My classmates were businessmen, office workers, teachers, and shopkeepers. They were very dedicated, hard working, and smart. I was the youngest student and had the most time for studying during the day; therefore, I was always a step ahead of the others, and ready to assist my classmates. In return, they treated me well and respected my intelligence. During our evening breaks and on holidays I discussed many topics with my older friends. The conversations we enjoyed were very valuable to me. Throughout the year of night school, I never experienced any discrimination.

Each morning I opened the store at 8:00am and prepared for the day. During the course of the day I worked in the store, ran errands, and studied when I could. My father felt comfortable and at ease in leaving the store at any time because he trusted my ability to manage things. It became common for him to disappear for hours at a time during the slow time of day. He became more and more distracted and less interested in the business.

Later that year, the Iranian economy fell into a deep recession and many storeowners were hard pressed to keep their businesses going. My father had to layoff all our workers and rely on just the two of us. The absence of customers allowed me the time to focus on my studies and excel at school. At the end of the school year I obtained the highest scores on the tests given to the students in all of the regional night schools.

The slow business had another effect: It encouraged middle-aged Muslim women to spend an unreasonable amount of time in our store, simply talking and passing the time of day. Often I had to ask them to please leave so that I could study and complete my homework. There were times when the presence of those beautiful women became overwhelming, and I could not always subdue my sexual urges.

Later I found out that many Jewish storeowners all over Tehran faced the same "difficulties." The most common gossip was about young handsome Jewish men who fathered children with Muslim women. I never could get a Jewish man to talk directly about his own experiences, but they were more than willing to talk about *other* Jewish men. Perhaps the most well kept secret among Jewish men of Tehran was their sexual relationships with Muslim women. Traditionally, the age difference between a Muslim man and his wife was approximately fifteen to twenty-five years. These Muslim men—especially clergymen and those who had immigrated to Tehran from the villages—often had much younger *sigheh*, "temporary wives," and were not interested in their older wives.

Young Jewish shopkeepers sold merchandise to Muslim women; this gave both Muslim wives and Jewish men a means to become acquainted with each other, and chance encounters sometimes resulted in sexual intimacy. Also, there were money collectors like me who appeared on women's doorsteps during the day, while husbands were at work and children were at school—sometimes a collector would be invited inside. With the ever-present possibility of a tryst, a Jewish man had an incentive to be always clean, shaved, and dressed in nice, well-pressed clothes. (And a bottle of aftershave was always kept in a bag in his store or on his bicycle.)

Despite the risks, Muslim wives would look forward to visits from their Jewish lovers. The Jewish men were always meek and quiet, allowing the women to feel comfortable and superior. These relationships developed slowly, with the woman always in control. Typically, the Muslim wife would spend time talking to her Jewish lover about her problems, wishes, and desires. She would share her most secret and intimate thoughts and feelings with her sensitive and trusted visitor. Jewish men would never dare speak to anyone about their Muslim lover, or treat her roughly. Rather, they were always responsive and tender.

Once a Muslim wife allowed herself to become intimate with a Jewish man, she would share her unholy but exciting experience with her closest friends, thus creating a chain of dishonest, impious relationships. It must be understood that while these women were happy to allow their bodily fluids to mingle with those of their Jewish lover, once the sex act was complete, the Jew was again *najes!*

One day I asked my father, "How many Muslim brothers and sisters do I have?" He looked at me with a serious expression. After a long silence he replied, "A gentleman never talks about these subjects." I gathered my courage and asked my mother what she knew about this, and she replied with no hesitation, "As long as your father comes home and he is a good father and a good husband, I love him and accept him as he is. As for you, young man, try to be as good a husband and father as your father."

Salsabil Neighborhood
Southwestern Tehran, Iran
Summer 1964

Another summer brought another attempt at entrepreneurship. I decided to try to make some money by selling fabric. I talked my father into lending me several bolts of low cost cloth, enabling me to start a business with no start-up capital.

I tied the bolts of fabric to my bicycle and pedaled to a neighborhood of high pedestrian traffic. Once I found a good location, I spread a blanket on the sidewalk and arranged my wares attractively. Then I began to shout my prices at passersby—prices that were much lower than my father charged at his store. Soon potential customers stopped and asked me questions and felt the cloth. Within a few hours I sold everything I had and made a small profit. I continued this business for almost six weeks, until the local shopkeepers started to complain. They finally kicked me out of their neighborhood.

No longer having a way to make my own money, I visited my good friend, David S., for advice. "How are you making money these days?" I asked him.

"Very simple," he answered. "I buy lottery tickets at a discount and sell them at a normal price. If I don't sell all the tickets, I pray that one of the unsold tickets will be a winner!"

"That doesn't sound like a very good business model to me," I laughed. "But I have nothing else going on, so I guess I'll try it." I attempted to sell lottery tickets for two weeks, but I lost money and gave it up. Thus ended my summer of entrepreneurship.

My Uncle Hanoukh Yomtoubian's House
Northern Tehran, Yousef Abaad Neighborhood
Early Autumn 1964

Late in the summer of 1964, my family was informed that Manouchehr, my older cousin, had returned to Iran from Los Angeles, California. He was the first member of the Yomtoubian family who had studied abroad, receiving a degree in electrical engineering at the Pomona campus of California State Polytechnic University. All the cousins were looking forward to hearing about the dreamland of America. The entire Yomtoubian family gathered at the Mehrabad Airport in Tehran to welcome him home.

The dapper twenty-six year old arrived wearing nice American clothes: a pressed pair of pants with a sport jacket, a beautiful pair of sunglasses, and a leather camera bag hanging from one shoulder. Each family group brought him either a small gift or a bouquet of flowers. When Manouchehr finally checked out of customs, everyone rushed over to hug and kiss him. After our overpowering display of affection, Uncle Hanoukh declared that we should all return to our own homes, but come to his house the next day to visit with Manouchehr. We respected the fact that my uncle's family needed to be alone with their son for at least a few hours.

Before Manouchehr was allowed to enter his parents' house, his mother performed a ritual to ward off the Evil Eye. As she swung the metal basket containing hot charcoal, she added handfuls of herbs. She muttered prayers as she directed the smoke to flow in all directions in front of the house.

"Mamon, why are you doing this superstitious ritual?" Manouchehr asked, somewhat embarrassed.

"Shh! I am protecting you," his mother retorted. "You think you are a modern American, but you need to be protected from the Evil Eye. You never know who might be jealous of you."

"Jealous?" asked Manouchehr, incredulously.

"*Baleh*! Yes! The neighbors, who knows, someone might be jealous of your achievements, my son. I must not take any chances."

Manouchehr shrugged with indifference, allowing his mother to assuage her anxiety.

The next evening, my parents traveled by bus to the wealthy Yousef Abaad neighborhood in northern Tehran, where my uncle lived. I rode my motorcycle and met them there. We were excited to see my "American" cousin. As we approached my uncle's modern house, I noticed blood on the sidewalk, all the way to the front door. This was the blood of a sheep that my uncle had sacrificed on his front steps to show *Ha'Shem,* the Lord God, his happiness and the fullness of his heart.

We walked through the house into the courtyard where many chairs were set up for guests. The fountain in the center of their pool was spraying water high into the air. A long chain of colored lights was stretched back and forth, crisscrossing the entire courtyard several times. Fresh flowers had been planted in the flowerbeds surrounding the pool, adding to the festive ambiance. The smell of delicious food hung in the air. My uncle, his wife and all their children wore their nicest clothes. They happily greeted their guests, offering trays of *sabzi, gondi,* fruit, sweets and glasses of tea. We felt as though we were attending a wedding or some sort of festival! There was an abundance of whiskey and *arak* with which to make toasts.

When Manouchehr came into the courtyard to welcome the guests, he remembered some of us, however, he had forgotten the names of the younger cousins. He had gone to America six years before, when I was just a nine-year-old boy; when he came home to Tehran, I was a fifteen-year-old young man.

Manouchehr spoke Farsi with an accent and used many American forms of speech. For example, when we asked him a question, he replied saying, "Uh-huh," and "Yeah," instead of *"Baleh,"* meaning, "Yes." He also seemed to have forgotten *ta'aroff,* Persian etiquette: When he offered us a glass of tea, we politely said, "no, thank you" as was the Persian custom—and he took away the tray! This behavior was completely unexpected and confusing to us. (Persian *ta'aroff* has been practiced for centuries; it is used to show respect, humility, and politeness. When offered a cup of tea, for example, one would politely refuse; after the tea is offered several more times, one would finally say "thank you, thank you" a number of times, and accept it. Another example: When a cab driver is asked, "How much do I owe you?" his first response will be, *"Gha'abe lee nada'areh!* Nothing! It is not worthy of you." After the passenger insists that the driver accept his fare, the cab driver will eventually accept payment.)

Manouchehr was wearing his beautiful Western-style clothes. He gathered us boys around him and, while drinking his coffee, he tried to impress us with subjects totally unfamiliar to us. We sat in rapt attention, awestruck, as he spoke frankly about his wonderful life in the United States. I had many, many questions for him. What exactly did an electrical engineer do? How did he get started in America? Where did he live? How did he support himself while attending school? What university did he attend? How did he learn the technical language in his field? How did he practice his Jewish faith? Was he back in Iran to stay?

"How did you survive so far from home, without the support of your family?" I asked, impressed with his audacity and independence.

"Ha! I wish I had received some support from them!" he answered with bitterness in his voice. "Some financial help would have been most welcome, but you know my father—no water drips from his hand—he is stingy! You see, when I left home my father had little money, but as the years passed he made some excellent investments in land here in Yousef Abaad. He never sent me so much as a *toman*! I had to perform all sorts of unsavory jobs, including cleaning toilets, to put myself through university."

"But you succeeded. That's the important thing," I reflected.

"Yes, I did succeed! In America, everything is achieveable. Believe me, the American Dream is a reality," Manouchehr passionately declared.

"So, tell me something about America. What is the government like there?"

"In America the entire government, the entire country, is based on mutual trust. For example, when you earn money as a salary or commission or sell goods, you are expected to pay taxes, a percent of your earnings, to the government." This concept was completely foreign to us. We never paid any money to our government! He continued, explaining that every working person has to report all his income once a year to the government. It took him at least thirty minutes to explain income, sales, gift, and real estate taxes. He emphasized that American taxation was a volunteer system based on total trust!

"How do Americans choose their leaders?"

"They vote for their leaders. There are always several candidates running for a particular office—mayor, governor, judge, congressman, or president. The adult citizens, both men and women, enter a private voting booth, one at a time, and mark a paper ballot."

"How did you buy food in America?" one of the younger cousins asked. "Did you buy sheep and slaughter them at home?"

"Are you kidding? Americans don't slaughter their meat at home!" Manouchehr said with disdain. "They have the most wonderful grocery stores in America, loaded with more beautiful edible items than you could imagine!" He animatedly described not only the quantity and quality of the food, but the fact that shoppers could walk through a store without anyone watching over their shoulders, take their time and examine everything, then choose items by placing them in a cart. "Buyers weigh or count their own items and finally approach the cashier, where they usually pay with a check," he informed us.

"What's a "check"?" asked my cousin Mousa.

"Actually, it's a promissory note from a particular bank, promising to cover whatever amount of money you write on it," he answered. "Of course, you have to put money in your bank account to cover your check."

Manouchehr took another thirty minutes to explain the shopping habits of Americans. He shared all sorts of information about the process of buying goods, such as the fact that shoppers can return merchandise to exchange it or get their money back. "The concept of trust in business dealings is paramount," he explained, as we listened in wide-eyed wonder. "Americans believe in standing behind the quality of their goods. In America the customer is always right." The concepts of fairness and trust in business were foreign to us. We decided that Americans must be very naïve and simple-minded when it comes to business.

Next he told us that when you walk down the street it is customary to greet strangers. "Americans are generally very polite and friendly," he told us.

Then he shocked us by telling us how proudly he declared his Judaism in America, with no fear and no discrimination. He had non-Jewish roommates who celebrated both Christian and Jewish holidays with respect and dignity. "In America, we have no college classes on *Shabbat* (Saturday) and Sunday. We celebrate the Israeli Independence Day in temples and synagogues, the same as Hanukkah and other Jewish holidays," he affirmed.

He told us how American Jews and Persian friends—some Jewish, some not—helped him learn English and assisted him in learning how to function at the university. He amazed us with a description of how the American education system is based on choosing many of your courses and not being dictated what to choose. The concept of dormitories, especially the co-ops, was introduced to us.

Finally, he told us about the need to own a car if you want to work off campus, go on a date, shop, or attend services on *Shabbat*. "But," he reminded us, "in America there is plenty of work, and as long as you are willing to work hard, you can support yourself and still get a good education. It may take you more than four years to get your engineering degree, but by working hard, you will succeed."

"Enough about all that," I said with a dismissive wave of my hand. "I want to know about the girls!"

"The girls in California are the best!" Manouchehr animatedly declared. "Here, let me show you some photos." He proceeded to pull a small stack of photographs out of his pocket. All of us cousins abandoned our chairs and gathered around him, ogling the photos of young, beautiful blonde women wearing bikinis on a beach. All of us began talking at once, pointing out the impressive attributes of each woman. America was looking better and better to us. We were salivating!

"You can hold a woman's hand in public in America," Manouchehr informed us. "And on rare occasions you can even kiss her on the lips in public! When you ask an American woman for a date, you do not need her parents' permission. Dating in America is quite honest and simple."

As the festivities began to wind down, we realized it was getting very late and we had to leave. All the young cousins had been greatly influenced by Manouchehr's informative stories. His descriptions of America, a truly amazing place beyond our *koocheh*, inspired us.

A few weeks later, we heard that Manouchehr had decided not to remain in Iran, but intended to return to America. His parents were determined to find him a bride before he left Iran. Within a few days, many Jewish families knew that Manouchehr, an America-educated engineer and son of Hanoukh Yomtoubian, was looking for a wife. It turns out that Manouchehr met a respectable Jewish family at a party and was introduced to their daughter. It took only two months for him and the young woman to be married. A day after the wedding, the bride and groom left for America.

Manouchehr became our idol—he was "a man of the world." He

was the one all of us wanted to follow. Many other young Persian men completed their studies abroad and returned to Iran to find their brides. On the other hand, many Persian Jewish families with eligible daughters sought to find American graduates to become their sons-in-law. It became common when visiting Jewish families in Iran to be shown photographs of their sons-in-laws and daughters who were living in America. There were also photos of their American grandchildren.

Almost all my friends started dreaming about America. Some of us purchased guidebooks with the Statue of Liberty on the cover and enrolled in night classes to learn English. America was the ultimate destination for us—the magical place where everything is possible and life can be lived without fear.

Ollum School
Iranshar Street, Takhte Jamshid Neighborhood
Tehran, Iran
Autumn 1965

Mr. Zamani was a Muslim teacher of history and literature at Kourosh High School who taught his students about the Holocaust. He was promoted to the position of principal, an assignment he held until he resigned in order to establish his own private school. Mr. Zamani recruited me to come to his new school, called Ollum (meaning "wisdom" or "knowledge" in Arabic). He recruited many other Jewish students, including my friend Bijan, who attended Ollum from the 9th through 12th grades.

Twelfth grade was a pleasure! I cannot say enough about the high quality of Mr. Zamani's classes. Even though he was Ollum's chief administrator, he lectured brilliantly on many topics in literature, history and philosophy—and he rarely used notes. He was the epitome of the intellectual.

Mr. Zamani was also very inspirational. Many times he lectured with the intention of encouraging us to attain our full potential. "Get out in the world," he would say to us. "Don't stay in the shadows! Make a mark on your country and the world!" He also reminded his students, both Jewish and Muslim, that the Jews had saved the Farsi language and traditional Persian music from the Arab conquerors who brought Islam to Persia. The Arabs had tried to eradicate the Persian culture by imposing their Islamic values. During the Safavid Dynasty, *Shiah* Islam became the official religion of Iran, thus making Iran a "religious" country. Individual freedoms and civil laws allowed under Zoroastrian rule were destroyed.

Zamani was a believer in democracy and the rights of the individual. He was a humanist and a big supporter of the initial decrees of the Shah's White Revolution—the Shah's attempt to modernize the government and the culture—which had begun in 1962. Zamani approved of the Shah's decrees on land reform, voting rights for women, the formation of the Literacy Corps, and the establishment of the Health Corps. He also was encouraged by the establishment of the Houses of Equity, the Shah's attempt to reform the justice system. Zamani lectures fostered in me an increased awareness of political and social issues in Iran.

> **Elsewhere in the world in 1966:**
> -The groundbreaking takes place for the World Trade Center in New York City, New York.
> -The U.S. has a total of 190,000 troops in South Vietnam.
> -An anti-Nasser conspiracy is exposed in Egypt.
> -Mao Zedong begins the Cultural Revolution in the People's Republic of China.
> -Saudi Arabia and the United Arab Republic begin negotiations in Kuwait to end the war in Yemen.

Jewish Cemetery
Esfahan, Iran
Early Spring 1966

It was the time of *Norouz*, the Persian New Year, which is celebrated each year on March 21st. For six months my cousin Mousa and I had planned a trip to the Jewish ghetto in Esfahan, and it was finally time to go. My grandfather's father Agha Baba—and at least seven generations before him—lived and died in the city of Esfahan. My grandfather Eliyahu was born in Esfahan, but he moved to Tehran in 1946, once my father's business was established there.

The inhabitants of Esfahan called their birthplace *Esfahan Nesfeh Jaha,* which means "Esfahan is Half the World." Why? The exquisite architecture, the verdant parks and the breathtaking Islamic art made it the most beautiful and romantic city in Iran. My grandfather and his ancestors, however, had been required to live in *Oudlajan*, Esfahan's Jewish ghetto—and the ghetto was not an attractive place: The narrow, winding streets were unpaved and the ancient, deteriorating houses were unhygienic. Even so, there was a time when the population of Jews in Esfahan was so large that the city was once known as *Dar-Al-Yahud* ("House of the Jews") or *Yahoodieh* (City of Jews), and it remains to this day a repository of Jewish lore.

Mousa and I arrived in Esfahan by bus at 5:00am and went directly to a public bath to refresh ourselves. Next we hailed a cab to take us to the ghetto, but the Muslim driver could only take us as far as the gates. To enter the ghetto we had to walk down a stairway, through a long, dark tunnel, and finally through a huge gated doorway. We walked with our suitcases, randomly knocking on doors that displayed *mezuzahs*. The one- or two-storied homes were very large and contained twenty or thirty rooms. There were twenty or so families living in each house; if you were a prominent family, you might have two or three rooms for your own private use.

We walked up to a house at random and knocked on the door. The door was opened by a very old, short, heavy-set woman. She had long, gray hair, a plump pink face, and brown eyes shaped like almonds.

"Shalom! Peace be upon you!" we greeted her. "We are Isaac and Mousa Yomtoubian. We are your cousins from Tehran. My grandfather is Eliyahu Yomtoubian, the son of Agha Baba, and my grandmother was Khanom Leah, daughter of Leah and Asher," I told her.

"Aye! Come in! Come in! My house is your house! May your steps be upon my eyes! I am your Great-Aunt Shoshona!" she exclaimed. "The Yomtoubians are here from Tehran!" she shouted to the rest of the inhabitants of the house. "Come and see your cousins from Tehran!" My Great-Aunt Shoshona was a widow, and very poor. To earn money she produced baby powder by crushing talc stones with a hammer, straining the powder with a sieve, and then bottling the result. She also made thread out of wool.

Everyone in the house welcomed us with many hugs and kisses and we were given an elaborate breakfast. After eating, we were escorted by Esfahani cousins on a tour of the ghetto. We visited the city's oldest synagogue, the Ezra Yaghoub Synagogue, where my grandfather and his ancestors had worshipped. It was very beautiful.

"As you may already know, our great-uncles were very scholarly," said my Esfahani cousin. "They knew Farsi, Hebrew, and Persian-Hebrew (Farsi written with Hebrew letters). They translated the *Torah* into the Judeo-Persian language. They also wrote Persian poetry with Hebrew letters." [See references, V. B. Moreen.]

"Why did they write Farsi with Hebrew letters?" asked Mousa.

"When they wrote for Jewish readers, they used Hebrew letters to write Farsi words because Jews knew the Hebrew letters and how to read the Hebrew alphabet in order to *doven* (pray)," our cousin answered. "Did you know that the Persian language was saved by Persian Jews?" our cousin continued. "When the Arab Muslims invaded, they tried to get everyone to speak and write in Arabic. As a matter of fact, they destroyed all the documents written in Farsi that they found. But the documents written in Farsi with *Hebrew* letters were not destroyed because they were thought to be holy books—however, some of the books were actually about mathematics, medicine, history, and poetry."

"For instance, my father is fluent in writing Farsi with Hebrew letters, and his math skills are very advanced," I said. "The irony is that the Arab Muslims thought the Jews were illiterate because they didn't use the Farsi alphabet!"

Together the three of us visited many tourist attractions in the city of Esfahan: the famous mosques, the ancient bazaar, and the beautiful bridges. That night we returned to our relatives' house. Before we fell asleep, Mousa and I reflected on the difficulties of Jewish life in previous generations.

Isaac (left) and Mousa at the Jewish school in Jewbar'eh, in Esfahan's Jewish Ghetto.

Before my grandfather Elyahu's time, life in the ghetto was terrible due to the awful living conditions and the restrictions that were imposed by Muslims. Most Jews were extremely poor and very limited in their vocations: They were not usually allowed to work outside the ghetto; they were forbidden to work with food or food products, meaning they could not be involved in agriculture or the grocery business. Jews had to make their living at something that didn't require education, such as shoe repair, cleaning the streets and septic tanks, peddling goods door-to-door, and anything involved with thread or fabric, such as a tailor or fabric salesman. During that time there were bakeries and butcher shops opening in the Jewish ghetto of Esfahan that dealt with only a Jewish clientele. Jewish women, especially widows, cooked inexpensive meals (such as lentil soup or bean and barley soup) in huge pots and they sold bowls of soup on the street. Women who had sewing skills made beautiful *tallit* cases and other religious items, using silver thread and expensive fabrics. There were other small businesses making thread out of wool, and then weaving the thread into fabric. It seemed as if everyone became involved in the struggle to make a better living for themselves and their families.

For many years, Jewish peddlers had a very limited territory for their business because they weren't allowed to own a donkey. Then, around the time my grandfather was born, restrictions were relaxed a little and Jews were allowed to own a donkey. Three or four Jews joined together and bought a donkey so they could go from village to village to sell things. They could cover a wider territory than they could on foot, and they would be away from home for a longer period of time.

My grandfather Elyahu and three other friends, Metat, Shmuel A., and Dychi B. shared a donkey. They sold fabric to several villages, including the hamlets of Kirkband, Nijeer, and Mobarakeh. This is how they traveled: The first day they would leave Esfahan and travel about 30 km southeast to the small village of Linjan; there they passed the night near the shrine of Serach Bat Asher, where there were places to sleep out of the weather, with fresh spring water to drink. The second day they traveled from sunrise to sundown, finally arriving at Mobarakeh. Sometimes they remained in Mobarakeh for several days and returned home for *Shabbat*, but most of the time the four partners rented a room in a Muslim farmer's outbuilding and remained for months at a time, finally returning home to Esfahan to purchase more fabric. The men brought chickens, eggs, yogurt and cheese to their wives, celebrated *Shabbat* or some other holiday, and returned to life on the road. As they prospered they purchased more donkeys, until each partner owned one.

My grandfather's donkey, the family's most valuable asset, became the center of attention. During the winter, especially when snow covered the entire yard, Baba Joon (as grandfather was affectionately called) would bring the donkey into the rented room that served as home for his wife and six children. Baba Joon didn't want the donkey to catch cold, but the room was extremely small for eight people and a large animal! On cold winter nights when the front door was shut, fresh air became a rare commodity. During the night, without fail, the donkey would release a blast of gas into the already-malodorous air. And every night the donkey would let loose a stream of warm urine onto the stone floor, which would splash onto the faces of the sleeping family.

Mousa and I listened with wide-eyed fascination to our relatives' stories about Jewish life in Esfahan in "the old days."

The next morning, Mousa and I traveled by bus on a very bumpy, unpaved road to the village of Linjan to visit the Jewish cemetery, known as Pir Bakran. I vaguely remembered visiting the cemetery with my father and his father when I was five years old. I recalled that my grandfather proudly led us among the graves, pointing out the resting places of many, many ancestors going back at least seven generations—finding the graves of even earlier relatives was almost impossible, though Grandfather knew such graves existed somewhere on the cemetery grounds. "Our family has been in this country for 2,500 years!" he exclaimed with pride. "And this cemetery has been here for at least 2,000 years."

This ancient Jewish cemetery is situated in front of the mausoleum of Muhammed ibn Bakran, and contains tombs inscribed from the second century CE. Mousa and I walked over stony, dry, hard-packed earth. There were tufts of scrubby grass here and there in small patches, scattered among the thousands of stone grave markers. The carved grave markers were made of large, flat slabs of stone lying horizontally on the ground; some of them were nearly flush with the earth, partially covered with dirt, while others lay on top of the ground, revealing their entire two to three-foot thickness. There was a special section for foreign Jews, and I could see hundreds of stones bordered with carved flowers and elaborate work, inscribed in Hebrew as well as English, Italian, German and Dutch—some dating back hundreds of years.

In days gone by, Pir Bakran was considered a place of asylum for the Esfahani Jews during the Persian version of pogroms. It used to take a week by horse and wagon in the winter to reach the cemetery for burial. At one time the cemetery contained huge buildings where whole families would stay for major holidays or at the *sal* (*yahrzeit*), the annual observance of a family member's death. These large structures were like *caravansaries*, temporary dwellings for people and their animals.

Mousa and I looked for the tomb of Serach Bat Asher, the daughter of Asher and granddaughter of Jacob, the Patriarch. She had arrived in Esfahan with the exiled Jews from the tribe of Judah over 2,500 years ago. Many Jews make a pilgrimage to her tomb in Kookooloo, an area near the cemetery. We entered the courtyard of a small synagogue. A dog was asleep at the base of a mud brick wall. There were two large, empty oil drums lying on their sides near the dog. Here and there we saw some shrubs and a few unhealthy looking trees. We entered a dark, narrow, tunnel-like corridor and found ourselves in cave-like room with windows high up, near the roof. Stone ledges were built into both sides of the walls to accommodate the burning of memorial candles. Mousa and I lit candles and chanted a Hebrew prayer for the dead.

Mousa and Isaac visit Kookooloo, a site frequented by Jewish pilgrims. Photo taken near Serach Bat Asher site near Esfahan, 1966.

Entrance to the tomb of Serach Bat Asher, the grand-daughter of Jacob, a holy site for Jewish pilgrims. Isaac (left) and Mousa. Spring 1966.

Mousa and Isaac inside the elaborate "Mosque of Shah," today known as Masjed-e Imam. This huge, beautiful mosque is an architectural marvel; the perfect acoustics within the mosque enable hundreds of worshippers to clearly hear the prayer leader. Esfahan, Iran, 1966.

Isaac and Mousa visit Menar'eh Jomjom, the amazing towers (there are actually two towers) that sway, near Esfahan. Thousands of tourists visit these amazing towers annually. Spring 1966.

While on vacation in Esfahan, Isaac (left) and Mousa took a day trip to Shiraz and visited Persepolis. Spring 1966.

Isaac and Mousa visit Persepolis, also known as Takht-e Jamshid or Shehel Minar. It was the ceremonial capital of the Archaemenid Empire (ca. 550-330 BCE). To the ancient Persians, the city was known as Parsa, which means "The City of Persians." Persepolis portrayed the height of the Persian Empire (which was destroyed by Alexander the Great). Photo taken in Spring 1966.

Isaac (left) and Mousa touch the relief named after the mythical hero Rostam. Naghshe' Rostam, about ten kilometers northwest of Persepolis, is an archaeological site which dates to 1000 BCE It is the site of the tombs of Darius the Great (522-486 BCE), Khashayar I (reign 486-465 BCE), Ardeshir I (reign 465-424 BCE), and Darius II (reign 423-404 BCE). There is also an unfinished tomb that might belong to Ardehir III or Darius III (reign 336-330 BCE), and the cube of Zartosht (Zaratustra) that dates from the 5th century BCE. Spring1966.

My Father's Store
Malek Street, Near The Gates of Ghazvin
Tehran, Iran
Late Spring 1966

After ten years of dreaming about emigrating from Iran to Israel, my father finally decided to sell everything he owned and make the move. Mr. Habib [a different man than Hajj Habib in a previous story] was a client and dear friend of my father for twenty-five years. He came to our store to talk to my father about his decision to leave Iran. I happened to be in the store the day that Mr. Habib paid my father a visit.

"*Chakeretam*, I am your servant," said Mr. Habib as he entered our store. His face was red with anger and his voice trembled with emotion.

"*Ghorbanat beram,* may I be your sacrifice," politely replied my father.

"Ebrahim-the-Jew! I don't think it is right for you to take your family to the poor country of Israel. There is nothing there but trouble! I will do anything—even pay for your children's education—if you don't take them away from Iran to a country that can't provide them a prosperous future." What I witnessed next was very surprising: Mr. Habib reached into his pockets and pulled out a stack of documents.

"What's all this?" asked my father.

"These are my ownership papers for all the houses and lands that I own, my friend. Take these houses and these lands and use them! Use them to support your family, but please don't leave Iran to go to Israel!" Mr. Habib exclaimed.

"Habib, how can you make such an offer to one you call 'Ebrahim-the-Jew'?" my father retorted. "We have known each other for over twenty-five years, and you are better than a brother to me. During those many years we have eaten each other's bread and salt. Why must you call me "Ebrahim *Johood*"?

"*Mokhlesam*! But you know I have a deep respect for you, Ebrahim," answered Mr. Habib incredulously.

"An injury by tongue is worse than an injury by sword," insisted my father. "I realize that in Iran sometimes a Muslim and a Jew can become friends, but only in Israel will I have peace and security."

"I don't understand how you can leave the place of your birth and go to a foreign land." Mr. Habib shook his head in disbelief.

"It is true that my roots are here, in Iran, but the Jewish people also have deep roots in Israel," my father reminded Mr. Habib. "When I visited Israel in 1956, I saw farms, egg and chicken packing plants, vineyards and orchards—all owned and operated by Jews. I saw Jewish soldiers walking proudly in the streets, and the Israelis were not afraid of them. My heart was happy when my feet touched the soil of the Holy Land."

"But who will your children marry? Don't you want them to marry *Persian* Jews? And what about their schooling? You know that Iranian schools are the best!"

"What you say is true," admitted my father. "It was not easy for me to make this huge decision."

"So, you will not reconsider your decision?"

"No. The knife has reached the bone. I must leave Iran."

During the last weeks of my father's business prior to my family's emigration to Israel, I asked my father to hold a weeklong, high profile, "going out of business" sale. During the week of the sale, we sold more fabric than we had ever sold in ten months of regular business! Before the week was over, my father started to go to the bazaar to buy more fabric for his "going out of business" sale. The success was unexpected and overwhelming: Customers waited by our doors for us to open, and in the evenings we had to lock our doors to keep them from entering. My father began to understand the opportunities he had lost by not pursuing this sales practice much earlier. He realized, too late, some of the things he should have done to maximize his business.

For a few moments I thought I saw my father weaken in his resolve—but no, he could not endure the humiliation of changing his mind at that late date. Besides, the fabric shop was already sold and the family was in the process of packing to leave the country.

Mrs. Robab's House
Tehran, Iran
June 2, 1966

While my family was making preparations to leave Iran, I decided to visit the Robab family for what turned out to be my final visit with them. Several years before, they had sold their farm and moved to another house, a house as modest as the one I visited when I was a little boy. Hassan was the only son who was not yet married; all his older brothers had families of their own and worked in the local factories. Hassan was the only one who finished high school, and he planned to attend a technical school to become a mechanic. Mr. Robab had died a year or so before my visit, and Mrs. Robab was now very ill. I brought her a gift from my parents.

"Isaac Joon, my son! You have brought light into our home! What's this I hear about your father, that he is moving to Israel?" Mrs. Robab asked with great concern after hugging me. "I think your father is a very stubborn and headstrong man to think of leaving Iran," she admonished.

"His mind is made up," I shrugged.

"Here he has everything! A home, a store, money, uncles, cousins, and many friends! What is he going to do in a strange land? How will he support his sons and daughters and wife in a country where he does not even know the language? Who will marry his daughters, strangers? How can Ebrahim leave the country that has given him so much? He is ungrateful!" she cried.

I gave her a hug and told her that in Israel my family would not be called *Johood* or *Najes,* and that Israel was our Jewish homeland. "If I decide to follow my family to Israel, I will no longer be afraid of Muslims chasing me to beat me," I reminded her. "In Israel, I will be able to walk anywhere at any time, and no one will call me names. In Israel, there is no limit on what Jews can achieve—we can become lawyers, judges, anything we choose. In Israel, my brothers and sisters will replace humility with pride. We will walk with our heads up!"

"But you will miss Iran. You will become sick at heart," Mrs. Robab warned me.

"*If* I decide to go to Israel, I will certainly miss you and all my friends and neighbors. I will miss my neighborhood with all its shops and parks. I will miss Persian holidays and Persian music and art. But I have not yet made the decision to leave."

"You must not leave," she sobbed, hugging me again. "You must not leave Iran."

#24 Koocheh Sharaf, and around Tehran
Tehran, Iran
Throughout the Summer 1966

When my family left for Israel, I remained in Iran living in our home. The house had been sold, but was waiting for the "closing" and transfer to the new owners. So there I was, residing in a large seven-bedroom house. I supported myself by riding my motorbike to collect funds that hundreds of Muslim families still owed my father. His book of accounts receivable totaled almost $250,000!

I was very popular among my friends because I had a furnished house all to myself, with plenty of cash in my pocket. Also, I knew many of the owners of nightclubs, movie theatres, and restaurants. Being young and virile, I knew many middle-aged Muslim wives; their elderly husbands were businessmen, army officers and clergymen—

and were often out of town. Soon I became the confidant and lover of many of those women. Life was wonderful!

I threw many parties and my house became so popular that even distant acquaintances claimed to be my best friends. The parties often became so wild that my neighbors would complain, but my friends and I were young, healthy, proud, and happy! Many of us young men were waiting for the glory years of university to begin. Our multi-cultural group blossomed. My circle of friends included all those I knew from the Muslim elementary school, Kourosh (the private Jewish high school), the private night school, as well as many of my neighbors and family members. My parties were so famous that boys in other neighborhoods soon demanded to be invited.

My Muslim friends insisted to come with me on Friday nights to visit the clubs. Although there was no official age limit, the club owners made sure you had cash and didn't let young men get too drunk or sick. The southern part of Tehran, especially around my father's store, was the center of the opium and hashish trade. In this neighborhood one could easily purchase any amount of drugs. Young men of northern Tehran, especially students, would get their "hits" in the local restaurants after dinner, before visiting a prostitute.

During the day, when I wasn't collecting money from my father's former customers, I visited the popular library of the University of Tehran and attended various youth organizations to discuss politics, the economy—and share the dating stories that young people like to tell each other. Among these groups were *Ha'Khaloutz* and *Kouroshe Kabir*, both of which I attended to keep myself active with Jewish youth. I also took classes in the history of music. My circle of friends, however, increased exponentially and grew to include Baha'i, Zoroastrian, and Armenian people.

I was definitely living "the good life" during the spring and summer of 1966.

My Uncle Morad's House
Tehran, Iran
July 1966

At 7:00am one July morning, my friend David S. hurried to my Uncle Morad's home to wake me up. The entrance exams for the University of Tehran were going to be given that morning and we had to hurry—there was no time for washing or breakfast. David and I hopped on my motorcycle and headed for the university.

We were both accepted to the University of Tehran, Mechanical Engineering Department. I was also accepted to attend the newly established University of Ariamehr, Civil Engineering Department. I chose to attend the University of Tehran because it had a very large student body, which included my friend David, and was located very close to my house. During the orientation and the first week of classes I realized that my Muslim classmates were the same type of people as my former friends Akbar and Jalaal, and many of my father's customers: They were arrogant and tried to make me feel humiliated and inferior. I felt like "Isaac, son of Ebrahim the Jew." Even though radical Islamists were not the majority, they were certainly the most vocal.

There seemed to be no way to escape the fact that I was a second-class citizen in a country where my family had lived for 2,500 years.

Ab-e' Ali Resort
Alborz Mountains, 75km northeast of Tehran
Early August 1966

The "Four Friends"—David, Mousa, Bijan, and I—decided to take a trip to the Ab-e' Ali Ski Resort. Even though it was summer, the resort was a beautiful place to visit. The magnificent vistas of the majestic Damavand Mountains, the sight of snow on the high peaks, and the fresh, cool air made the visit exhilarating.

For this excursion we did not pack food and supplies, as we did

The trip to Abe-Ali, the last trip the four friends took together. Mousa (left to right), Bijan, and Isaac relax at a typical teahouse. (David took the photo, late summer 1966.)

on all our earlier outings. This time we had enough money to eat at the restaurants and teahouses at the resort. Unlike on previous trips, we were quiet and subdued. We knew in our hearts that a chapter of our lives was ending, and that this was likely our last outing together. Without really verbalizing it, we understood that now was the time to say goodbye to each other. As we hiked the mountain paths, we discussed our plans for the future.

"If I can avoid being drafted into the Iranian army, I want to go to California," Mousa declared.

"I'd like to go there, too," stated David, wistfully. "But I've already been accepted to the University of Tehran to study mechanical engineering. When I'm finished with my studies, I definitely plan on getting out of Iran."

"As for me, I've got one more year of high school to finish," sighed

Bijan. "Because mean old Mr. Azimi flunked me in Islamic studies back in Kourosh, I'm a year behind the rest of you guys. When I finish high school I'll probably have to serve in the army—then I'll go to the U.S. for college studies."

"I've already been accepted to the University of Tehran," I said quietly. "Normally I would be celebrating about that, but I'm not sure I really want to stay in Iran."

"What would you like to do instead, Isaac? I know you've been active in Zionist youth groups," offered Bijan.

"I'd like to go to Israel, I think," I confessed to my friends. "Maybe I could live on a kibbutz, where everyone is equal. I want to spend time with beautiful, young Israeli women who let their long hair flow in the wind and wear shirts that bare their arms and show the shape of their breasts. I also want to study to become an engineer. I am restless here. In my heart, I feel that I must leave Iran."

We made no judgments of each other's decisions. We all knew that our lives were about to change and that each of us was about to embark upon a different path.

"Let's not be sad," insisted Mousa. "Here's to our future! May we all be together somewhere again, in the future!"

My Great-Uncle Asher Nejat's House
Tehran, Iran
Late August 1966

Since my immediate family no longer lived in Iran, it was expected that I spend Friday nights and Saturdays with my uncles and their families. One Friday night I met the Israeli representative to Iran, Mr. Manoucher Omidvar, at my great-uncle Asher Nejat's house. During *Shabbat* dinner, Mr. Omidvar found out I was the best student in my region and was accepted to attend the University of Tehran. He also learned that my parents and all of my siblings, except Ruben, were in Israel. Mr. Omidvar vehemently stated that it was ridiculous for me to remain in Iran.

Mr. Omidvar and my uncle talked to me till late at night. They told me about Technion, one of the best engineering universities in the world, where Albert Einstein had been offered the presidency. Many famous, world-class scientists were teaching there. I expressed my concern about leaving my country to study engineering in a language I did not know, with little money and no job. "Don't worry about any of that. You must go to the Technion Institute!" Mr. Omidvar declared. "I will work out the details," he assured me.

I was told to take copies of all my school records to the Jewish Agency, where Mr. Omidvar worked. After a thorough review of my records, it took Mr. Omidvar less than five minutes to tell me that I *must* go to the Technion Institute, and that the Jewish Agency would make all the arrangements. He said I would be provided with Hebrew translations of all my documents, a passport, and a one-way El Al plane ticket to Tel Aviv.

I was given one week to get ready to leave the country! I spent the night thinking about whom I should tell of my departure. I had insufficient time to visit with many of my Kourosh friends, to inform them of my decision. I did not even inform Tehran University—or my father's customers who still owed him many thousands of dollars—that I was planning to leave the country very soon.

What should I do first? What should I pack? I tried not to think too much about my Muslim friends (including the Muslim women whose secrets I kept) who I might never see again. How would I remember the narrow streets, the crowded bazaar, the shopkeepers, and all those who inhabited my past? *How could I take the beauty of Tehran with me?*

The next morning I decided it was time to inform my relatives of my impending departure. I decided to make a list of items to be packed. I selected books that I knew I would need and those I simply could not leave behind: books of history, philosophy, Persian art and Persian poetry. Next I carefully packed my violin and music books, Persian art works, a photo album, my stamp collection, and numerous record albums. Later that day, I purchased a beautiful, hand embroidered *tallit* case and *kippah* from some Jewish ladies in the Tehran ghetto.

My next stop was the home of my Uncle Morad, who lived on Koocheh Ensaf, off of Sheikh Hadi Street. After I gave my familiar whistle, my young cousin Albert opened the door. My uncle, my aunt Pouran, and my three cousins were in a state of shock when I told them about my plan to leave Iran and study in Israel. Uncle Morad reminded me that I had always claimed to be an Iranian first, and Jewish second. He admonished me to remember that attending the Civil Engineering Department of the Tehran University was my dream.

"You have so many friends here in Iran, and they all love you!" Uncle Morad declared.

"When you become an engineer, any Jewish father in Tehran would love to have you marry their daughter!" insisted Aunt Pouran. "How can you leave the comfort you have here? *You are chasing after a mirage!* You are leaving your ancestral home and all those who are buried in the Jewish cemetery. You are leaving the culture and customs you cherish!" she cried.

"Isaac, you don't understand Hebrew as a spoken language. It will take years before you will be proficient enough in Hebrew to enter an Israeli university," my Uncle Morad warned.

"But I never will be an equal here," I protested. "I must search for true liberty and equality. I need to live where there is nothing to inhibit me from the best opportunities. Besides, I will be joining my family."

When my uncle and aunt realized that my mind was made up, they hugged and kissed me. I promised my motorcycle to my cousin Albert, who always asked me for rides. He knew how to take care of the bike.

After I left Uncle Morad's home, I decided to visit my Great-Aunt Eshrat Khanom. My aunt, my six cousins, and I had a discussion similar to the one that had just taken place at my uncle's house. I finally convinced everyone that I would be much happier in Israel.

"You have several Persian rugs of your own, don't you? It will be difficult to pack all the rugs, Isaac Joon. You should go to Mr. Yashar's rug store on Ferdowsi Street to exchange your rugs for one special rug to take with you. Yashar is the most trusted rug dealer," advised my great-aunt.

I took my aunt's advice and tied my Saroogh and Naein Persian rugs to the back of my motorbike and headed to Mr. Yashar's store, where I exchanged them for the most beautiful silk and wool rug I had ever seen: It had a dark blue background and multi-colored designs in the center and the corners. A famous Esfahani designer had signed the 3' x 6' rug. Then and there I made a promise to myself that I would keep the rug forever as a reminder that someday I will return to Iran, my home—and kiss the ground and breathe the air once more!

On my way home from Yashar's rug store, I decided to visit Hassan, the son of Hajj Ashi. Hassan worked for his father in a store that was close to my father's store, near Darvazeh Ghazvin. Hassan and his brother Fazlollah joined us Kourosh boys on our trips to Damavand and the Caspian Sea. Over the years, Hassan and I had spent many Thursday nights together enjoying salami sandwiches and beer, while discussing our weekly struggles. We always shared our failures and successes with girls and women—the drama and excitement of being young, healthy men.

When I arrived at his father's store, it was lunchtime. Hassan rushed to welcome me and invited me to the *kababi* place next door. I gladly accepted his invitation. We ordered our lunch: *chello kabab* with *doogh*, plates of *sabzi*, warm *sangak*, and our usual Majid beer. The loudspeaker of the mosque across from my father's store broadcast the call to noon prayer, drowning out the noise of the heavy traffic. I deeply inhaled the thick BBQ smoke that hung in the air, trying desperately to imprint the smell of it into my memory.

After our normal chitchat, I told Hassan about my decision to leave Iran. He could not believe his ears. With wide-open eyes, he yelled, "Where can you have a better life? Here we have peace, a good economy. You have been accepted into the best university, in the best academic field—and you are just starting to date the most gorgeous girls! What more do you want?" He stopped for a moment to catch his breath, and then continued to harangue me. "In Israel there is always war. You have no idea what is going on there! You don't know the language and you will never be an Israeli. *You will always be Iranian!*"

"I will take my chances. May the chips fall where they fall," I responded. "How many Muslims would eat lunch with me and would respect me as I respect them?" I asked. "Your parents still call me Isaac-the-Jew," I reminded Hassan.

"Big deal! So what if you are called a Jew? After all, you are a Jew, so what's the big deal? The most important thing to remember is that here in Iran we protect all minorities, including Jews."

"How dare you continue to call Jews a minority! Your people come from Rezaiyeh and have Turkish roots. I am more Iranian than you!" I replied.

"Isaac, we should not argue with each other this day," he said quietly. He smiled and shook my hand, whispering, "I guess birds of the same flock have to fly together: pigeons with pigeons and eagles with eagles. We had many great times together and we will always share many fond memories."

"May our friendship remain strong and flourish in the future," I responded with sadness.

Late in the evening, I met with my friends at *Ha'Khaloutz*, the Jewish Zionist Youth Club, and we all celebrated my decision to move to Israel. It had become a ritual to celebrate the departures of Iranian Jewish youths, and sometimes the festivities would last until late at night. The club leader, an Israeli representative named Mr. Hanasab, would make a short speech on each of those occasions, emphasizing how important it was for young Jews to emigrate to Israel, and he stressed the opportunities waiting for them there. In my case, he explained how wonderful was the *kibbutz* of my choice, Gan Shmuel. My *kibbutz* was located near Hedera, a small city about forty miles north of Tel Aviv. We all knew about the social life on a *kibbutz* and how great it was for young people: There was a mixing of boys and girls in the activities of daily life, unlike in Iran. As if that weren't enough, on the *kibbutz* there was no need for money and no daily worries. It sounded like heaven!

The next day I decided to visit as many of my father's customers as possible, in order to collect money for the last time. Some customers expected to see me, but many more were surprised to see me at their homes on a day that was not their usual collection day. All the customers, with no exception, said they were sad to see me go. Some were angry with my father, who had already left, and some resented the fact that Iran was losing its brightest youth to Israel.

Most of them would ask me, "After all this country has given you and your family—air, water, bread, schooling—how can you desert us for a country that has nothing to give you but poverty and war?" Others offered to assist me if I would stay in Iran and complete my studies; they truly acted like members of my family.

I felt compelled to visit the Khaleghi family in southeastern Tehran. Mr. Khaleghi, very well educated, was extremely wealthy. He owned several farms and small villages and had real estate holdings all over Iran. Mr. Khaleghi had been my father's very first customer, and rumor had it that Khaleghi's wife had been in love with my father before her marriage.

Mr. Khaleghi was a seventy-five year old man, but still an imposing six feet in height. He had gray hair and a pleasant face. He had been a high-ranking officer in the army and was now retired. His wife, also very tall, was from a very wealthy Azerbaijani family. She was a friendly, plump woman with a round face and large brown eyes, and was at least twenty years younger than her husband. The Khaleghis were very modern people, very liberal in their thinking.

The Khaleghis had been my father's best customers. They bought fabric for all their workers almost weekly. They had one child, a daughter named Maryam, who studied music and played the piano. She was two years younger than me. My siblings and I used to play with Maryam during our summer visits to one of the villages her father owned east of Tehran. I used to play chess with Mr. Khalghi and, before each game, I made sure his waterpipe was properly prepared with his favorite tobacco. Mrs. Khaleghi had a special affection for me, and Mr. Khaleghi always called me "son," never "Isaac-the-Jew."

When I told them I was leaving Iran, they were horrified.

"How can I entice you to stay?" asked Mr. Khaleghi.

"Perhaps he would consider marrying our daughter Maryam?" suggested Mrs. Khaleghi to her husband. "After all, they have known each other all their lives and have always been good friends."

Her offer took me by complete surprise. Perhaps she was still thinking about her love for my father and decided that her daughter should marry one of his sons. Or perhaps it was just a case of Persian *ta'aroff,* Persian flattery. At any rate, Maryam was only fifteen years old, in the ninth grade at school. Certainly, I thought to myself, the Khaleghis were much too modern to marry off their daughter at such a young age!

"An excellent idea!" exclaimed Mr. Khaleghi. "You can stay with us and supervise our farms while attending Tehran University. We have always needed a son! You can be the son we never had."

I still thought their offer was *ta'aroff,* a form of exaggerated praise and a sign of their respect for me, rather than a serious offer, but who knows? Mr. and Mrs. Khaleghi might have been serious because they had always honored and respected Jews. They knew that Jews were trustworthy, had a strong work ethic, and treated their wives very well. They also knew that I had many Muslim friends and had recited the Muslim prayers for conversion to Islam in school many times—therefore I was *almost* a Muslim in their eyes. It is possible that they would have accepted me as an equal.

In spite of their offer, the Khaleghis could not change my mind.

My flight was scheduled for Thursday morning at 10:30am. By Wednesday, I was packed and ready. My friends kept dropping by my uncle's home to leave me gifts. David S. brought me a yellow and black tie, and Bijan brought me several pairs of men's black nylon socks. Many others wrote me lovely cards, wishing me the best. Manni R., my music classmate from Kourosh, brought me several record albums and books.

I was troubled that there still remained some of my father's debts I had not collected. "What shall I do about the money still owed us?" I asked Uncle Asher.

"It's gone! Forget it! It died on the birth!" he advised me with a shrug. "Don't worry about it, for God gives and God takes!"

Late Wednesday afternoon I went to a *sarraaf,* a Jewish money-exchanger, at the bazaar. I brought all the money I had accumulated by selling most of my father's fabric and other personal assets. I wanted to convert *rials* into dollars and knew that I would receive a fair rate of exchange, without having to disclose my transaction to any officials. The *sarraaf* were very discreet, very efficient, and very honest.

Wednesday night became the longest night of my life. As I lay in my bed in the empty house in which I was born, my mind was flooded with memories and scenes from my childhood: The comfort and warmth of my home on Koocheh Sharaf with the continuous noise of seven children; the sound of my mother's calm voice inviting us to come and have our meals; the wonderful aromas of rice, saffron, chicken soup, fresh ripe fruit, and so much more delicious food. I recalled the Friday nights, the holidays, and the times when all my relatives visited us and I happily played with my many cousins.

Of course, I thought about my friends in the neighborhood—Ali, Soli, Younai, Jalaal, Akbar, Maseod—and many others. How many times I gave rides to my friends on my green tricycle! How many times we quarrelled over silly disagreements!

I closed my eyes and remembered the heavenly fragrance of cherry trees blossoming in the spring. I sighed when I thought about the hot summer nights when the entire neighborhood slept on the rooftops. As I finally fell asleep, I thought I could hear the beautiful sound of *golha,* traditional Persian music, carried along on the night breeze.

Early Thursday morning, I called a cab and picked up my suitcases and packages from my Uncle Asher's house. The next stop was Mehrabad Airport. I was very sad, but content. It was not until I entered the plane and took my seat by the window, that I suddenly felt alone. When the plane took off I experienced both deep pangs of sorrow and great excitement. As my homeland disappeared beneath me, I struggled to think of a prayer that would be fitting for this momentous occasion. Tears filled my eyes as I pictured the Land of Milk and Honey, the land promised to me by God, to which I was now heading. I began to whisper the familiar prayer, *She'Hekyanu*: Praised are You, Lord our God, King of the Universe, for granting me life, for sustaining me and *for helping me to reach this day*!

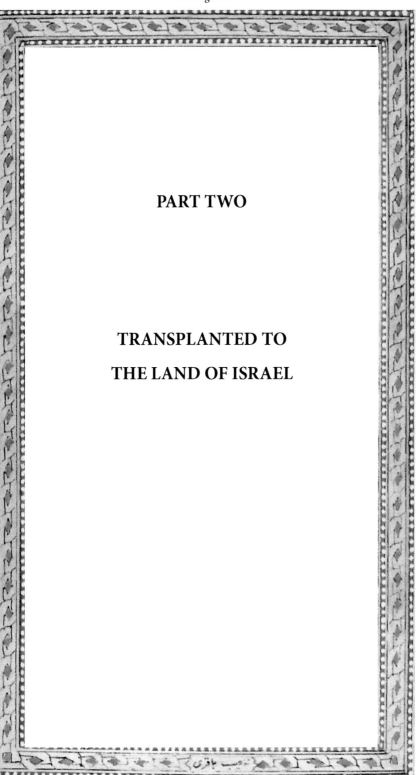

PART TWO

TRANSPLANTED TO
THE LAND OF ISRAEL

I will bring your children from the east and gather you from the west...Bring my sons from afar and my daughters from the ends of the earth...

—*Isaiah 43:5*

I will bring them out from the nations and gather them from the countries, and I will bring them into their own land. I will pasture them on the mountains of Israel, in the ravines and in all the settlements in the land.

—*Ezekiel 34:13*

Kibbutz Gan Shmuel
Near the town of Hadera, Israel
September 1966—Spring 1967

In 1966, when I arrived in Israel, I had no idea about the status of Persian Jews living there. It took only a short time to discover that *Parsim*, Persians, were considered lower class citizens because we possessed little knowledge of European culture. There were only a few Persian students in Israeli universities, and there were very few Persian doctors, engineers, lawyers, politicians, military officers, teachers and *rabbis*.

Most educated and wealthy Iranian Jews chose to emigrate to Europe or America; those Iranian Jews who went to Israel were from the lower economic level and tended to have very little education. Unfortunately, the Israeli government had no plans or programs in place to encourage or empower the new Iranian immigrants to enter into the universities or the highly skilled jobs. Indeed, the Israeli system encouraged the new immigrants to quickly enter technical schools and begin working in factories and farms. The older generation of Iranian Jews continued their practice of entrepreneurship in Israel and became independent shopkeepers and small business owners. The younger generation followed the path of least resistance and attended technical schools, and then entered the labor force. A small number of Iranian immigrants chose to live in *kibbutzim* or *moshavim* and work in agriculture.

My parents were living in the city of Netanya, not far from Tel Aviv. My father knew only how to be a shopkeeper, so he opened a store and sold pots, pans, and other household goods. When I arrived in Israel, the country was in the grips of a severe recession. My father's business was not doing well, so my mother had to get a job for the first time in her life. She found work in the 778 Jelly Factory, a plant that made kosher jelly.

I reported to Kibbutz Gan Shmuel, near the town of Hadera. Immediately I became aware of an enormous "culture clash": When I reported to my bedroom, I found out that I was supposed to share it with a woman! I was so confused and agitated that I didn't sleep that night. The next day I was given a male roommate. Because I was used to the behavior of reserved Iranian women, I was amazed that women on the *kibbutz* greeted men with a hug and a kiss. I couldn't get over the fact that men and women were allowed to dance together.

In the beginning, I loved *kibbutz* life. I was learning Hebrew as a spoken and written language. I was meeting Jews from every Eastern European country, also Greece, Egypt, Turkey, and South America. There was one immigrant from the U.S. and several gorgeous women from Scandinavia who volunteered to work on the *kibbutz* for one month. I realized that European Jews typically spoke their minds, while Jews from the Middle East were much more quiet and reserved.

Isaac in his work clothes, Gan Shmuel Kibbutz, near Hadera, Israel.

I enjoyed the work on the *kibbutz* because there was always something different to do. I worked picking and packing olives, apples and avocados. I packed chickens for transport and milked cows. My least favorite job was killing weak chicks by twisting their necks; the kibbutz couldn't afford to feed chicks that most likely would not survive. My favorite job—and one in which I rose to a managerial position—was collecting the garbage! I enjoyed collecting the trash because it involved riding a large, imposing tractor. Eventually I became a supervisor in charge of assigning jobs to other people, making sure to rotate everyone from job to job. The girls on the *kibbutz* begged to be assigned the task of scrubbing the toilets and showers because those chores took little time to complete and the girls could relax the rest of the day.

I arrived in Israel an ardent Zionist, but gradually my feelings began to change. Little by little I grew to dislike the socialist mentality of the *kibbutz*. We could not choose the films that were shown; we were given free cigarettes, but no pocket money; there was one car for the use of all members of the *kibbutz* and it took months of being on the waiting list before anyone could borrow the car. I also came to despise the long list of restrictions, which included limited hours for swimming at the pool. I became very disenchanted. I left Gan Shmuel in the spring and headed for Technion to take a special course designed to prepare me for the entrance exams.

Technion Israel Institute of Technology
Haifa, Israel
Early Spring 1967

Isaac's Identification Card for Israel's Technion University, Institute of Technology, Department of Civil Engineering

When I entered the Israel Technion Institute of Technology, Iranian students made up less than 1% of the student body. Discrimination against non-Europeans was a common aspect of life.

I met Yosef Eimani in the fall of 1967, in a special dormitory called *Maonot Shderot Um* (the English translation: "dormitory on United Nations Boulevard"), for foreign students. He was a quiet, bashful, kind Iranian from a small town—and he was very smart. He and I were among about forty pre-college students housed together in one dormitory on United Nations Boulevard. We were all trying to learn to read and write Hebrew proficiently so that we could eventually take the entrance exams and begin classes in our chosen field of study. Many nationalities were represented at Shderot Um, including Iran, Turkey, Greece, Morocco, Egypt, Libya, Tunisia, Iraq, France, the United States, South Africa, Russia, and Romania. Two students were assigned to each 10x15 room; each room contained two beds, a sink, and a closet. All tenants of the dormitory shared the kitchen, showers, and bathrooms.

Yosef and I were very poor and we struggled to cover the cost of our living expenses and still have money to buy food. He and I studied constantly so that we could enter a Technion degree program and reach our goals. I realized that I was very lucky to have him as my friend during a difficult time in my life.

Kibbutz Sha'ar Ha'Golan
Jordan Valley, at the foot of the Golan Heights
Mid-May through the end of Summer 1967

It became apparent that a war was imminent. A busload of young men from the Shderot Um dormitory volunteered to go to Kibbutz Sha'ar Ha'Golan; Yosef Eimani and I were among them. First we all donated blood, and then we traveled northeast to a location near Lake Tiberias, in the valley between Jordan and Syria, called the "Gate to Golan." Only fifteen of us made it to Kibbutz Sha'ar Ha'Golan—the other fifty men had been dropped off at other locations along the way. We were all excited to be part of major defense activities against the millions of enemies! Amazingly, we had no fear and were anxious to receive the necessary training that would enable us to enter the war.

Upon our arrival, we were given uniforms and guns with no bullets. The next day at 4:00am we were ready to get our assignments.

"Here is your daily schedule!" a young female sergeant yelled. "Starting at 4:30am, you will dig tunnels. At 7:30am, you will quickly eat your breakfast, and then serve breakfast to all the soldiers and other members of the *kibbutz*; you will then clean up the dining room and put all the dishes in the main dishwasher. At 8:30am, the dining room will be closed, and shortly after all the guests have gone, you will wash all the floors and organize the kitchen and dining room. At 9:30am, you will feed the cows, and all the other animals; you will then feed the chickens and collect all the eggs. At 11:00am, you will resume digging the tunnels. At noon you will help serve lunch and complete all clean up tasks by 2:30pm." She stopped talking for a moment and glanced at us over her clipboard.

"At 2:30 sharp, my assistant and I will meet you for two hours of training, which will include target practice," she continued. "At 4:30pm, you will drive yourselves to the banana, apple, and avocado orchards to collect all the fruit you can. At 7:30pm, you will assist in serving dinner and complete all clean up tasks by 9:00pm, and then you will assist milking the cows and cleaning all the animal stalls. You should be done with all your chores by 10:00pm. You will dig tunnels from 10:00pm until 11:30pm, at which time you may retire." She sternly surveyed all of us with piercing eyes. "Any questions?"

It took us two days to figure out that our volunteer job did not include any actual war activity. There would be no fighting for us. We were there to take care of the *kibbutz* members and make sure the tunnels were ready for use by the soldiers and members of the *kibbutz*. We had no time to read, write letters, hang out, listen to music, or take long showers. We noticed that all of the *kibbutz's* men between the ages of seventeen and fifty-five were in the army, somewhere else.

One week into our stay, all of our training was cancelled because they needed us for other tasks. We were assigned to listen to small transistor radios to keep up on the hourly news reports. As we listened to the rhetoric and propaganda coming from the Arab news broadcasts, we realized that Israel was threatened by nearly all the Arab countries, including Egypt, Saudi Arabia, Jordan, Syria, Lebanon, and Iraq. Egypt declared that all the Jews in Palestine would be pushed into the sea. Syria announced that from the Golan Heights they would be able to shoot at every Jew as far as Tel Aviv. Nasser, the President of Egypt, closed the port city of Sharma el-Sheikh to Israeli ships; this cut Israel off from the Red Sea.

We listened to reports of the neighboring Arab countries placing their armed forces on alert; they were readying themselves for a very long war. We were so busy with our volunteer work that we had no time to think. Because our Hebrew was not fluent, and we were new immigrants, the members of the *kibbutz* and the soldiers ignored us.

On Saturdays, we were allowed to rest from digging tunnels. We found time to discuss the political and military situation with each other and some of the elders of the *kibbutz*. We had no phones and no way to call our families. During this time of great uncertainty, Yosef and I became very good friends. We discussed politics and our religious beliefs. The entire country exhibited—justifiably—a "bunker mentality," and there was fear in the air. We all knew that a war was imminent.

I think it was during the night of June 5th that we first heard the sound of bombs exploding. We were all sleeping in underground bunkers when we were awakened by the sensation of our beds shaking. The bombs fell all night, several minutes apart. The lights in the bunker flickered and we could hear the terrible noise outside. No one talked.

Finally, I climbed down from my upper bunk and sat next to Yosef on the bed below. "Here we go, this is a war and we are in it," I whispered.

"Maybe they will finally let us do some real war work now. We can help," Yosef responded in a quiet voice.

Soon all the guys in the bunker gathered around Yosef and me. No one doubted that Israel would be victorious, but we all had opinions about the length of the war: Everyone figured the war would last six months, maybe a year. We decided that we might as well get along with each other, accept the fact that our college plans were delayed, and resign ourselves to the fact that there were no eligible women around—they were all in the regular army.

We waited eagerly for the dawn. As the sky became light and the smoke from the bombs cleared, we came out of the bunker, one by one. After a quick look at the outside world, we entered the tunnel system that we had dug all over the *kibbutz.* These tunnels connected all the buildings and bunkers to each other. We had no plans to take a shower, shave, or even eat. We waited, anxiously, for our orders.

Around 6:30am, our female sergeant called all of us to meet her in a bunker way in the back of the *kibbutz.* When we arrived at her bunker, we found it was air-conditioned and well stocked with food, water, and several refrigerators. There was also a great variety of radios and communication equipment.

"We are at war," she declared tersely. "Your first obligation is to stay alive. You must wear your uniform, helmet, and boots at all times. You must stay with your group at all times. You are still required to do kitchen chores, but no one will be eating in the dining room; you will deliver food to *kibbutz* members in the bunkers. You must still feed the animals and milk the cows, but the fruit on the trees will have to wait. Also, when supplies arrive, you will assist the *kibbutz* members and place supplies in the kitchen and/or the bunkers. I must remind you that no one is allowed to take photos, or use any shiny or reflective material, such as mirrors or binoculars. Now let's go to the kitchen and start our day!" she ordered in an authoritative voice.

When we arrived in the kitchen, we found that hundreds of boxes had been delivered: water, fruit, vegetables, and other food items. Our job was to organize and store everything. The cooks began preparing breakfast as we volunteers began to reorganize the dining room. All of us worked at a feverish pace, ignoring the bombs falling nearby.

Within an hour, everyone had eaten breakfast—children first—and the kitchen was cleaned up. All the *kibbutz* adults helped us take care of the animals, which was a first. We returned to the kitchen at 12:30 to prepare lunch and found many more boxes had been unloaded; these were gift boxes that Israelis had shipped to us for the soldiers. We tried to sort and store all of the donated items: cigarettes, candy, gum, cakes, socks, underwear, sun glasses, magazines, music tapes, comic books, newspapers, T-shirts, prayer books, stationary, aftershave, playing cards, etc. There were so many gifts that we didn't know what to do with them all! I must confess that we gained many pounds because of the delicious treats piled everywhere.

For three days the bombs that fell on the *kibbutz* caused no damage. On the fourth day, however, a bomb hit the dining room and damaged two of the walls. Fortunately, no one was in the dining room at the time. Later that day, a bomb fell in the banana field causing a major fire. The volunteers were assigned to put out the fire while the *kibbutz* members fixed the damage in the dining hall. The *kibbutzniks* were no longer arrogant towards us volunteers from Technion. We were treated like family. Everyone was focused on the tasks at hand.

The night of the fourth day of war, we gathered in our bunker, exhausted, but unable to sleep. We exchanged ideas about our work for the next day as bombs continued to fall outside. The sounds of explosions and the smell of smoke became our new reality, and we learned to ignore them. We had no idea that Israeli forces had destroyed the entire Arab air force during the first six hours of the war. We did not know that the Egyptian army had already surrendered.

Listening to the radio on the fifth day of the war, we heard the heavenly song, *Jerusalem of Gold*, by Naomi Shemer. A new Israeli song, *Sharm A-Sheikh* kept playing over and over, commemorating the recent capture of Sharam el-Sheikh, which is situated on the southern tip of the Sinai Peninsula. We also listened to the sound of the *shofar* being blown at the Wailing Wall, as an announcer shouted with great excitement, "Here comes General Moishe Dayan and his officers! Here come Israeli soldiers! They are all walking towards the Sacred Wall!"

We could not believe our ears! The music and announcements on the radio sent chills through our bodies. How was it possible that the tiny Israeli army had prevailed over the Arabs in only five days? King David was alive and Goliath was dead! Jerusalem was in our hands once more, and Jews were once again at the wall of the Temple. Tears of great joy flowed uncontrollably down our cheeks and we were too excited to sleep that night.

Early on the morning of the sixth day, a steady parade of tanks, heavy artillery, trucks, and hundreds of soldiers made its way through the *kibbutz*. The men, weapons, and supplies were headed for the fighting in the Golan Heights. We were ordered to go about our work and not stop to gawk, but it was very difficult to prepare breakfast with all the soldiers marching through.

No one was really interested in eating breakfast, so we joined the *kibbutzniks* outside, shouting encouragement to the soldiers and patting them on the back. Even the most non-religious members of the *kibbutz* offered blessings as the soldiers passed by. It was as if we were no longer Orthodox, Conservative or Reform Jews; it didn't matter whether we were immigrants, volunteers, soldiers, civilians, young or old: We were all one family and we cared deeply about each other. We all wanted to live in peace. Our generals and leaders hated the fact that Israel was forced to kill so many young men on the opposing side. I remember a speech in which Golda Meir said, "We can forgive them for killing our young men, but we cannot forgive them for forcing us to kill theirs."

As the sun rose, we could see a huge black cloud of smoke covering the entire Golan Heights. The bombs began falling like rain and we had no choice but to seek shelter in the bunkers. While we waited below ground, we wished that we were soldiers on the field of battle. We felt cheated. Our hearts pounded and we suffered in the intense heat of the day, but we knew the war would soon end. Yosef and I hunkered down and nodded knowingly at each other. What could we do? This was war.

Isaac (standing in rear, wearing white hat) with a crew of surveyors, taken in the Golan Heights after the '67 War. Walking only twenty feet ahead of Isaac, one of his fellow crewmen (the man standing in front, second from right) stepped on a mine that blew off one of his legs. (Notice bullet holes in the building.)

Technion Israel Institute of Technology
Haifa, Israel
Early Autumn 1967

Yosef and I both took the entrance exam and were accepted to pursue our studies at Technion. My chosen field was civil engineering. I spent all my time studying and working partime jobs; I was not offered any financial counseling and had no idea about scholarships or loans. Eventually, I applied for scholarships and found out that the Ashkenazi (Eastern European Jews) students had obtained all the available funds. The fact that no scholarships were made available to Persian Jews was a form of discrimination.

Isaac in front of his dorm at Technion. Photo was taken by his Nigerian roommate. Students from many developing countries received scholarships to be trained as engineers.

Four years later, after Yosef and I completed our degrees, we faced great difficulty finding jobs. I understood clearly that Persian Jews were looked down on: I was called *Parsi*, a derogatory epithet for a Persian. I became fed up with the subtle and not-so-subtle forms of discrimination. I had had enough of being a second-class citizen in Iran! I wrote to my brother Ruben and described my unhappiness. "Come to the United States," he advised me. That sounded like a wonderful idea, though it took several more years for me to get there.

Dior Le'Oleh
Netanya, Israel
November 1968

In November of 1968, I came down with a bad case of the flu and had to leave Technion and go home to Netanya. My parents lived in the Dior Le'Oleh neighborhood, a community of new immigrants in the southern part of Netanya. My family lived in a two-bedroom row house, next to immigrants from Turkey, Morocco, Libya, Iraq, Egypt, and Iran. Two elementary schools were located in the neighborhood, one Orthodox and the other secular. Lydia, my youngest sister, attended the non-religious school.

Isaac's sister Lydia, Netanya, Israel, 1972

I was sick in bed when I heard my baby sister enter the house sobbing. I asked her why she was crying and she said she was upset because all the children hated her and called her *"Parsi! Parsi!"*—the derogative word for Iranian Jews.

I was fed up with the intolerance of Israelis. This was the last straw! I jumped out of bed and assured my sister that we lived in Israel, not Iran, and this behavior did not have to be tolerated. Wearing my pajamas and slippers, I ran outside to find the children who had offended my sister.

Two boys walking down the sidewalk, classmates of Lydia, saw me and became very frightened. They ran into a small grocery store. I ran into the store, grabbed the boys, and sat them on the counter. I held their heads against each other and yelled, "Boys, we are all Jews no matter where we were born! We must love each other! But, if you do not have love for your classmate, at least have respect for her and accept her." The boys were terrified and the customers and owner of the store were in a state of shock.

There I was, in my pajamas, my face red with fever and anger. I took a deep breath and set the two boys on the floor. Then I kneeled and told them, "You must ask Lydia to forgive you, and you should also apologize to your parents for the way you behaved. I will speak with your parents and advise them to stop this intolerance in our schools and our neighborhoods."

A week later, after I recovered from the flu, I returned to the grocery store. The owner of the store hugged me and said that all the parents in the neighborhood were in agreement with me.

[Years later, in 2011, when Lydia attended her elementary school reunion in Netanya, the entire class remembered the incident. Her former classmates assured her that today young Israelis accept and cherish Jews of all cultures. — The Author]

Tel Aviv, Israel
October 3, 1971

I walked into the American Embassy with fear and doubt. As I answered question after question by the embassy staff, I kept thinking, here we go again, no visa for me. This was my third attempt to obtain a visa to visit the United States. I found out that obtaining a visa to travel to the U.S. was extremely difficult, much more difficult than any other country. I had to assure the American officials that I planned to return to Israel to study for an advanced degree.

"Why are you going to the United States?" the bureaucrat asked.

"I wish to see my older brother, who I haven't seen for seven years. Besides, I am in love with the USA and I can't wait to see the greatest land on the face of the earth!" I responded enthusiastically.

"Where are you going to stay while in the United States?"

"With my brother, in Lincoln, Nebraska. Here, his address is 2222 Vine Street, apartment #7."

"How long are you going to be in America?"

"Just two or three weeks," I quickly replied. In my heart I knew I wanted to stay longer. I needed time to convince my brother to return to Israel with me.

"Are you planning to stay in New York City before traveling to Nebraska?"

"Oh no, I will go straight to Nebraska to be with my brother."

"Do you have money?"

"Yes, I have several thousand dollars. Besides, my brother is a successful electrical engineer and he will pay for all my expenses," I assured the official. I guess my answers were convincing because after an hour of waiting and holding my breath, a loud voice called my name. When the clerk handed me my Iranian passport (I never applied for an Israeli passport), I noticed a piece of white paper had been inserted in it—this was my visa!

The sun shone brighter and people's faces seemed radiant. I floated, as if on air, down Yarkon and Hertzel Streets. An old friend of the family called me into his store and asked me why I was walking with my eyes raised to the heavens, laughing and talking to myself. With a huge smile, I explained that my dream was finally realized: I was going to America! "Ever since I could read, I learned about America. I watched American movies, imagined seeing the Statue of Liberty in person, and have been very curious about the incredible document known as the Bill of Rights," I told him.

When I left the store, I found the TWA office and purchased my airplane tickets. There were no direct flights to Nebraska. I decided to fly to New York, and then continue the journey by bus. I was sure I would be able to find a place to stay in New York for a few days. I called an old friend and classmate and asked him for his brother's address in Queens. After several calls, Eli D. finally found his brother's address on an old envelope, but Eli didn't know whether the address was accurate or if his brother was still residing at that location. I wasn't concerned.

When I returned home to my parent's apartment in Netanya, I began to pack and organize my belongings. How long will I stay in the America? What clothes should I take? As I deliberated these matters, I heard my mother's voice calling me to come and drink my tea.

"We have a date for Alon's *brit milah*, now that he's healthy enough. It will be next Sunday," my mother informed me.

"It is too bad Alon's *brit milah* had to be postponed because of illness." Alon was my first-born nephew, the son of my sister Homa. "Mamon, that will be a lucky day for Alon—just one day before I leave for America," I added happily.

On Sunday, all the members of the family gathered at Hedera Hospital to celebrate Alon's *brit milah*. Everyone knew I was leaving Israel the next day and they wished me well. I accepted the family's hugs and kisses, proudly wearing the pinkish-brown Italian-made corduroy suit and the white shirt I was planning to wear to New York the next day. My new high-heel, brown leather boots were fashionable, but not so comfortable.

In my heart I was still an ardent Zionist, but in my soul I loved America. Somehow my father knew about my conflicted loyalties. He hugged and kissed me and gave me his blessing, and then he held me by my shoulders and looked deep into my eyes. "Don't be afraid, Isaac," he advised me. "Go for it, with your full strength!"

The love in his eyes made me tremble. He knew I was not coming back to Israel to live.

PART THREE

AMERICA: THE ULTIMATE LAND

There are different wells within our hearts—
Some fill with each good rain,
Others are far, far too deep for that.

I have learned that every heart will get
What it prays for most.

—Hafez

New York City, New York
October 10, 1971

The following day, after an uneventful flight, I arrived in New York City. I was carrying two heavy suitcases and a shoulder bag, uncomfortable in my tight, double-breasted corduroy suit and tight leather boots. I sported a mustache, side-burns to my jaw, and an imposing Afro hairdo—what a sight I was! It was 6:00pm and I needed to get to an address in Queens, an address I was not sure of.

After taking several buses, I was no closer to the mystery address. It was now past midnight and I was fearful of getting mugged. Finally, with some kind assistance, I found myself in front of an old building at 2:00am. I walked into the vestibule of the building and knocked on the door. No answer. I was sweaty, exhausted and miserable. My feet inside the tight boots were numb. I knocked again and still there was no answer.

I walked outside and shouted at the open windows, "It's Isaac Yomtovian, from Israel! Let me in!" A face appeared in the window yelling, "Go away! We have no more room! There are already so many people here that we sleep in shifts!" I picked up my suitcases, walked back inside the building, and ducked under the stairway that led to the first floor. I sat down and soon I was asleep.

I awoke the next morning with a start. A large black man was kicking me in the feet. I struggled awake, gathered my belongings, and began my odyssey to find the bus station. First I needed to make a phone call to Ruben, to let him know I was already in New York and on my way to him. I found a pay phone, but did not know how to make a collect call. I asked three different people, but I still did not understand how it was done. Everyone kept saying, "Put in a dime!" but I had no idea what a "dime" was—I thought they were telling me to put a "diamond" in the phone. I became more and more desperate. I stopped a lady and asked once more. I emptied my pocket and displayed all the change I possessed. She quickly grabbed a coin and declared, "Dime! Put dime in slot, dial "O" and tell the operator what you want." I made the call.

Somehow, I had to find Lincoln, Nebraska and my brother Ruben. I figured the best way to reach my destination was to ask directions. "How do I get to the bus terminal?" I asked someone on the street.

"Go one block, then turn left and go one block, and then turn right and go straight one block," the man told me with a heavy New York accent.

I didn't understand his rapid speech and decided to ask someone else.

"Go one block straight, turn left and go one block, and then turn right and go straight one block," the second man replied in a hurry.

I was totally confused. The directions sounded simple enough, but I did not know what a "block" was. I had learned only classroom English—*British* English—and to me a "block" was a "brick." It took several more tries before I finally understood that a "block" meant the distance between intersections. I finally knew how to get where I needed to go!

Exhausted, I arrived at the bus terminal and tried to buy a bus ticket to Lincoln, Nebraska. The ticket seller at the window had never heard of Lincoln, Nebraska. I decided that if I kept repeating my destination in a loud voice, the clerk would somehow grasp my intention. It didn't help.

Finally, a manager was called over to assist. He unfolded a large map of the United States and located Nebraska. This was a good start.

"There is no direct service to Lincoln, Nebraska," he informed me, looking at me as if I wanted to go to the moon. "You'll have to go through Chicago," he said, pointing at the map again.

"Will I arrive in time for dinner?" I asked hopefully, for I was very hungry.

"It will take several days, young man. Don't you see how vast this country is?" he replied, sweeping his hand over the map, from New York to Nebraska.

I purchased the necessary tickets using the last of my money. I would have to fast all the way to Nebraska.

2222 Vine Street, #7
Lincoln, Nebraska
Autumn 1971

I almost lost my packet of bus tickets in Chicago, but a nice person saved the day and a catastrophe was averted. Finally, I arrived in Lincoln, Nebraska on October 13, 1971—exhausted, grimy, and reeking of sweat. I stayed with Ruben and his two roommates, Frank and Dick, one mile east of the University of Nebraska campus. During the first few days of my stay, I only had the energy to eat and sleep.

After I was sufficiently rested, Ruben and I spent all our time catching up on the news of our family members in Israel. When I told Ruben that I intended to bring him back to Israel with me, he was shocked. I told him that all Jews belonged in Israel and that he was a defector. We had many heated conversations. Gradually, we became reacquainted with each other. We hadn't seen each other for several years and we became close friends for the first time in our lives. We forged a strong bond in Nebraska.

I had many questions for Ruben about America and the American language. "Everyone acts as though they know me; they're so friendly! What is this word *hi,* and what does *you betcha* mean? And when I say *you're welcome,* the other person says *uh hum.* In Iran it is rude to say *uh hum.*" Ruben tried to explain everything to me, and so I began my American education.

A few days later, I decided to walk through the campus and visit each department. As soon as I left the apartment, every pedestrian passing me on the sidewalk greeted me with a hearty "Good Morning!" This warm greeting was very pleasant, but also very surprising to me because in Iran and Israel, people who do not know each other rarely smile at strangers and wish them a good day.

I found the Civil Engineering Department and visited with graduate students who informed me of the new Water Resources Research Institute. The director of this institute was a well-known engineer, Dr. Warren Veissman. I decided to meet Dr. Veissman at his office in the Agricultural Engineering Building on the east campus.

A gray haired man with a friendly smile rose behind his desk and offered me a seat. "What can I do for you?" he asked.

"I only wish to introduce myself," I explained. "I am a graduate of the Civil Engineering Department at the Technion Institute of Technology in Israel."

"What branch of civil engineering?" he inquired.

"Hydrology and hydraulics, under Professor Jacob Bear," I responded.

"Professor Bear! How is his handbook coming along? Has he finished it yet? Did you work for him?"

I was shocked that he knew my department chairman and favorite professor. After fifteen minutes, Dr. Veissman knew exactly what I had studied and who my instructors were.

"Would you like to get a Masters Degree in your field, here at the University of Nebraska?" Dr. Veissman asked me, leaning forward in his chair. "I am offering you an assistantship."

"I will get paid to study and receive a degree?" I asked in disbelief.

"Yes, you can start right now!" he answered with a smile.

"Of course! I would love the opportunity!" I exclaimed without hesitation.

Dr. Veissman walked over to his bookshelves and filled a box with several books on hydrology and hydraulics, and a large stack of volumes of the *Journal of the Water Resources Research Association*, which included many of his own articles. We shook hands as he told me to return when I had read all the materials he had given me. I was in total shock as I lifted the box and walked slowly out of his office. I couldn't believe what had just happened! I had presented no transcripts, no documents, and no resume—yet I now had the opportunity to work for one of the best known authorities in my field, obtain a graduate degree, and remain in the land of my dreams. And, best of all, I would also get paid! I could not have planned this any better—this was assuredly my destiny, as decided by the Creator!

Several weeks later, towards the end of November, I was sitting in Ruben's apartment listening to the album *Jesus Christ Super Star*, when the phone rang.

"I wish to speak to Yomtovian," stated the voice on the other end of the line. "I am Dr. Grace Hanson, and I am calling to invite you to my home for Thanksgiving dinner."

"What is this Thanksgiving and who are you?" I asked in confusion.

"I realize that you don't know me, and you may not know what Thanksgiving dinner is all about. Let me explain. I received your name from an agriculture-engineering professor who knows you have just arrived from abroad and have nowhere to go to celebrate Thanksgiving."

"But I also have a brother," I stated.

"Well, both of you are invited. My address is 28 Apple Street, just across from the East Campus."

When I told Ruben about the invitation, he told me the story about Thanksgiving's origins. "This is a great American holiday," he concluded with a smile. "It is customary for Americans to invite students who have no place to go for the holiday."

I could not fathom the great difference between Mrs. Grace Hanson and virtually any Muslim person in Iran. How could a woman invite to her home a total stranger from a foreign country, who also happened to be Jewish?

On Thanksgiving Day at two o'clock in the afternoon, Ruben and I rang the bell at 28 Apple Street. A tall, slender, white-haired woman opened the door with a smile and welcomed us into her home. The delicious smell of turkey, cranberries, cornbread and freshly baked pumpkin pies filled the entire house. A large dining table was decorated with colorful plates and napkins. There were several plates of raw vegetables and dip. Mrs. Hanson introduced Ruben and me to her son and his family from Seattle, and her neighbors. There were twelve people seated around the table.

Mrs. Grace Hanson, the lady who introduced Thanksgiving to Isaac, and later on became his landlady. (left) Faramaz, Bijan's cousin and Bijan. Lincoln, Nebraska.

A large TV was strategically placed so that all of the guests could watch the football game between the University of Oklahoma and the University of Nebraska. Everyone in the room was talking about the game and the players. I had no idea what was going on around me. Mrs. Hanson's son offered me a tall glass of beer and announced, "We will make you into a real American! Let me explain the game of football to you."

That cold, snowy Thursday afternoon was carved into my heart forever. I began to understand the generosity and kindness of the American heart, and the values cherished by all Americans: trust, humility, and friendship. How could my fellow Iranians believe that America is the Great Satan?

University of Oklahoma
Mewbourne School of Petroleum and Geological Engineering
Norman, Oklahoma
Summer 1972

I had some vacation time, so I decided to visit the Petroleum Engineering Department at the University of Oklahoma. I had taken some courses in that field while at Technion and still had some interest in it—petroleum engineers made very large salaries. During my visit to the Petroleum Engineering Department, I ran into Sharokh Amini, an Iranian graduate student who was studying there. I asked him if, by any chance, he knew my two Muslim friends Fazlolah, son of Hajj Ashi, and Akbar Shikholislami—and he did! I explained that I was always to know what had happened to those guys, and Sharokh gladly shared with me what he knew.

"Sadly," Sharokh said, "Fazlolah's father, Hajj Ashi, has died and Fazlolah is working on a graduate degree at a German university in Munich. Akbar remains in Iran, where he has had a difficult time dealing with the Shah's regime, and is in and out of jail."

Home of Uncle Mordechai Jacobson
Fargo Street
Lincolnwood, Illinois
September 5, 1972

Every so often, Ruben and I would go to Chicago to visit our Great-Uncle Mordechai Jacobson. Early one morning in early September, we packed Ruben's car with sandwiches and enough clothes for a long weekend, and set out. Uncle Mordechai and his wife Miriam were our only family members who lived relatively close to Lincoln, Nebraska. (Everyone else lived in New York, Los Angeles, or Israel.)

That evening after dinner, Uncle Mordechai settled into his comfortable chair in the living room, lit his pipe, and became very quiet and thoughtful. Ruben and I knew that our uncle was in the mood to tell a story, and he was an excellent storyteller.

"Isaac, shortly before you were born, my older brother Najat asked me to take over his medical practice in Esfahan, just for a few days, while he attended a medical conference in Tehran. I was very honored that he asked me, a mere medical student, to stand in for him. You see, Najat was the most famous Jew in Esfahan! He was an honored professor of medicine, and perhaps the most respected physician in the entire city. Because of his esteemed position, Najat had many important Muslims among his patients: High-ranking military officers and even Muslim clergymen sought his attention. They respected him so much that they trusted him to care for their wives and children also.

"The morning I arrived in Esfahan to take over Najat's clinic

because I consider myself a Zionist, yet refuse to live in Israel?

The truth is, I love America and the freedom I have here. I hope that one day in the near future I will find my ideal Jewish woman here in America so that the decision to remain here will be obvious!

How prophetic the last line of my letter proved to be.

Cornell University
Ithaca, New York
Spring 1975

A reception for the Shah's sister, Ashraf Pahlavi (wearing suit and gloves), at Cornell University. Isaac is standing directly on her left, as a representative of the Persian Student Club.

I went to Cornell to finish my doctoral program in environmental engineering, and in the spring it was time for me to defend my dissertation. (I had already taken all the necessary coursework and completed all the requirements.)

The day arrived for me to stand before a group of professors and answer questions about my thesis—or so I thought. My advisor had been very specific: He told me to be prepared to respond to detailed questions regarding my dissertation, and that nothing more would be required. Consequently, I walked into the designated room with confidence. I was convinced that no matter how detailed the inquiry, I would be able to do well.

How wrong I was! Instead of asking me about my dissertation, the professors proceeded to ask me to regurgitate information I hadn't looked at in years: formulae and equations I had memorized years ago, but could no longer remember because I had not used them in a long time. I froze. I became paralyzed. My throat tightened up and I could not speak.

The professors repeated the questions, however, I was in total shock. I felt as if I were standing in front of an Islamic tribunal, with stern-faced clergymen asking me why I had transgressed against Allah! Apparently the years of living in Iran had taught me to be meek and fearful when confronted by authority of any kind. After what seemed like an eternity, I was able to move my legs. I turned and hurriedly walked out of the room.

I was sweating profusely and my heart was pounding. I felt totally confused and humiliated. (I had always excelled in academics—that had been my only way to fight against the feelings of inferiority caused by Muslim domination.) Now, for the first time in my academic life, *I had failed.*

I phoned my brother Ruben, who had moved to Minnesota. I told him what had just happened.

"Go back in there and defend yourself!" he shouted. "Tell them you were misinformed! Ask the professors to reschedule the test and give you a second chance. Do not submit yourself to them just because they are big shots! This is not Iran! In America you have every right to argue with authorities."

"I can't. I won't. I'm done with this," I said quietly. I had been conditioned to feel inferior by years of Islamic arrogance and abuse.

"Come to Minneapolis, Isaac," he advised me. "You can stay with me."

Shortly after moving to Minneapolis, I began to have nightmares. Terrible nightmares. In my sleep I relived the doctoral dissertation fiasco, and how I had been unable to defend myself when asked questions for which I was not prepared. In one dream, I clearly remember standing in front of a firing squad, defenseless. I woke up shaking and trembling, amazed that I was still alive.

> **Elsewhere in the world in 1976:**
> - Apple Computer Company is formed by Steve Jobs and Steve Wozniak.
> - The United States celebrates its bicentennial.
> - Palestinian extremists hijack an Air France plane in Greece and force the pilot to fly to Entebbe, Uganda, where Israeli commandos storm the plane and free the 258 hostages.
> - The Syrian Army conquers Beirut, Lebanon.
> - Jimmy Carter is elected President of the United States.

University of Winnipeg
Winnipeg, Canada
Winter 1976

I attended a lecture given by Sharokh Amini, the same Iranian petroleum-engineering student I happened to meet back in 1972, at the University of Oklahoma. Now he had his doctorate degree and was very important in his field. Like the last time I saw him, I asked him about my friends Fazlolah and Akbar. Sharokh invited me to join him for lunch, since he had a lot to share with me.

When we arrived at the restaurant, Sharokh told me he had a job offer for me. He invited me to return to Iran and work with him in the Iranian petroleum industry. He offered an unbelievable salary and benefits. He told me that the demand for professional Iranians was very high, especially in the fields of hydraulics, hydrology, petro-chemistry, and petro-engineering. "Isaac, it no longer matters that you are Jewish. The economy in Iran is booming! There is so much money in circulation that we don't now how to spend it all! You will be paid $20,000 per month to start, plus a house, a car with a driver, and much more," he informed me. "Furthermore, I will make sure you will be paid for all of your moving expenses. What do you say?"

Though I found his offer to be very tempting, I was non-committal, and shrugged my shoulders in a gesture of indifference. I asked again about Fazlolah and Akbar.

"Fazlolah is back in Tehran. He is running a number of companies and is doing very well. As a matter of fact, he has brought many German, French, and American engineers and technicians to

Iran to work for him. Fazlolah has established entire modern communities, high-rise buildings, factories, and office complexes," said Sharokh, as he counted all of Fazlolah's accomplishments on his fingers. "He married a very beautiful woman from one of Iran's wealthiest families, and has converted his father's soup restaurant into the largest soup kitchen for the poor and needy in Tehran," he continued. "And if you agree to return to Tehran, I will make sure to bring you to see Fazlolah. I guarantee you will have lunch with him every week!"

"And Akbar? What of him?" I asked.

"He has obtained a law degree and has become a member of the clergy. He is deeply involved in the Islamic movement and politics. Akbar has married the daughter of a highly respected *ayatollah* and is working between Tehran, Mashhad, Qum, and Najaf," Sharokh informed me, with a wink of an eye. "You see how he is getting ahead in the world, that Akbar!"

Somehow I was not surprised that Akbar, a very conservative Muslim, had chosen the path he was now following: He had always lectured me on the importance of once again making Iran a holy Islamic state, with the clergy in total control of the government and people's lives. It was clear to me that Akbar was working diligently to attain the goal of taking Iran backward to the time of the Safavid Dynasty.

I also thought about the fact that Fazlolah was so successful, and the offer of returning to Iran and possibly collaborating with him was very tempting. Looking deep into my heart, I realized that nothing could convince me to leave the land of the Bill of Rights and the Constitution. My answer to Sharokh was a simple, "no thank you."

Minneapolis, Minnesota
Autumn 1977-Summer 1978

I met Roslyn Kaplan, a young medical intern, at Temple Adath

Jeshurun one *Shabbat* evening. At first I thought she would be an excellent match for my brother Ruben, but they didn't seem to hit it off. On the other hand, Roz and I seemed to like each other, so I asked her out. Our first date proved to be very inauspicious. Even though I had a bad case of the flu, I took her to a fancy restaurant for dinner. That was a mistake. I spent the entire evening in the restroom, vomiting.

The second date didn't go much better. Roz was a Yankees baseball fanatic, so we got together to watch a game on television. Roz was glued to the game, giving us no opportunity to talk to each other.

Our third date began as unpromising as the first two. We went to see a movie that was so terrible we left after only ten minutes. Luckily, we stopped by the Lincoln Dell Restaurant afterwards, and for the first time, we actually engaged in a conversation.

Our relationship seemed to become serious very quickly, even though I was not really looking for a wife. Soon we decided that we should try living under the same roof, to see if we were compatible. Roz insisted that there would be no "hanky-panky." After one month of living together, Roz invited her mother to come from New York City to meet me. Mrs. Kaplan stayed at my apartment for one week and we got along very well. Now that I had met her mother, Roz became very serious about getting married. I was not sure that I was ready for such a commitment.

"My parents and my other relatives don't know you, Roz, and in Iran both families must meet and get to know each other before a wedding can take place," I insisted. I was stalling.

"That's fine, I'll go to Israel with my mother," Roz declared.

Soon thereafter, I received a phone call from my father in Netanya, Israel. "Isaac, we have here visiting us a young Jewish-American woman and her mother. They are very nice people and we like them, but what are your intentions for this woman?"

"I'm not sure, Agha Joon," I answered him. "I don't know."

"It's either yes or no! Can you put your head next to her head for the

Isaac and Roslyn dating in Minneapolis, Minnesota, 1977.

rest of your life? You must make a decision!" my father demanded.

"OK, yes," I agreed.

"*Mazel tov!*" my father said, and hung up.

Before Roz and her mother returned to the States, my father threw a huge party to announce my engagement to her. He bought Roz a ring and my grandfather Elyahu presented it to her at the party! Roz returned to Minneapolis as my fiancée.

In May, I received my temporary American passport, and in August of 1978, Roz and I went to Israel to get married.

Paper money is placed on Roslyn's forehead to ensure prosperity in her future life.

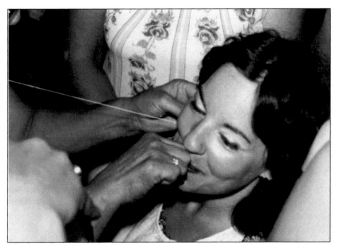

Band Andazoon literally means, "removing the hair." During Band Andazoon, a celebration that occurs several days before her wedding, a bride is prepared for her groom. Traditionally, women used threads to remove facial hair. It is said that for each plucked hair, the bride must receive a gift. In the past, single women were not allowed to remove facial hair or use cosmetics—indeed, women wearing lipstick were known to be married.

Singing for the bride-to-be, Grandfather Elyahu (standing, left) joins in.

During Band Andazoon, the henna party a few days before her wedding, Isaac's father places candy on Shahnaz's forehead to ensure her a sweet marriage. Shahnaz was married during the same week as Isaac and Roslyn. Netanya, Israel; August 1978.

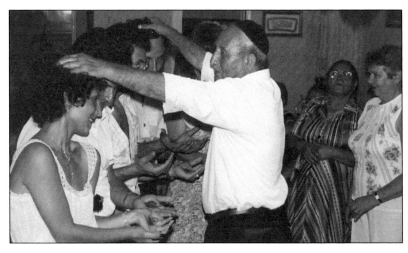

Women and men with henna in their up-turned palms (henna ensures good luck) receive a blessing from Eliyahu, Isaac's grandfather, at the Band Andazoon party for Shahnaz and Roslyn (Isaac's fiancée). Netanya, Israel; August 1978.

The wedding day, August 22, 1978, in Netanya, Israel. (left) Roslyn's mother, Mary Kaplan and Isaac's mother, Ezat, look on as Isaac lifts Roz's veil, as tradition allows, making sure he is marrying the right woman! Netanya, Isreal.

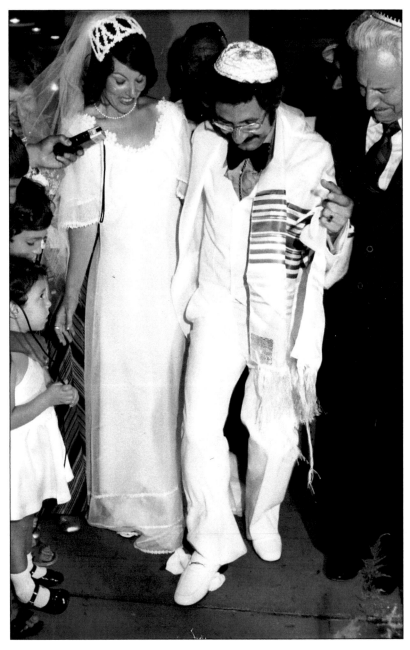

Isaac, following Jewish tradition, stomps on a glass at the end of the wedding ceremony.

Isaac and Roslyn proudly display their ketubah, the traditional Jewish marriage contract that outlines the rights and responsibilities of the groom, including the prenuptial agreement. The ketubah is given to the bride's mother to keep. (Roslyn's mother stands at left, rear; Isaac's father, at right) .

My parents and all my uncles and aunts had "arranged marriages." They learned to love their partners as a result of shared experiences and obligations. They developed tenderness and affection for each other over the course of time. Respect for family unity and the expectations of the community were the strong forces that kept couples together—the survival of the community depended on this.

In reality, a marriage is a union of two families. The phenomenon of strong, durable marriages is typical for Jews. Ghetto living, with limitations forced by external forces, created an environment in which such values as obedience, patience and acceptance were the norm. These values became important when my father was ready to marry.

At the age of twenty-four, several years after he moved to Tehran, my father fell in love with a Tehrani Jewish woman named Azizagha. He could not disclose his love for Azizagha to his parents because his mother insisted that she would choose the right wife for him from the Jewish Esfahani community.

As a young, single man, my father worked over twelve hours a day, so he had no time to take care of himself. He purchased a small house in Tehran's Jewish ghetto, in partnership with the Yashar family. Azizagha, the young, beautiful, and educated older daughter of Mr. Asher Yashar, chose to take care of my father by preparing warm dinners, washing and ironing his clothes, and advising him on things that he should buy: nice shoes and clothing for himself, and beautiful sets of dishes and silverware for his future family. (My mother kept the rose colored dishes and used them for Passover.)

My father was smitten by Azizagha's beauty and her unconditional love, but refrained from showing any affection for her. His mother had instructed him that touching a woman would rob him of his intellectual ability and that kissing a woman would cause pregnancy. He believed his mother.

During the High Holy Days (*Yom Kippur and Rosh Hashanah*) my father visited his family in Esfahan, bringing gifts for all members of the family. This ritual was especially important to my grandmother who considered my father to be her richest son because he lived in the metropolis of Tehran. My father finally found the courage to tell his parents about the woman he planned to marry. His mother threatened to commit suicide, and his father became determined to find a suitable wife for his lonely son as soon as possible.

During the ten days between *Rosh Hashanah* and *Yom Kippur*, while my father was visiting friends and neighbors in the ghetto of Esfahan, he noticed a tanned, trim, black-haired young woman wearing a pretty green dress. She was running into a neighbor's house, doing errands. My grandfather noticed my father looking at that young girl and decided to find out all about her. Within a few hours, my father's father had met my mother's father and discussed a potential match (*shidduch*) between their children.

My mother lived with her parents and a younger sister on a farm far from the Esfahan ghetto. She was able to visit her four older siblings who lived in the Esfahan ghetto only during holidays. Her family was probably the only Jewish farming family in the entire country! Her father loved to farm and raised lambs, chickens, turkeys, goats, and other animals. He had left his oldest four children in the ghetto and moved with his wife and two younger daughters to an isolated farm, and lived among Muslims.

Since the Jewish schools were in the ghetto, my mother never had the opportunity to attend school. She remained illiterate growing up, with no friends and no relationships with her older siblings. According to my mother, she could only speak the Jewish Esfahani dialect. She learned Farsi after her marriage, after she moved to Tehran.

When my mother was told that she had a suitor—a potential husband—she prayed to be saved from the farm. The questions, Who is this man? How does he look? What is his job? How old is he? were not important. She knew that arranged marriages were the custom and that it was up to the family to decide. My father was simply told, "We have picked someone out for you!" and my parents became engaged within the week.

As I said before, in Iran a marriage is much more than the union of two people: It is the union between two families. The backgrounds of both families are examined and the financial prospects of the groom are assessed. Before the actual engagement takes place, there is a "meeting of the minds"; some small gifts and sweets are exchanged, and the potential bride and groom are allowed to get to know each other—while the families supervise, of course. Next the men in the bride's family take the groom to a physician to make sure he is capable of producing children. The female members of the groom's family examine the bride in the nude at the public bath; they must attest that the young woman is free of physical defects— the groom therefore cannot reject her for some unsightly blemish after they are married.

The extended families of both the bride and groom get together for a big party at the bride's house. If both families get along, and everything checks out to everyone's satisfaction, the groom's family is invited back for another party, called "the asking for the hand," or the "engagement party."

At the engagement party the Persian custom of the Seven Trays is observed. Many gifts are carried through the streets on trays, from the home of the groom to the home of the bride, accompanied by singing and dancing. These gifts must include bread, water, silver and gold coins, sweets, *sabzi*, a mirror, and jewelry. After the engagement, more presents are received and negotiations for the bride's dowry are conducted.

Once the amount of the dowry is agreed upon, the terms are written in the *ketubah*, the Jewish marriage contract. The dowry consists mainly of household items: dishes, towels, sheets, nice clothing and jewelry. The cash gift is treated as a separate item. All the gifts are then displayed and priced by the bride's family—the price for each item is greatly inflated so that a huge number would be written in the marriage contract, often two or three times more than the agreed amount of the dowry.

The next celebration is called *Pagoshah* (literally, "the opening of the feet"), which officially opens the way between the two soon-to-be-united families. The *Pagoshah* takes place at the bride's house and allows both families to socialize and have fun together. More gifts are exchanged and the *khacham* (Jewish "wise man" or religious leader) sets the date for the wedding.

After the *Pagoshah*, my father had to return to Tehran to attend to his business. During the ten-hour bus ride, he kept rehearsing what he would tell the Yashar family. By the time he arrived in Tehran, he had decided to sell his share of the house to Mr. Yashar and rent a room for himself and his future bride. And so he did.

Father never shared with me his final conversation with Azizagha. However, shortly thereafter she married a nice Jewish Tehrani man named Nemat. My father became the best friend of Nemat's family, and he provided the best fabric to Azizagha and her two beautiful daughters, Pary and Shaheen. (Years later Mr. and Mrs. Yashar convinced my grandparents to allow their youngest daughter, Pouran, to marry my Uncle Morad.) Several years later, when Azizagha's husband was accidentally electrocuted and died, my father remained a good friend to the family.

My parents married in 1943 in Esfahan. My father was twenty-four years old and my mother was just seventeen. The religious part of the wedding took place during the day at the home of the bride, in the courtyard. The *khakham* was present and the bride and groom's immediate family were in attendance. The ceremony was very simple: The groom took the ring and recited a blessing in which he declared, "You are holy to me. I place this ring on your finger and according to the laws of Moses and Israel, you are my wife." After the ring was given to the bride, the Seven Blessings were recited. The necessary papers were filed with the civil authorities.

That evening, the groom's family hosted a party that lasted far into the night. Guests bearing gifts attended. The guests danced (men and women danced separately) for the bride and groom, and for the happiness and enjoyment of the newly married couple. There was music and delicious food to share.

After the wedding, the bride and groom were taken to their bedroom by the elders of the families. A special blessing was recited over the bed that expressed the desire for a male child, and then the couple was left alone.

Following the wedding, there are the "Seven Days and Nights of Blessing" during which the bride and groom were supposed to spend all their time together, in bliss. The bride was not allowed to cook or do chores, so each day a different member of the family invited the new couple for meals. (In the case of my parents, this wonderful custom was not observed because they were in a hurry to return to Tehran.)

In Persian Jewish culture, the newly married couple attended synagogue on the first *Shabbat* following their wedding. The fact that the entire congregation recognized the union cemented the spiritual aspect of their wedding. At this point the newlyweds were officially soul mates. Their marriage was sealed in heaven.

Within a few days, my father and his bride left Esfahan and moved to my father's rented room in Tehran. As I mentioned before, my grandmother had taught my father that kissing was the cause of pregnancy. This kissing concept kept my father from consummating his marriage for over a year after his wedding night! My mother once told me, "your father was always a great kisser." It took my mother over two years after her wedding night to give birth to her first child, Ruben—an unusually long time.

After the birth of my sister Homa, my father realized that a one-room rented living space was not sufficient for his growing family. He purchased a two-story, seven-bedroom house located in the prestigious neighborhood of Agha Sheikh Hadi, near the Shah's Marble Palace. This was where Jews who could afford to leave the ghetto migrated.

My mother learned to love my father and my father fell in love with my mother. They raised seven children and never, in their sixty-two years of marriage, did they question each other's loyalty and commitment. Although I never heard either of them say the word "love" or tell each other "I love you," it became a fact and unquestionably true that they were totally in love.

All of my elder family members had similar marriage experiences. They all had marriages arranged by their families, with no sexual experimentation allowed prior to their weddings. They all learned to fall in love with their spouses over time. If questioned, they would all, without exception, claim that as long as you marry within your community, an arranged marriage cannot fail.

This brings to mind something I once overheard Uncle Mordechai say to his own children: *"If a woman loves you beyond your expectation, and you only like her, your marriage will be successful because you will learn to fall in love."* I believe this is true.

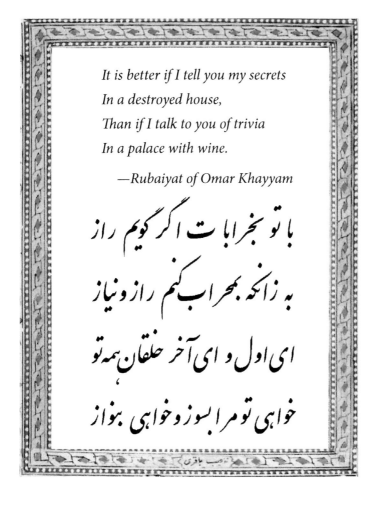

It is better if I tell you my secrets
In a destroyed house,
Than if I talk to you of trivia
In a palace with wine.

—*Rubaiyat of Omar Khayyam*

با تو سخن را با ت ا گر گویم راز

به زانکه بمحراب کنم راز و نیاز

ای اول و ای آخر خلقان همه تو

خواهی تو مرا بسوز و خواهی بنواز

Fortunately for me, I was not ignorant of the act of sexual intercourse or the ways in which to please a woman. I remember with great fondness the lessons taught to me by my Muslim Persian friend, Layla Daneshfar, who I met while I was attending Cornell University. She was a young graduate student in the Agricultural Engineering Department.

Layla was born in Yazd to a family of educated and observant Muslims; her father was a military officer and her mother a school principal. Layla was an outstanding student and winner of a special scholarship that allowed her to continue her graduate studies in the United States. She was married to a well-respected veterinarian who lived in Mashhad.

Back in 1975, three years before I met my future wife, I shared some classes with her. Soon we became study partners and I realized her exceptional intelligence and knowledge of life. Since her husband was in Iran, it became important for her to become involved in the Persian Student Club's activities. It was during those activities that we would discuss history, religion, philosophy, music, and memories of Iran.

We also talked about our families. She told me all about her engagement, wedding, and wonderful married life. She explained to me how women differ from men in their affections, feelings, and thought process. Layla emphasized how important it was for a man to be sensitive to the needs and desires of his wife, and that lovemaking actually began hours before going to bed, with kind words and gentle touches offered during the day.

Layla explained that a woman appreciated a bouquet of flowers more than an expensive gift, and a hand-written love note or poem was valued more than an evening out. Above all, she told me, a woman wants to be appreciated and feel loved. "Once in bed, do not rush!" Layla advised. "And do not worry about going to sleep after you make love, even though you must get up early to go to work. If you cannot be playful and have fun after intercourse, you may as well consider your wife a sporting tool and yourself a selfish athlete. Remember to always thank your partner for the pleasures

226

she gives you."

My friend and I enjoyed a chaste relationship. She was always loyal to her husband, in thought and deed, but her honest advice and discussions were enlightening and powerful.

Eventually, Layla's husband visited her at the university, and she became pregnant. In her joy she told me that in Persian literature, love is often explained using the metaphor of a butterfly and a candle. "A truly love-drunk butterfly throws itself into the flame of the candle and is completely consumed. That is the only way to truly know what love is." She was very wise.

Netanya, Israel
August 23, 1978

A dear friend of mine, Morad Rostami, arrived from Iran for my wedding—a day late! (I met Morad years ago when I attended classes at Kharazmi Night School. In those days he lived in south Tehran and was a lowly clerk in a bank; he was highly motivated to improve his education and we often studied together.) Morad was sorry that he missed the ceremony, but I assured him I didn't like him any less. It was very good to see him. Morad had become a buyer for a large company that acquired construction machinery, and so he made frequent trips to Germany, England, and Japan. Morad also had the opportunity to meet with many businessmen and bankers in Iran, Europe, and Southeast Asia. He and I spent many hours discussing the political turmoil in Iran, and his information proved to be very unsettling to me.

"Isaac, I have to tell you that the influential men I speak to in Europe and Iran—all over the world—are in agreement: The Shah has lost his control over the Iranian government and people. He is finished!" Morad informed me.

"Really? How can that be? I thought the Shah's White Revolution was going great!" I was completely shocked to hear Morad's words.

"Those same influential men have concluded that the Shah's family and close friends keep him in the dark. They have hidden the people's discontent from him. His latest decree, price control, has caused inflation to go sky-high. Corruption is rampant, and the regulatory agencies are out of control!" The expression on Morad's face was one of extreme worry.

"Tell me more, Morad. I want to understand what is happening." My head was reeling.

"It's simple. The Shah has lost the support of almost everyone but the military. The peasants and farmers, who were once great fans of the Shah, have been forced by inflation to migrate to the large cities, where there are no jobs, and no housing, and they have had to rely on the clergy for assistance.

"The intellectuals are also abandoning the Shah," Morad continued. "They are emboldened by men who have graduated from foreign universities, men who have tasted freedom in the United States and Europe. These teachers, doctors, journalists and engineers are speaking up and criticizing the Shah.

"The labor unions, factory workers, and salaried people are also expressing their discontent with the Shah, both in the mosques and in the streets. The clergy provide safe havens for these people. And finally, the businessmen and the *bazaari* (shop owners in the bazaar) are fed up. The daily harassment of regulatory agents, and the corrupt enforcers of the Shah's policies affect them all. High inflation and total instability of the economy have thrown the businessmen and *bazaari* into a panic." Morad stopped talking and waited to see my reaction.

"So, things are very bad in Iran," I conceded. "The *bazaries* are very conservative Muslims and have always had a strong affection for the religious leaders. The fact that the Shah's attempt at price control has upset the *bazaaries* is not to be taken lightly. They wield a lot of power."

"Yes, that's true," agreed Morad. "Also, it looks like foreign companies are beginning to pull out of Iran, and the Israelis have been the first to leave," Morad continued. "The largest Israeli construction company, Solel Boneh, is leaving; they are already pulling out their equipment and machinery. The Israeli engineers and advisors have been warned to leave Iran."

"I can't believe that Mossad (the Israeli Secret Service and Special Operations) knows the Shah is in danger and does nothing," I protested. "The Mossad could penetrate the SAVAK (the Iranian Secret Service) and provide honest and accurate information to the Shah," I suggested. "Also, the leaders of the Israeli army have a very close relationship with the Iranian army—Israeli generals should push the Iranian generals to inform the Shah of his dire situation."

"I think it's too late," said Morad with a shrug.

"The Shah's own inner circle knows he is in trouble, and no one tells him," I said in disbelief. "The Shah is living in the dark, totally in the dark. His advisors have fed him lies for so long that even they are believing the lies they tell!"

"It reminds me of the Mullah Nasruddin story I learned as a child: The *mullah* stands on a street corner and tells everyone that passes by to go to the bazaar where they are giving away free soup. He tells dozens, maybe hundreds of people to go get the free soup. Of course, he has invented the entire story. But human nature being what it is, the *mullah* starts to wonder if indeed they are giving away free soup, and he grabs his bowl and spoon and runs to the bazaar to get some!" said Morad with a laugh.

"Yes, if a lie is repeated often enough, the liar believes his own lies," I said in agreement. "But when all is said and done, the Shah is a good Muslim and still believes that his fellow Iranians love him. Unlike his father, the Shah has always accepted Islam and its clergy, and he never stopped supporting the religious leaders—in fact, he has always placated them."

"The Shah has always trusted the clergy," Morad agreed. "He never treated them with disdain, like his father, Reza Shah. Reza Shah never viewed the clergy as an asset to the country and he did everything he could to diminish their power. The Shah's father realized that religion has no place in government."

"Reza Shah was right! Trusting the religious leaders is a huge mistake. Unfortunately, his son, our present Shah, has always been weak: He should have had Khomeini and his followers executed, but didn't have the stomach for it. Instead he had Khomeini deported to France," I observed.

"The Shah should have taken control back in 1963, when the first riots occurred. The Iranian army and the secret service begged him to give them the power to stop the riots, but he refused," Morad declared.

"He does not want to shed the blood of his people," I said quietly. "His mercy and pity are now the cause of his destruction."

St. Cloud, Minnesota
Spring 1982

I have learned some news of my old friend from Technion, Yosef Eimani. Evidently, he accepted a job in Haifa after graduating with an electrical engineering degree. He married Rashel and later, when great opportunities became available in Iran, he returned to Tehran and accepted an excellent position as an electrical engineer, earning a high salary.

By the year 1979, when the Islamic Revolution succeeded and Ayatollah Khomeini became the Iran's leader, severe limitations and constraints were imposed on the Jewish population. Yosef and Rashel decided it was time to take their two daughters and their son and emigrate back to Israel, or maybe try to enter the U.S. or Canada. At any rate, their main objective was to leave Iran.

Since the Islamic Republic would not allow entire families, especially Jewish families, to leave the country, Yosef decided they would escape illegally to Turkey. He made all the arrangements, paid the smugglers, and drove with his family northwest towards Tabriz and the Turkish border. Unfortunately, the plan failed and the family was arrested. Rashel and the children were allowed to return to

Tehran after a significant amount of money was paid in bribes. Yosef, however, was put in jail and accused of trying to escape the country. This offense carried a minimum one-year sentence.

Ironically, while Yosef was kept in jail, his guards and the prison authorities demanded that he practice his Jewish faith! They provided him with prayer books, a copy of the Torah, a *tallit* (prayer shawl), and *tefillin*. Every morning, noon, and evening the prison guards kicked the door of his cell to remind him that it was time to pray. On Saturdays and all Jewish holidays, the guards made sure that Yosef performed all his religious obligations. During Passover, they supplied Yosef with *matzohs* and all the required foods. By the time he was released, he was a devout and learned Jew! (The Islamic Republic has respect for religious and observant "People of the Book." However, the government has *no* respect for modern, secular, or reform Jews and their liberal practices. When Yosef Eimani was serving his sentence, the Muslim guards and prison administrators intended to improve his character and rehabilitate him by forcing him to practice Orthodox Judaism.)

(Left to right) Ruben, Isaac's brother; Isaac; Yosef Eimani and his wife Rashel. After the 1979 Islamic Revolution, Yosef was imprisoned in Iran for almost a year.

After about one year in prison, Yosef was freed and he and his family tried to escape once more: This time they made it to the Pakistani border and ultimately to Italy. Once in Italy, an international relief organization assisted Iranian-Jewish escapees to sustain their lives until such a time as the U.S., Canada, or Israel was ready to accept them. While in Italy, Yosef became a teacher of Jewish studies. Eventually, Yosef and his family were allowed to emigrate to Toronto, Canada.

"Wake up! Isaac, wake up!" Roz was trying to shake me awake.

"What? Where am I?"

"You were grinding your teeth and flailing your arms. I can see your heart pounding!" Roz was alarmed and anxious.

"I'm sorry I woke you up. It was another nightmare. This time I was trying to protect myself and my father."

"From the Muslims?"

"Yes, the Muslim bogeymen, again," I sighed. "They invade my dreams. They ruin my sleep."

"You've been thinking about your friend Yosef Eimani a lot lately," Roz observed.

"Yes, I have. Perhaps thinking about him and the way he was harassed by Muslims has released some more of my bad memories. In my dream, I was trying to defend my father. Men with sticks were attacking him, but I couldn't lift my arms—they were useless! Finally I picked up a gun, but then I could not make it shoot."

I lay in bed, staring at the ceiling, feeling like a victim all over again. Afraid. Angry. Humiliated.

Isaac asks Chayim, his maternal grandfather, for a blessing. A visit to Afoula, Israel, 1984.

My third daughter Leah visits Israel to meet her great-grandfather and receive his traditional cohanim blessing, 1985.

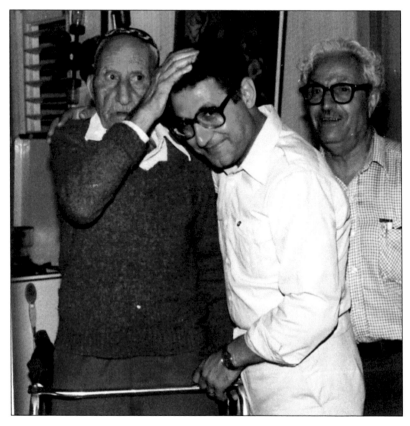

Isaac's grandfather Elyahu gives him the traditional elder's (cohanim) priestly blessing on each and every visit. The Yomtoubian ancestors had sworn not to ever marry a Cohen, because the daughter of a Cohen (descendents of Moses' brother Aharon) must never be disrespected—the husband may not even raise his voice in anger. Since Roslyn was a daughter of a Cohen, Isaac had to be forgiven for not honoring the Yomtoubian promise. Isaac's father is in the background. Netanya, Israel, 1985.

St. Cloud, Minnesota
September 10, 1986

This morning I put Misha, my eldest daughter, and Ezi, my second daughter, on the school bus. I couldn't help thinking about how different things were in my Sheikh Hadi neighborhood: I had to chaperone my younger sisters on the walk to school each morning or they would be harassed by the local Muslim boys. Actually, the harassment of Jewish girls was worse than that of Jewish boys. Typical torment involved blocking a girl's path and verbally taunting her or grabbing her book bag and running away with it—nothing too serious, but it was very frightening. The boys knew they could get away with their bad behavior.

Thank God, my daughters are safe and they are never accosted or annoyed by anyone. Misha and Ezi love the Montessori school they attend, and even though there are only ten or twelve Jewish families in St. Cloud, my girls are never faced with derogatory name-calling or discriminatory behavior.

After school or on the weekends, my daughters play with neighborhood friends. Unlike what I experienced in *my* childhood, they are welcome inside their friends' homes. Most often I was only allowed in my friends' courtyards, but not in the interior rooms. If the mother or other female family members were home, I had to be very careful not to look at them if they were not covered with a *chador*. The same Akbar or Maseod who freely studied and played with me at school, treated me as inferior when I visited their homes. Thankfully, my daughters do not experience prejudicial behavior.

Home of Uncle Mordechai Jacobson
Fargo Street
Lincolnwood, Illinois
Spring 1988

Roz and I were on our way from St. Cloud, Minnesota to Cleveland, Ohio. Roz had secured a job as a pathologist at University Hospital and we decided to make the move. Once we started driving east, we figured we might as well stop and visit my uncle and his wife in Chicago.

"I'm glad that Uncle Mordechai's children, my cousins, won't be at his house during this visit," I said quietly. "I am relieved that I won't have to deal with their attitude."

"Why is that?" inquired Roz. "I thought you'd be happy to see them."

"I don't have a particularly close relationship with them. They have an air of superiority about them and they always act very arrogant towards newly arrived Iranians. I think they don't like my heavy accent." I explained. "This is typical behavior of children of immigrants, especially when the immigrants exhibit little pride in their cultural heritage."

"Why do you think that's so?"

"They think they are superior because they were born in America, Roz. Also, my uncle taught them that everything Iranian is bad. He went out of his way to put down Iranian culture—he even expressed his distaste for *Jewish*-Iranians, especially Orthodox Jews. It is humiliating for me to be around my cousins. They look at me as if I were a vulgar, inferior person!" I stated with agitation.

"Well, your uncle is always very kind to you, Isaac," Roz reminded me. "He is very proud of you and Ruben because you both are college educated—and you did it on your own."

Uncle Mordechai was happy to see us. He invited us to stay for lunch. After the meal, he excused himself and seemed to disappear. I began to talk with Aunt Miriam about the master's thesis she had written about the Jews of the Esfahan ghetto. A short time later, Uncle Morechai re-emerged and joined his wife in saying good-bye to Roz and me.

As we drove away from Chicago, Roz looked at me and said, "Isaac, there is something I think you should know. After lunch, while you were talking to your aunt, I went to the bathroom. I thought I heard quiet Persian music coming from a room down the hallway,

Misha, Isaac's first-born, cuddles with her great uncle Dr. Mordechai Jacobson. In later years, Uncle Mordechai and his children became close friends of Isaac and his family.

so I peeked in. There sat your uncle, with his head close to a radio, listening to *golha* music! His head was down, so he didn't see me watching. Isaac, he was sobbing."

Tears came to my eyes. "No matter how often my uncle tells me that he hates Iran and everything Iranian, I don't believe him. *I know for a fact that no matter how much you try to leave Iran, Iran never leaves you.*"

Pepper Pike, Ohio
Spring and Summer 1988

When Roz and I arrived at our new home in Pepper Pike, Ohio there was a basketful of flowers waiting at the front door. The enclosed card said, "Welcome from Bahman and Maheen Akbari, your neighbors." I recognized their names to be Iranian-Muslim.

When I was in my garage the next day, I heard two women speaking Farsi! I ran to the neighbor's house and introduced myself, and Maheen and her mother welcomed me with smiles and hugs. It felt so good to see someone from my homeland, someone with whom I could share memories and culture. The Akbari family and the

Yomtovians began a journey together which spanned many years and included many family events. We shared good times and bad. When Maheen's mother came to visit she met my father, who was visiting from Israel. Our parents got along so well that the two families' relationship was cemented forever.

I was looking forward to celebrating my fortieth birthday in August. My wife and I had no extended family in Cleveland, and except for the Akbaris, no friends either. I did not yet have a job and my wife had just started her new position at University Hospital. We had three daughters who were enrolled in private schools about which we knew very little. It was the start of a new chapter in our lives.

I decided to find a way of making as many new friends as I could. Roz and I decided to hold a housewarming party and invite as many neighbors as possible. I asked Maheen to assist me. We printed invitations, requesting a RSVP. We addressed the envelopes with no names, since we did not know anyone, and put the envelopes (illegally) in the mailboxes of as many neighbors as we could. We expected to receive about fifty RSVP's, but within a few days we received over two hundred! Even my sister-in-law from Israel and my youngest sister from California decided to join us. We needed to move the party to the back yard, under a large tent.

Of all the guests, to my knowledge only my youngest sister Lydia was unmarried. Out of the blue, a young man appeared who declared himself to be "Dr. Michael Frankel, single." An unmarried Jewish doctor! This news caused Maheen and another neighbor, Dr. Halina Podlipsky, to grab him and bring over to meet my sister. "Lydia is returning to California tomorrow night," Halina informed Michael. "Get to know this lovely girl—fast!" Three months later, Michael proposed to Lydia and she accepted. Maheen threw a pre-engagement party for them at her home, and we all had a most pleasant time.

We celebrated many Friday nights, holidays, anniversaries, and birthdays together. Maheen's and my family enjoyed a deep friendship, and yet certain subjects were taboo: Whenever I attempted to bring up the topic of religion or Israeli politics, Bahman and Maheen would tactfully—and quickly—change the subject. How did they reconcile their private feelings about Judaism with the demands of social etiquette? Attending synagogue with us to celebrate the *bat mitzvahs* of our daughters, they politely smiled and seemed to enjoy the experience—Bahman even volunteered to wear a *kippah* (*yarmulke*, or skullcap). They opened prayer books and followed along, commenting favorably on the 23rd Psalm. At the end of the service the congregation offered the prayer for the sick, followed by a prayer for America. Bahman and Maheen nodded their approval of those prayers, whispering, "What wonderful prayers!" If they felt uncomfortable to be in a Jewish house of worship, they didn't show it.

When Bahman lost his mother, we were there to help him memorialize the loss. When their son or daughter needed rides, we were there. A few times when Bahman and Maheen could not attend their children's school events, we substituted for them. Every year when Maheen's mother or other relatives came to Ohio to visit, they were welcomed in our home as if we were the extended family.

But, in reality, we were not quite family. There was always the barrier of religion between us. Just below the surface there were feelings that divided us and issues that were never resolved.

Pepper Pike, Ohio
Autumn 1988

Ever since the Islamic Republic was established in 1979, I have wondered what has happened to my two friends, Fazlolah and Akbar. Because I had been following the career and scientific writing of Shahrokh Amini, I found out that he was presenting a paper at an international seminar in Canada. I succeeded in contacting him, also securing a safe telephone line so that he could speak freely.

At first, Shahrokh and I talked about our families, and then he told me that he was happy to work in a high position in the petrochemical industry run by the new Islamic regime. He informed me that he was a very observant Muslim, but that he was at peace with himself and his life. He continued by explaining that he was working hard to make the Iranian petrochemical industry independent of foreign engineers and technicians. I asked him about Akbar and Fazlolah.

"Oh, Akbar now has a very high position in the government," Shahrokh informed me. "That's very ironic, eh?"

"I always expected Akbar to go far when the Islamic fundamentalists took over," I answered. "I am not at all surprised."

"He has many regulatory agencies and offices under his management now," Shahrokh continued, obviously impressed with Akbar's accomplishments. "And he has become *hajji* (made a pilgrimage to Mecca), Isaac. He has always had an air of superiority and arrogance about him, but now he deserves to be arrogant! As for Fazlolah, all his factories were confiscated by the new regime, and the government also took his many homes. After serving a brief period in a state prison, and a thorough investigation into his relationships with foreigners, he was forgiven by the state judge. He became a devout Muslim and operated his free soup kitchen while working in a government office, earning a decent salary."

"So, Fazlolah is now a bureaucrat under the Islamic regime?" I inquired, amazed at how far Fazlolah's standard of living had fallen.

"He is no longer in Iran. In 1983 or '84, he and his family left Iran to live in Europe. I think they may be now living in France," added Shahrokh. "I have not heard from him since he left Iran."

I have given much thought to the fact that Akbar has become a zealous, radical Muslim, agreeing in principle with those people who have the innocent blood of young Iranian protestors on their hands. I think also about Fazlolah, who made a vast fortune and then lost it and went into exile. So far, I have not been able to make any direct contact with either Akbar or Fazlolah.

Jewish Community Center
Beachwood, Ohio
Winter 1989

Yesterday morning it was bitter cold and snowy outside—what better day to cook a pot of *ashe reshteh* soup? My mother made *ashe reshteh* whenever we asked for it, since it was one of our favorite winter meals, though traditionally it was prepared by Persian women to celebrate a baby's first tooth or the fulfillment of a wish. There is nothing complicated about preparing *ashe reshteh*: I cook chickpeas, navy beans, kidney beans, lentils, and spinach altogether. Noodles are added near the end of the cooking and the soup is served with fried onions. It is a complete meal in one pot!

Recently, I joined the local Jewish Community Center (known informally by its initials, JCC). I am finding many enjoyable activities and amenities there, especially the steam room. After getting the *ashe reshteh* started, I decided to go to the JCC and warm up in the steam room.

No sooner did I enter the steam room and settle myself on the wooden bench, than I began to relax. I leaned back against the wall and closed my eyes. I inhaled deeply and allowed the steam to fill my lungs—and suddenly I was aware that I had experienced this sensation before, an overwhelming sense of déjà vu came over me: All at once I was back in Tehran's public bath with my father, inhaling the same hot humid air I inhaled when we shared our weekly bath every Friday morning.

My father! How I missed my dear Agha-Joon, living so far away in Israel! As a boy I heard how my father had left Esfahan for Tehran at the age of sixteen, and I thought what a brave and determined young man he was. He began his own business carrying bolts of fabric on his shoulder, walking through the streets and *koochehs* shouting, "Fabric for *chador*! Fabric for shirt! Fabric for pants!"

I recalled how he expanded his business when he was able to buy a bicycle, and then finally, he opened a store. His "Malek Fabric Store" was on the corner of Malek and Ghazvin Streets, very near

Darvazeh Ghazvin, a huge intersection. This wonderful location was also several blocks from the gate to the "New City," a busy, prosperous neighborhood of famous nightclubs, restaurants, and houses of prostitution.

On Friday mornings, sometimes as early as 4:00am, my father shouted for my brothers and me to get dressed and accompany him to *Hammam Estakhr* (Estakhr Public Bath). Once inside the bathhouse we undressed, hung our clothes in wooden lockers, and then wrapped a large piece of red cotton fabric, called a *loong*, around our waists for the sake of modesty.

We followed an attendant down a white-tiled hallway—the walls and floors were all white—to our assigned cubicle. Each private cubicle was numbered. We waited in the hallway while the attendant sprayed permanganate inside the cubicle to disinfect it, followed by a spray of water to rinse it. Once inside our little room, we filled a pitcher from a large tub and poured the hot water over our heads.

While we waited for the attendant to return, we cleaned our feet with a pumice stone and scrubbed our fingernails with a soapy, rough fabric. The attendant finally returned and scrubbed each of us raw with a rough, course fabric; his purpose was the removal of dirt and dead skin, but he also removed some living skin during the rubbing and scouring!

Following the exfoliation, we rinsed ourselves and waited to be washed with soap and extremely hot water. One by one, we sat on a tiled bench while the attendant washed our hair and body with a very powerful soap. I clamped my eyes shut to avoid the stinging suds. After each of us had been soaped and rinsed, my father tipped the attendant for his efforts.

The last step in the cleansing process was taking a shower. (This was the only time we were completely nude.) After showering, we yelled for towels: one for our upper half and one for the bottom. By this time we were over-heated and dehydrated. My father would shout, "Rosewater in #14!" and an attendant would arrive at our numbered cubicle with a tray. On the tray were glasses of ice-cold water containing sugar and rosewater.

After regaining our energy, we dressed and returned home. We ate breakfast and then my father went to work at his store. During the years that I attended Muslim elementary school, I had Thursday afternoon off to play and have fun. (My siblings who attended Jewish school did not have the afternoon off.) Women and girls were allowed at the public baths on Thursday afternoons; my mother and sisters went to the bathhouse after my mother finished washing the family's laundry.

Pepper Pike, Ohio
Winter 1989

"Wake up! Wake up!" Roz shouted.

I woke up with a violent jolt, as if I had been thrown to the earth from a great height. My heart was pounding so hard that I could see my chest quivering with each beat. I could hear the sound of my heart in my ears, thumping like a drum. For several minutes I didn't know where I was.

"Try to take a few deep breaths. You're safe now," Roz consoled me.

It took time, but finally my heart calmed down and I was able to fully wake up. I wiped white foam from my lips with the back of my hand. Roz turned on the bedside lamp. "Can you tell me what frightened you?" she asked.

"The beginning of my dream was quite enjoyable: I was walking to the public bath, like I did many times—looking here, looking there—when suddenly I heard the sound of people running. I turned around. Not far behind me were a dozen large men carrying clubs. Somehow I knew it was me they were after, and I began to run.

"I sensed that the men were getting closer. I could hear their angry shouts. The next thing I knew, I was on the roof of the public bathhouse—how I got up there, I don't know. As I dashed along the rooftop, I dodged between row after row of beautiful red *loongs*, the red fabrics we wrap around ourselves at the bathhouse, that were hanging on clotheslines. There were dozens, maybe a hundred, of those large red fabrics billowing in the breeze, back and forth, like kites, like flags. I ran in and out among those *loongs,* trying to evade the men who were chasing me. I knew they wanted to throw me off the roof."

"I remember you've told me how you were chased many times by Muslims who wanted to beat you." Roz was wiping my face and chest with a towel. "They are still chasing you."

"My God, in my nightmare *I felt such fear!* Total fear, like an animal that is hunted—like a rabbit chased by a wolf. My whole body was swept along by the sheer terror of being caught and killed, Roz. There was a sensation of imminent death, a primordial feeling. I felt dehumanized. I was like a rabbit, without pride. My stomach wants to retch at the thought of it."

Cleveland, Ohio
March 1991

Roslyn Yomtovian, Isaac's wife, admiring the haft seen table for the Hafez Foundation's Norouz celebration in Pepper Pike, Ohio.

I have become involved in several Iranian groups in the Cleveland metro area. In March of 1991, I assisted the Hafez Society to celebrate the Persian New Year, Norouz, in one of the local hotels. Over 450 guests participated in this celebration, including dignitaries, county commissioners, mayors, state representatives, and senators. We discovered that many Persian doctors served the Cleveland Clinic, University Hospital, and several other healthcare institutions. We also invited men who were former officers in the Iranian military, university professors, engineers, and business owners. Many cultural events have been planned and successfully implemented in the Cleveland area.

How do Jews and Muslims relate to each other at these events? We acknowledge that certain topics of conversation cause tension, so we avoid any discussions of religion or Israeli politics. When I remind Muslims of the Jews' 2500 years of history in Iran, they seem unimpressed. When I bring up the fact that many Muslims are relative newcomers to Iran, they still insist that Jews are Jews and should not be called "Iranians." Even my most learned and intelligent Muslim friends are incapable of accepting the fact that Jews living in Iran have been unreasonably discriminated against, and that especially during the last 500 years (since the Safavid Dynasty), Jews have been treated as subhuman, third class citizens. "If you don't like the way Jews are treated in Iran, you should go back there and work to change the laws and the Iranian constitution. We don't think discrimination is a big problem there," declare Muslim émigrés in America.

Perhaps the most sensitive issue among Muslim immigrants is the fact that their children form relationships with American Jews and Christians. The new generation, born in America, is not under the tight control of their parents and grandparents. Many young Muslim men marry Catholic Americans, claiming that at least their wives are God-fearing and have strong morals. A large number of American Muslim daughters have married Jewish men. When I ask these young women why, they claim that they specifically looked for Jewish men because they are loyal, kind, intelligent, and respectful of their wife and family. Roz and I are often invited to dinners hosted by Muslim families whose daughters have married Jews—especially when the Jewish in-laws are also invited: Roz and I are supposed to show that the Muslim family already has Jewish friends, and therefore should be granted the seal of approval. Usually, however, the tension between the families remains palpable.

I have learned that present-day Iranian politics is another taboo subject. When pressed, Muslim Iranian immigrants praise the Islamic Republic's theocratic policies, including the strict religious laws imposed on the population, especially women. The fact that they defend the Islamic Republic is a paradox because it is contrary to the American values of democracy and human rights! I cannot understand how they can justify this point of view.

"Since you love the Iranian government so much, why not pack up and move your entire family back to Iran?" I ask them.

"Our children live here, our jobs are here, and we're comfortable here. It is to our advantage to remain here," most Muslim immigrants respond. "We go back to Iran from time to time to visit, but we have built lives in America."

"You must admit that living in a democracy is much better than a dictatorship," I suggest. When my Muslim friends and acquaintances dismiss my statement with a shrug, I usually persist by asking, "Do you at least admit that the government of Iran does not represent the needs and wishes of the majority of its citizens?"

"You are wrong, Isaac. Most Iranians understand that democracy is strong in Iran and they support their government. The government of Iran is no better or worse than any other government," they answer. "Iran is not perfect, but America is not perfect either! Look at the poverty and crime in America. Look at all the drug and alcohol abuse. And all the homosexuals! They're even marching in the streets and demanding the right to marry each other. Shameful!"

"Yes, there are problems in this country," I concede, "but America does not hide the truth: Everything, the good and the bad, is out in the open. Americans don't hide their social problems, but the Islamic regime attempts to do so. In Iran, the religious leaders deny the existence of vice and depravity; they are hypocrites and liars. Don't you think the people of Iran would be better off if the Islamists allowed modernization and reform?"

"Things are fine the way they are in Iran," they insist. "Iran is *not* like Saudi Arabia, Syria and Libya. You are naïve, Isaac. You think the U.S. government is so wonderful, but the President of the United States listens to the oil industry! Look at recent history, please: The Americans got rid of Mohammad Mossadegh and put the Shah in charge after Mossadegh nationalized the Iranian oil industry. When the Shah became too independent and began to raise the price of oil, they got rid of *him* and caused a horrible war between Iraq and Iran. And now America wants to get rid of the Islamic Republic! Listen, Isaac, all the power is in the hands of the oil industry. The President of the United States has limited power and must be careful not to antagonize the countries that it counts on for oil."

Lurking just below the surface of the immigrant Muslim's psyche are strongly held conspiracy theories that cast America as the great Satan, always taking advantage of Iran. [See: Part IV] It is their belief that America has acted like the imperialistic regimes of Great Britain and Russia, raping the resources of the country. "How can Muslims equate America with those countries?" I ask my Muslim friends and acquaintances. "It is a historic fact that Russian and Britain invaded Iran and seized the oil, but America did not invade. In fact, there were periods in which America actually brought stability and economic growth to Iran." I am unable to convince them of this. Facts don't seem to matter, regardless of their level of intelligence and education.

And so it seems that we always arrive at an impasse. End of discussion.

Pepper Pike, Ohio
September 19, 1993

My eldest daughter Misha approached me with an important request. "I want to go to the Homecoming Dance with Jason."

"You're much too young to go on a date," I responded. Misha was only in the eighth grade.

"I'm thirteen, almost fourteen!" Misha protested.

"We did things differently in Iran," I informed her.

"In case you haven't noticed, we're not in Iran!" she shouted.

"Settle down a minute and let me tell you how things went between girls and boys in *my* teen years: We had a very nice, no-pressure way to meet members of the opposite sex." I knew I was in for an argument.

"I imagine that whatever went on, the parents were in complete control," said Misha angrily. Her dark eyes flashed.

"Listen and you'll understand, Misha-dadi. You see, on warm Saturday evenings, after celebrating the end of *Shabbat*, Jews left the center of Tehran by bus and rode to a resort area located at the base of the Alborz Mountains called Shemiran. The ride to Shemiran took about an hour and the ticket was twice as expensive as a regular bus ticket," I explained.

"So you're telling me that only rich people went to Shemiran?" asked Misha.

"No, at that time Shemiran was a destination for the middle-class," I responded. "Jews went there to visit the ice cream parlors and restaurants on Tajrish Square. It was a place for families to relax, have fun, and eat. And there was a secondary purpose for those weekly excursions: It was a place for young Jewish men and women to meet each other and for their families to socialize and perhaps begin the process of match-making."

"How did this match-making work?" asked Misha, suddenly interested.

"First of all, the families would promenade the plaza several times, then the parents would go to teashops, sweetshops, or ice cream parlors to talk. Meanwhile, groups of boys and groups of girls continued to promenade, checking each other out, sometimes talking to each other. But they always remained in groups. The only time a young man and a young woman could hold hands and walk together was when they became engaged—such behavior signified a public announcement of an engagement."

"I still don't understand how the match-making occurred," declared Misha.

"Morvarid Khanom, Mrs. Morvarid, was always available on Saturday nights in Shemiran. And she always had her little book with her."

"What was in her book?" asked Misha.

"Many things! She kept a record of all the Jewish families that had eligible sons and daughters. She knew the names, ages, and level of education of each young person, and she was always updating her information," I replied.

"So, I guess you liked going to Shemiran, Daddy," teased Misha.

"Oh yes, I always looked forward to going there. Sometimes I went there with my family, but by the time I was fourteen years old I went with my friends from Kourosh. We would save our money so that we could afford bus fare, a sandwich, and beer. I remember how delicious those egg and potato sandwiches were! But there were some Muslim-owned restaurants that posted signs (*Vijeh Musalmanan*, "Muslims Only") warning non-Muslims that they were not welcome."

"That's not right!" said Misha with indignation.

"No, it wasn't right—and the restaurants that discriminated against Jews lost lots of business because the majority of visitors to Shemiran were Jews," I added. "I also remember that buses were available for the return trip from Shemiran until 2:00am, unlike most service which stopped at around 10:00pm."

"You were allowed to stay out very late," observed Misha. "You won't let me even go on a date."

"I was a young man; you are a girl," I said defensively. "I think you're missing the point, which is that *parents* make the decisions."

"I'm not looking for a husband, I just want to go to a dance," argued Misha.

"Dating is not something that girls from good families did," I countered. "But boys and girls were allowed to meet at the synagogue, under certain circumstances."

"What circumstances?"

"During *Rosh Hashonah* and *Yom Kippur*, a tent was set up in the center of the courtyard at Kourosh, our high school. All the Jewish young people of both sexes would congregate in the tent and socialize and look each other over. The boys would then talk among themselves and say, 'Look at Pary! She's all grown up! Look at Fereshteh! She's gorgeous!' Meanwhile, the girls would get together and compare notes regarding the boys: 'Look at Morad! He's so handsome! Did you hear that Parviz wants to go to America to study engineering?'"

"What happened then?" asked Misha.

"When a son met a girl he liked, he told his mother. The mother went to find Mrs. Morvarid, the *shadchanit* (matchmaker), to gather information from her and then, hopefully, make a *shidduch*, an introduction between the two young people."

"It sounds like Mrs. Morvarid was very busy."

"She was one of the principal matchmakers and very much in demand," I agreed. "Anyway, the young man's mother went to Mrs. Morvarid and asked about a particular girl. Mrs. Morvarid pulled out her book and said, 'Oh, *that* girl is the daughter of Yakov and Sara Eliyahu; her brother married a girl from Esfahan and her older sister married a young man who is now a physician.' The mother listened carefully to all the information about the girl's family, and then asked, 'So, is this a good match for my son?' Mrs. Morvarid would think it over and respond, 'Yes! It is a good match!' or, 'No! Forget it! The girl's family and yours will not be compatible.' That's the way it was done."

"You still haven't told me whether or not I can go on a date to the dance," Misha reminded me. "You've told me all about girls and boys in Iran, but you haven't given me a straight answer. I think you're trying to change the subject, and hoping I forget what I asked in the first place."

Misha was too smart for me. "I can go along with you hanging out in a group and getting together with friends for an activity. That's OK. For instance, in Israel we danced as a group, in a circle. I cannot give my permission for you to go out one-on-one; this I don't agree with. You are too young for dating." [Misha grew up to be a very accomplished, independent woman who lives and works in Manhatten.]

Pepper Pike, Ohio
March 20, 1995

It was time once again to celebrate Passover, a Jewish holiday that falls around the same time as the celebration of the Persian New Year. My fourteen-year-old daughter Ezi already knew a lot about Passover and the Israelites' exodus from Egypt, but she was very curious about the Persian holiday of *Norouz.*

"The word *Norouz* means New Light," I told her. *Norouz* marks the first day of spring and the beginning of the year on the Iranian calendar. It is similar to the Jewish holiday of Passover because both holidays symbolize the beginning of new life, the time of year the earth renews herself, when it's time to plant new crops," I continued.

I told Ezi that in Iran the refrain throughout the year was, "Wait for *Norouz!* You want something new? Wait for *Norouz!* You want new shoes, a new dress? Wait for *Norouz!*" Meanwhile, in Jewish homes, the refrain was always, "Wait for Passover!"

"*Norouz* is a happy time of year, isn't it?" asked Ezi.

"It is a very exciting time when everybody is happy and very nice to each other. Preparations for *Norouz* begin months before the actual day of March 21, and the holiday lasts for thirteen days," I explained. "On the thirteenth day of *Norouz* everyone in Iran goes outdoors to promenade in a park; it has always been a major day for match-making."

"Passover lasts for eight days," Ezi observed, "and I thought Passover was a long holiday!"

"On the day after the eighth day of Passover, Jews also go out to the parks. They have BBQ's and picnics, and bring along music so that they can dance. Passover is also a time to visit one's relatives; if a death has occurred, the grieving family is visited first," I said, continuing my explanation. I was happy that Ezi was interested in learning about *Norouz*. "When you visit an Iranian home during *Norouz,* you are presented with an amazing variety of sweets. And then there is something called *haft seen*, seven things that all begin with the letter "S" in the Farsi language, that everyone has in their house for the holiday. These seven things all have to do with health, wealth, love, and all the things we hope for in the New Year.

"I still don't really understand what *haft seen* is, Daddy," said Ezi with a confused look on her face.

I attempted to explain: "First of all, the women of the house would cover a large table with a beautiful *sofreh*, or tablecloth. And then a bowl of *sib*, apples, which symbolize beauty and health, would be set out. You would also have *sanjed*, the dried yellow fruit of the oleaster tree, which represents love; *seer*, which is garlic and represents medicine; *serkeh*, which is vinegar and symbolizes patience; *sabzi*, green vegetables, which symbolize green and rebirth; *samanu,* a sweet pudding made from wheat germ, which symbolizes affluence; *somaq,* sumac berries, which symbolize the color of the sunrise; and *sekeh,* coins to represent wealth."

"What else is put on the table, Daddy?" Ezi asked.

"There might be lentil sprouts growing like grass in a beautiful bowl to symbolize the season of rebirth, and colored hardboiled eggs, also to symbolize new life. Many Iranians also display a glass bowl of little orange or red fish, another sign of life. Candles, which stand for enlightenment and happiness, are set out. And I must not forget a crystal carafe of rosewater and a beautiful, ornate mirror," I concluded.

"That's a lot to put on the table!" observed Ezi.

"Yes, and I almost forgot to mention the bowls of dried nuts and raisins and the trays of pastries," I added.

"For Passover we have a special prayer book, the *Haggadah*. Do Iranians have a special book for *Norouz*?" asked Ezi.

"Good question! As a matter of fact, religious Muslim families display the Quran on the holiday table. More modern Muslim families display a book of Ferdowsi's *Shahnameh*, or perhaps a book of Hafez's poetry," I added, smiling.

"I think I understand now," Ezi said. "*Norouz* sounds very wonderful!"

"Yes, it was always a beautiful time of year!" I said wistfully. "I will always associate the smell of *sonbol*, little purple hyacinth flowers, with *Norouz*. And the delicious meals! A traditional meal was served of steamed rice with chopped chives, dill, and parsley, and fish. This meal was called *sabzi polo mahi*."

Ezi gave me a quick hug and ran off to help her mother prepare dinner. I walked to the window and watched a cold rain begin to fall. There was so much I wanted to teach my daughters about their Persian heritage.

Pepper Pike, Ohio
Early April 1996

It was pleasantly busy around the house. Preparations for Passover were in full swing.

The afternoon preceding the first *Seder*, my four daughters came home from school to find Roz and I setting the table.

"Tell me about Passover in Iran, Daddy," begged seven-year-old Ariela, the youngest. "I want to hear all about it."

"When my parents entertained guests for any occasion, or when we celebrated a holiday such as Passover and the High Holidays, we used the "guest room." The "guest room" was actually what Americans call a "formal dining room," and it was the most elegant room in the house. There was a large European-style dining table with many chairs, probably eight or ten. On the floors were the most exquisite Persian rugs that my family owned, and the walls were adorned with gold and silver plates engraved with Hebrew prayers and colorful paintings with Jewish themes. There were special cupboards in which we stored our best porcelain china and crystal glassware, and sideboards on which we displayed our best bottles of wine and hard liquor," I described.

"Was the special dining room big enough for everyone?" Ariela wondered.

"You see, my father had five brothers and one sister. When you add in the many cousins and other relatives, there would be forty to fifty guests coming to celebrate the first two nights of Passover! If the number of guests exceeded the capacity of the guest room, the overflow would use our main family room, and sit on the floor to eat," I said.

"On the floor, Daddy? I thought people only eat on the ground when they go on a picnic!" Ariela exclaimed with a giggle.

"My family almost always ate meals on the floor, Ariela. We would spread a *sofreh*, a tablecloth, on the floor and then set the plates and utensils on it. The tablecloth we used for everyday meals had no decorations and was made of plastic or a synthetic fabric. For Passover we used a special *sofreh* that could only be used for Passover. It was made of a lovely brown fabric and had beautiful Jewish artwork and Hebrew blessings embroidered on it. For the weekly *Shabbat* meal we used a lovely white *sofreh*, which was also embellished with designs and blessings," I explained.

"That's very different than in our home, Daddy," said Ariela.

"If you think our sitting on the floor was unusual, would you like to hear about how we made Passover wine?"

Ariela responded with a resounding, "Yes!"

"In the months prior to Passover, my father Ebrahim and his father, my grandpa Baba Joon Eliyahu, would uphold the tradition of making wine for the entire Yomtoubian family. Our courtyard was divided into two sections: One side was kosher for Passover, the other side was not. My grandfather would spread an enormous white sheet on the ground in the kosher section and pile hundreds of pounds of dark brown and black grapes upon it. There were also several large, deep metal containers, thoroughly cleaned and ready to receive the squeezed juice of the grapes," I said.

"What did you do to help?" asked Ariela.

"After my brothers and I had washed our hands and arms and tucked in our shirts, we were allowed to squeeze the grapes with our hands. We had a wonderful time! No food or snacks were allowed in this area, but the radio was blasting Persian music into the courtyard. I remember the sound of that music and the aroma of fresh grapes as we worked under the warm spring sun! After the grapes were squeezed, the metal containers were taken to the basement storage room, which was always dark and cool—a perfect environment for the fermentation of the grape juice.

"Our Muslim neighbors knew we were making wine. They eagerly waited for my father to give them a bottle of wine as a gift for Persian New Year. Even though the Holy Quran prohibits the drinking of wine, our Muslim neighbors gladly accepted it in secret. Jews, however, were allowed to use wine for their holiday celebrations," I explained.

"Passover was a busy, happy time of the year for your family," observed Ariela.

"Passover was almost like the New Year to us!" I exclaimed.

"How was that? I thought *Rosh Hashonah* was the New Year," said Ariela, wrinkling her brow in confusion.

"Passover was the time of new beginnings. It was also the time of receiving new clothing," I explained. "Everything you wanted had to wait for Passover! My parents would tell me, 'For *Pesach* (Passover) you will get your new shoes!' And when I protested that my shoes were too small, they insisted that I 'wait for *Pesach*' anyway. If my sister asked for a new book bag, because hers was falling apart, they'd tell her"—

"Wait for Passover!" Ariela chimed in.

"Yes! That's right!" I laughed. "And there is something else I should tell you about how my family celebrated Passover in Iran: Up until I turned thirteen or so, we baked Passover *matzoh* for all the Jews in the neighborhood!"

"Really?" asked Ariela in disbelief.

"Yes, of course," I assured her. My family's ancestors were bakers of *matzoh* for many generations: They baked *matzoh* in Esfahan, and then brought the tradition to Tehran."

"How did you do it?" Ariela pressed me for details.

"One side of our house was made 100% *glatt kosher*. We filled up the other side of the house with wood for the large clay oven. About three weeks before *Pesach*, dozens of fifty-pound sacks of flour were delivered. Two weeks before *Pesach,* the ten laborers showed up, some were men and some were women."

"Where did the laborers stay?" asked a wide-eyed Ariela.

"In our house, for two weeks! Our house was thrown into total chaos: The laborers slept on the floor, wherever they could find space, and arose to begin work at 5:00am. My mother had to prepare food and tea for all those extra people. The male workers were in charge of carrying wood outside and keeping the fire in the oven going. They also had the task of mixing the flour with the correct amount of water to make dough. Meanwhile, the women sat on pillows in the living room; they took pieces of dough, flattened them, and then put little holes in them. It was just like an assembly line!

"Next, one of the workers carried the flattened dough outside to the courtyard. Baba Joon Elyahu was in charge of baking the dough in the oven for one or two minutes and then removing it when it was baked to perfection. Grandfather removed each *matzoh* from the oven and placed it on a clean white sheet to dry. When the *matzohs* were dry, they were stacked in big piles. The work continued each day until 11:00pm.

"Two or three days before *Pesach*, the neighborhood Jews began to line up in the *koocheh*. All of our customers eagerly talked to each other and caught up on the news of the entire Jewish community. It was a chaotic scene! One at a time they entered our house to purchase the *matzoh*. The *matzohs* were huge, round—not like the smaller, square ones you are familiar with. My father set up a huge scale that hung from the second floor balcony on a chain. He weighed the *matzohs* and then sold them," I said happily.

"Can we make *matzoh* here in our house?" Ariela asked hopefully.

"I don't think so, daughter. It would be too much work and commotion. Your mother would never condone such a project," I answered, and kissed Ariela's forehead.

Isaac surprises Roslyn's mother, Mary Kaplan, with the Persian-Jewish Passover tradition of Daiyanu, in which celebrants are allowed to gently hit each other with green onions to symbolize the beating of the Jewish slaves by their Egyptian masters. This is the only time a person is allowed to "hit" an elder.

Isaac conducts the Passover Seder with great exuberance in his home.

Home of Dr. Abdolah Namazi
Cleveland, Ohio
Summer 1998

After the death of my Muslim friend, Dr. Abdolah Namazi, I was invited to come to his funeral and then sit with the family. The doctor's sons, grandchildren, and friends gathered and talked to each other for a while. (All three of Dr. Namazi's sons were married to Catholic women, and their children were raised in the Catholic Church.) After everyone had some time to visit with each other, the attending clergyman invited us to join him in the next room for prayers. The family asked me to follow them to the next room.

The clergyman asked us to move the casket and place it in front of all the guests, facing east, towards Mecca. Then he asked us all to remove our shoes and socks and sit on the floor. After he completed his eulogy, he began to lead the guests in prayer (*namaz*) in Arabic. At this point I became very confused and didn't know what to do: I was too embarrassed to leave the room, but I didn't want to perform the *namaz*, which I hadn't recited since childhood.

There I was, surrounded by many of my friends, and I did not want to offend any of them. As the clergyman recited the first verse, I automatically recited what I remembered. As I pronounced the words, I began performing the ritualized movements and gestures with precision, ending up with my forehead on the floor, my nose against the carpet, as I had been taught in elementary school.

At that moment, the vision of all my Muslim elementary school friends flashed before my eyes. In an instant I decided that I could no longer be coerced into appeasing Muslims, even those who were my friends. I gathered my shoes and socks, stood erect, squared my shoulders—and left the room. They finished their *namaz* without me.

Fort Lee, New Jersey
Summer 1999

When my father came to visit us in the States in the summer of 1999, he insisted that I find his first cousins Ester and Ardeshir who were living on the East Coast. Ardeshir's last name was Yomtoubian and Ester was married to a man whose last name was Farajian. After two phone calls to friends in New York, we found Ester's family and also Ardeshir's children in New Jersey. On a Friday afternoon, before *Shabbat* eve, we called Eshrat. My father talked to her as if they had left Esfahan yesterday. As expected, Ester insisted that all of us visit her and her children and grandchildren the weekend of my father's return trip to Israel.

My brother Ruben joined my father and I and we drove to New Jersey, just past the George Washington Bridge, and within minutes we were at the home of my father's cousin, Eshrat Farajian. She had invited her entire family, as well as the former wife of Ardeshir, Malakeh Khanom.

Ardeshir Yomtoubian was born in Esfahan. He completed the ninth grade and at the age of fifteen moved to Tehran, determined to become the wealthiest Yomtoubian. He was extremely handsome with a pleasant personality, an outstanding sense of humor, and endless energy. Within days of his arrival in Tehran, he secured a job at a barber/beauty shop on Nadery Street, one of the high-class commercial neighborhoods. By the age of eighteen he managed to establish an extensive network of wealthy Muslim and Jewish friends. He wore only the most expensive clothing: He became known for his Italian shoes, French suits, British shirts, and imported aftershaves. He made sure that Morvarid Khanom, the matchmaker, knew that he was seeking to marry a rich Jewish woman, regardless of her looks, education, or health.

Soon he married Malakeh Khanom, daughter of a respected, wealthy land developer and merchant. She was well-educated, very kind, short, average looking, and handicapped—one of her legs was shorter than the other—and she was older than Ardeshir. Eventually, Malakeh Khanom gave birth to two boys and two girls.

In the meantime, Ardeshir increased his wealth exponentially and established a large land development and construction company. In Iran in 1955, he was the only Yomtoubian who owned an American car, a huge white Buick. Shortly after he purchased the car, my family went to see it. Everyone exclaimed that the shiny automobile was a thing of great beauty. As I walked around the car, inspecting it from every angle, I noticed dried blood on one of the front tires. It was the custom to sacrifice a pigeon or a chicken or a lamb (whatever you could afford) and let the blood flow onto a newly purchased vehicle of any sort—car, motorcycle or bike—to prevent future accidents or mishaps. "The blood has already been shed!" the witnesses would exclaim. "No more blood will be shed, God willing."

Uncle Ardeshir also adopted the title *"mohandes"* (engineer) even though he never attended school beyond ninth grade. His most famous development consisted of expensive homes that he constructed on a huge tract of land; he named the streets in the subdivision after his children. His own home, modern and ostentatious, was located in this development. I remember that when I visited his house in the mid-1950s, I was amazed to see a Western-style bathroom, complete with a tub and shower and a flush toilet. (Before that, the toilets I had seen were the old fashioned hole-in-the-floor type.)

Shortly before the 1979 revolution, his wife and children insisted on leaving Iran to make their home in America. To protect his vast wealth, Ardeshir had to remain in Iran. On the advice of his attorneys, Ardeshir formally divorced his wife Malakeh Khanom in an Iranian court. He then sent his family to the United States, with considerable liquid assets.

After the revolution, the local cleric and a number of *mullahs* and *ayatollahs* informed Ardeshir that his vast real estates holdings would be confiscated if he remained a Jew. Ardeshir's attorney and a cleric with whom he was friendly advised him to convert to Islam, and he did. He changed his name to Ali Islami. Soon he found out that his conversion was not enough to save his wealth; he was advised to marry a Muslim woman who would hopefully bear a son. Under this arrangement, all his wealth could be legally transferred to his Muslim son, but nothing could ever be transferred to his Jewish children in America.

In 1982, Ahmad Islami, my Muslim second cousin and the son of Ali Islami—formerly Ardeshir Yomtoubian—was born. He grew up knowing that his father was a convert and that his half-sisters and half-brothers were Jewish. Indeed, Ahmad communicated with his Jewish brothers and sisters via telephone, letters, and lately through e-mail. Even the Muslim wife communicated with Malakeh Khanom and all her children and grandchildren.

In 1997, when Ardeshir was diagnosed with cancer of the liver, he decided to visit his Jewish family in the United States. He stayed with Malakeh Khanom and spent the summer with his children and grandchildren. During the visit he succeeded in transferring some cash to purchase a number of buildings in New York City. He also was able to strengthen the relationship between his Muslim and Jewish families.

Shortly after his return to Tehran, Ardeshir died. In his will he requested to be buried in the Jewish cemetery. His Jewish children were convinced that Ahmad and his mother would honor Ardeshir's last request, however, due to the requirements of Islamic laws and the Ahmad's desire to preserve his inheritance, Ardeshir had to remain Ali Islami, a Muslim, and he therefore had to be buried in a Muslim cemetery.

[In 2009, when I once more visited the Yomtoubians and Farajian, I was shocked to learn that Ahmad and his mother had filed a claim in the Iranian courts demanding the ownership of the properties in New York City. According to the Islamic laws practiced in Iran, the Muslim son shall receive the entire inheritance of the Jewish family member. So far, the courts in the United States have not implemented those Iranian Islamic laws.]

Los Angeles, California
December 2000

I first met Hossein Mohammadi in his professional capacity as an official for the Department of City Planning, in the summer of 1999, during a meeting in which I hoped to obtain building permits for a construction project. After the business meeting was concluded, I approached Hossein and asked him if he was Iranian, and he said yes. We immediately began to speak to each other in Farsi and decided to go to a coffee shop and get to know each other. I knew by his last name that he was a Muslim from southern Tehran.

It didn't take long for us to share the details of our lives with each other: where we had lived in Iran and which schools we had attended; how many children we had (he had two daughters), and how we had met our wives (his wife was an American Catholic). After a long conversation we shook hands and promised to stay in touch. We often communicated with each other on the phone or in person.

One frigid day in late 2000, I received a frantic phone call from Hossein. "Isaac, I need your help!"

"What's wrong?"

"I'm in hot water, Isaac. I've made big trouble for myself," he began.

"How so?"

"I was in a restaurant in Beverly Hills a week or so ago, and I got into an argument with a Jewish-Iranian who was eating there. I lost my temper and called him "Dirty Jew" and some other bad names, and now the man has a lawyer and is suing me!"

"I see," I replied. "So, you acted as if you were back in Iran? You forgot you are in America! Jews in this country don't have to take verbal abuse from a Muslim and let it go. In America, Jews are not conditioned to be submissive. Here we are not inferior."

"I know. I'm sorry. I forgot I am not in Iran and let my temper rule me," he admitted with contrition. "Now I am afraid I could lose my job, and my attorney told me that the *Johood* will probably win his suit—there were many witnesses. You must help me! Please, speak to the man I offended. Intercede for me, Isaac. Tell him that I am very sorry and that I want to apologize to him," Hossein begged. "I cannot endure a defamation lawsuit. I could lose everything!"

"I'll see what I can do."

A few days after Hossein's phone call, during my next business trip to Los Angeles, I made time to meet with the offended man. I assured the man that Hossein was very sorry for his behavior and arranged for Hossein to offer him a face-to-face apology. The apology was accepted and the lawsuit was dropped.

Pepper Pike, Ohio
September 11, 2001

What has happened to my beloved country, America? I cannot believe that such horror has befallen my cherished country! My eyes are filled with tears and my heart is heavy. I watch the Twin Towers fall again and again on the television, and I am overcome with emotion. To the radical Islamists, the Twin Towers were the idols of Western materialism, and the Quran is very explicit about idols: They must be destroyed.

Today I remember July 1, 1983—the day I became an American citizen at the courthouse in St. Paul, Minnesota. Immediately after the ceremony, I went across the street and bought a large American flag attached to a pole with an eagle on top, to display in my office, and a small flag to keep in my attaché case. I also purchased a flag pin to wear on my jacket.

Iranian Jews are very proud of America, their adopted country. My extended family sings *God Bless America* at every party and celebration. Always. We take our citizenship very seriously. Today is a day for all Americans to stand together and believe in our strength and survival. We are shocked beyond comprehension and outraged at the people who have done such a terrible thing.

Home of Hossein Mohammadi
Los Angeles, California
September 20, 2001

Not long after the terrible tragedy of 9/11, I accepted an invitation from Hossein to visit his home while I was conducting business in Los Angeles. After dinner he and I sat down in the living room to talk.

"Have you experienced any harassment since 9/11?" I asked him. "I wouldn't be surprised if you did. Americans are very angry now."

"No, no one has bothered me, but I am very nervous," he admitted. "I don't know what to expect, Isaac."

"Americans are level-headed. Once the shock of 9/11 has time to heal, reason will prevail," I assured him. "Unlike Iran, America is a democracy and you have rights here, regardless of what a few radical Muslims have done."

"I am thankful for the rights we enjoy in America, but you are wrong about Iran, Isaac," Hossein countered. "Iran is also very much a democracy! Iran has an Islamic *Shi'ah* Democracy!"

"Hossein, the term "Islamic *Shi'ah* Democracy" is an oxymoron! "*Shi'ah*" and "Democracy" are contradictory concepts. In a real democracy there is a definite, purposeful separation of church and state; Iran has no such separation. In Iran it is decreed that the government must be *Shi'ah*. You are under a delusion, Hossein. Iran is a theocracy, a pretend democracy. In reality, a theocracy is a form of fascism."

"No, that's not true. The laws of Islam serve to elevate the people to a higher moral standard. It is not a bad thing to defer to the learned clergy; they are the guardians of our culture and our laws," Hossein argued. "They are well educated and their entire lives are dedicated to God and the people."

"The entire premise of the Islamic Republic is that the citizens, and I use that word loosely, are like children and are not capable of thinking for themselves. Eric Hoffer, in his book, *The True Believer*, wrote extensively about the "herd mentality" of people who live under repression: People who must do as they are told are not free!" I insisted.

"But there are checks and balances in the Islamic system of government," Hossein pointed out. "The *mullah* reports to the *olama;* the *olama* reports to the *ayatollah,* who in turn reports to the *Supreme Ayatollah.* If the Supreme Leader, the *Valih-e-Fagih,* does not meet the people's needs, he can be impeached."

"Sure, he comes before a panel of clergymen that he has appointed himself! How likely is he to be impeached? Get real! Dissent is not allowed in Iran, so the people have no avenue to express themselves. Face it! The *Shi'ah* view of democracy is not the same as the democracy practiced in the West. You are comparing apples and oranges, my friend," I declared vehemently. "The only people in Iran who enjoy social justice are the *Shi'ah* Muslim males."

"Certain aspects of *Shariah Law* have been relaxed, Isaac. Iran's regime is giving the people more liberty, a little at a time," Hossein pointed out.

"Democracy in Iran is an illusion! I reiterated. "The *Ayatollah* has created *an illusion of freedom* while keeping his people in a box; granted, sometimes the box is allowed to expand a little, but it is still a box. In a real democracy, the government doesn't "give" the people freedom: In a real democracy freedom is an unalienable right! In America there is a Bill of Rights and no one can take that away; our rights are guaranteed. *The Ayatollah's democracy is a mirage built on sand. It is made of threats and promises."*

"But as I said, there is more freedom in Iran now," insisted Hossein. "The people might be in a box, but the box is larger than it has been for years! Women are now free to remove their headscarf in their homes, if they like. Women and girls are now allowed to swim with their husband, brothers, or fathers as long as they wear the proper attire and a headscarf. A woman can now walk in the street without a male relative and not be considered a whore. This is progress, Isaac."

Hossein's viewpoint angered me greatly. "That is democracy? So they allow a woman to show a little of her hair in public or maybe wear colored clothes—big deal! What about the young women who must cover themselves from the head down in public while playing soccer, volleyball and tennis? They are not even allowed to go to a sports arena to watch a game unless a man accompanies them. What about the rights of women who seek a divorce? How about highly educated, professional women who need to have their husbands' permission to travel out of town? And tell me, Hossein, who are the prisoners of Ghasr Women's Prison? According to someone I know who was imprisoned there, that horrible place is packed with women who are locked up for talking to men to whom they are not related, or for having parties in the privacy of their own home. Other women are imprisoned for merely playing music that is not allowed by the Islamic Republic!"

"Women are better off in Iran than Saudi Arabia," Hossein protested. "In Iran a woman can get a university education and enter a profession. They can drive cars."

I was not about to let Hossein win the argument of women's rights. "Even though women can obtain an education and drive cars, they do not enjoy the same rights and privileges as men," I declared with great vehemence. "For example, if a man and a woman riding in the same car have an accident in which they are both injured, the woman receives only half the damages that the man receives; as witnesses in a court of law, two women equal the importance of one man; the husband always obtains custody of the children in a divorce settlement; under the law, a nine year old female child is punished as an adult, even when capital punishment is called for, but for boys the age is fifteen."

"You bring up only the negative aspects, Isaac. But there has been progress."

"Progress? The Supreme Leader and his henchmen only make the box in which people are imprisoned a little bigger, that's all," I explained. "They don't allow real freedom; they operate only on the fringes of democracy—from time to time they throw the dissidents a bone to try and quiet them, and if that doesn't work, the regime throws the dissidents into prison. My good friend Fereidoon N. was imprisoned for four months in isolation. He was tortured—and for what? He wasn't even a dissident! His crime was a visit to Israel in the early 1970s! The regime accused him of being a spy."

"I'm not saying the Iranian government is perfect, but there is voting for various officials," Hossein pointed out.

"Yes, but the *Ayatollah* pre-selects two or three men and then he tells the people to go vote. No matter who wins, it is the Ayatollah's selection; in his eyes, the people are not capable of making decisions. I'll say it again: As long as there is an Islamic government run by a Supreme Leader, there is no democracy in Iran."

Hossein's eyes flashed with the intensity of his convictions. "It's true, a person has to watch his step in Iran, but change is possible within the structure of an Islamic regime, Isaac. Even the dissidents of the Green Revolution want to keep an Islamic republic, only with a "bigger box"—more freedom."

"All you'll get in an Islamic regime are crumbs, Hossein. Don't you see that? When the Shah tried to modernize the country, he failed. The biggest obstacle in trying to bring Western-style democracy to Iran is that *there is no cultural memory of democracy in Iran*; throughout Iran's history there have always been absolute monarchies and despotism. We Iranians have always sought a leader who will save us—the Shah, Mossadegh, Khomeini—it doesn't matter. Iran is a nation of followers who allow the Islamic Republic to censor art, literature, music, and even the content of history and philosophy classes. That is not the hallmark of a free society," I argued.

"Maybe some censorship is a good idea, Isaac. There is no point in filling the people's head with false ideas. You would be better off, Isaac, if you stop watching certain Persian TV stations that broadcast pro-West propaganda. Also, you must stop listening to Iranian liberals like Naser Engheta, Bahram Moshiri, Maziar Bahari, and Manouchehr Ganji."

"You are gravely mistaken, my friend. How can you be so afraid of the truth? The Islamists have brain-washed you."

"But Islam is a good religion, Isaac. If the clergy would keep their noses out of people's daily lives and discontinue *Shariah Law*, everything would be fine. The clergy should only be involved in religious matters, not every aspect of life. There should be civil courts in Iran, like in Europe and America, where the clergy have no power. Israel is a good example of a country that has religious political parties, religious laws, and yet is a democratic country."

"And how will the clergy be persuaded to give up so much of their power?" I asked. "They won't give it up willingly."

"Things will change for the better in Iran, you'll see," Hossein insisted.

"How will things change if Muslims in the Diaspora remain silent? The silence of moderate Iranians is not a sign of tranquility; it is a sign of fear. Silence exists in graveyards! You and I cannot call ourselves "good" people if we don't speak against tyranny in Iran. My friend, you have an *obligation* to speak up and make your voice heard!"

"I don't see how that will help," Hossein said quietly.

"Of course it will help! The apathy and indifference of the world's moderate Muslims tells the *Ayatollah* that they are in agreement with his policies of torture, repression, and humiliation. Silence is almost as bad as evil. Your silence convinces Americans that you condone the behavior of the *Ayatollah* and Ahmadinejad. Do you hate America?"

"Of course not."

"Do you despise Jews?"

"No, of course not."

"Do you condone the terrorist attacks of radical Muslims?"

"No!"

"Then you must say so publicly, at every opportunity! You cannot stand by and say nothing. America is waiting to hear your voice, Hossein!"

This clay pot, like a lover once in heat:
A lock of hair my senses did defeat.
The cold lip of that clay pot did I once kiss,
How many kisses did it take—and give!
                    —Rubaiyat of Omar Khayyam

این کوزه چو من عاشق زاری بودست

در بند سر زلف نگاری بودست

این دسته که بر گردن او می بینی

دستی ست که بر گردن یاری بودست

Pepper Pike, Ohio
October 2001

Every so often in life something occurs that changes everything forever. Several days ago, I found out that my beloved Roz has cancer, non-Hodgkin's lymphoma. Roz, a medical doctor and pathologist, diagnosed herself. She has been much braver than I am.

I sat at my desk a week after the diagnosis, looking at my daily calendar. I was unable to concentrate. My mind was turbulent and full of thoughts as I stared at my desk calendar again and again: "At 8:50am call Mr. H. At 10:00am the cleaning ladies will arrive. Finish the environmental report for the city of Euclid. Write checks. Pick up Ariela at 3:30pm. Have food ready by 4:30pm, when Misha arrives home. At 7:00pm attend JCC Board meeting and give report on summer camp program." There it was, a normal day's activities.

But life was no longer "normal." All of a sudden there was great uncertainty, and possibly a different future than we had planned. Would we be able to travel the world after our children were grown, perhaps visiting Iran? We plan, God laughs.

I took out a piece of paper and tried to write down my thoughts and feelings.

> *My eyes are for watching your beauty,*
>
> *your gracious movements, kind smiles.*
>
> *Not seeing your splendid face would be no different*
>
> *than being blind!*
>
> *My ears are for listening to your kind words,*
>
> *your warm and sensual whispers.*
>
> *Not hearing your voice would be no different*
>
> *than being deaf!*
>
> *My mouth is for praising our friendship,*
>
> *our limitless affection and love.*

*Not speaking of my devotion would be no different
than being dumb!*

The phone rang and interrupted my writing. I was forced to return to reality.

Pepper Pike, Ohio
Autumn 2002

According to Jewish law, all boys become *bar mitzvah* at the age of thirteen, regardless of whether or not they participate in a ceremony: To become *bar mitzvah* is a natural part of a boy's biological growth. Throughout Iranian Jewish history, this process of physical maturation has been celebrated according to the tradition of families in the particular city of residence; for example, in Esfahan a *bar mitzvah* boy was expected, at the very least, to recite the *Shema*, Judaism's main prayer. Some families expected a lot more from their boys. In the last century, the wrapping of the *tefillin* on one's arm was added to the recitation of the *Shema*.

As my daughter Ariela's *bat mitzvah* approached, I began to think about my own *bar mitzvah* in Iran. I fondly remembered my Hebrew teacher, Mr. Dilmani. He required us to attend early-morning services in the local Mashhadi synagogue to observe *Selichot*, the month-long preparation that precedes *Rosh Hashanah*. During those 4:00am services we all waited for the sun to rise, at which time all boys age thirteen and older would wrap one of their *tefillin* around their left arm and the other *tefillin* around their forehead, while reciting a special prayer. Later the entire congregation recited the *Shema* and many other prayers. On Mondays and Thursdays, selected *bar mitzvah* boys would recite in unison the special prayer before and after the reading of the day's Torah portion. Often one or two of the best students with pleasant voices were invited to read the day's Torah portion, sung in a particular melody.

Boys like myself, who had a minimal interest in reading prayers, recited only what was required of us and spent the rest of the time drinking tea, eating pastries, and talking to each other. (As a matter of fact, I didn't know how to wear the *tefillin* until I was twenty-one years old, and walking down a street in Manhattan—a young Chabad rabbi showed me how to wrap the *tefillin* and recite the appropriate prayers. I learned that the wrapping and wearing of the *tefillin* actually defines the celebration of *bar mitzvah* and the acceptance of the responsibilities of performing *mitzvot*, good deeds, required of a Jewish man.)

In Iran, our families did not celebrate or throw a party to mark the observance of our *bar mitzvot*. Today, in America, the situation is very different! The concept of celebrating *bar mitzvah* for sons and *bat mitzvah* for daughters has gained great importance; large sums of money are spent on elaborate parties, some as lavish as the most ostentatious wedding. As I prepare for the *bat mitzvah* of my youngest daughter, I realize that I am guilty of this mistaken behavior: I have spent a fortune to celebrate the *bat mitzvot* of four daughters.

The difference between my life (and the lives of other Iranian Jews of my generation) and the lives of my children is incredible: I had little material wealth growing up, while my daughters have so much. The paradox is that the more I try to give to my children, the greater the conflict between us.

I am beginning to realize that I am living under false assumptions. During my childhood, I saw that men were measured by their wealth and to some extent, their profession. I have striven to give my children everything I never had, but wished to have. In doing this I have also tried to force my children to want the same things I have desired, and to live in the same manner I have desired to live, with the same values. This is selfish of me, and I see that it causes discord.

Why has it taken me so long to understand that my daughters crave freedom from their father, as I did as a young man? My daughters desire the freedom to invent themselves and become what they wish to become.

When did I lose sight of the fact that showing off one's wealth does

Leaving Iran

not reveal one's spiritual development? In my heart I knew better, and yet I fell into the trap of trying to impress family and friends. I suppose I have needed to convince myself that I've come a long, long way from #24 Koocheh Sharaf to Pepper Pike, Ohio, USA.

A family portrait taken at Ariela's bat mitzvah. (Standing, left to right) Ezi, Misha, Ariela, Leah. (Seated) Isaac and Roslyn.

274

Pepper Pike, Ohio
Spring 2003

I was sitting in the sun, with my eyes closed, lost in reverie.

"Where are you, Isaac?" asked Roz, after watching me for a minute or two.

Startled, I opened my eyes. "I think I was back in Iran, in my old neighborhood."

"You seemed to be having happy thoughts."

"Yes, I was remembering spring time in Tehran. Have I told you how flower vendors carry large trays of pansies and snapdragons on their heads? It was a beautiful sight!"

"It must have been a lovely time of year," Roz agreed.

"A month before *Norouz* a lot of shopping was going on. People purchased new clothes and other things that they had put off buying until spring. There was excitement and happiness in the air! Everything "new" was introduced—new movies, new plays, new music—the entire country renewed itself."

"How exciting!" Roz exclaimed.

"The Shah gave gifts to his personal staff and also to some specially chosen citizens. During *Norouz* everyone was generous and in a good mood. My tips for wrapping fabric for our customers were much higher than those normally given: 'Here's *eidi*, a tip for the holiday,' customers would say."

"Time and distance make memories sweeter," said Roz quietly, as she placed a kiss on my cheek.

Pepper Pike, Ohio
Autumn 2005

I suffered another nightmare. In my terrible dream I was chased by men shouting, "Catch him! Beat the *najes*, filthy bastard!" As usual, Roz woke me up and comforted me.

Later that day I gave thanks to God for the comfort I always receive from my wife. Even though she struggles with cancer and suffers greatly, she is always there to lift my spirits and give me hope. I know that I can unburden my heart and soul to her. I composed a poem for her in an attempt to describe my love and gratitude, for she is the heart of our home.

> *At night I embrace you.*
> *My heart races, my blood rushes,*
> *My senses awaken,*
> *My eyes see only you.*
>
> *By day I dream of you.*
> *My eyes are open, but they do not see,*
> *For I am lost in reverie.*
> *My thoughts are only with you.*
>
> *When ice and snow cover the land,*
> *I will warm you with the heat of my breath.*
> *When summer's heat parches the earth,*
> *I will shelter you in the shade of my shadow.*
>
> *Without you I am dust,*
> *blown away by the slightest puff of wind.*

Pepper Pike, Ohio
September 24, 2007

I just saw Ahmadinejad on television speaking to an audience at Columbia University. In his usual, ridiculous manner he stated, "We don't have homosexuals in Iran." [CNN News]. I beg to differ with him.

Contrary to Ahmadinejad's claims, homosexual activities have been common practice throughout Iran in all sectors of the community, especially among the clergy: The all-boys religious schools were a breeding ground for homosexual activities. I have heard many stories about clergymen pouring *aragh* (vodka) into their samovars to embolden men and boys to engage in sexual activities. Indeed, I know for a fact that parents warned their young sons to avoid befriending members of the clergy.

Another well-kept secret is that homosexuality is very common in cities such as Ghazvin, Qum, and Mashhad; as a matter of fact, there are sections of these cities designated as places where homosexual acts are practiced for a price. Young boys bring high prices. I remember hearing wisecracks about homosexuality: "If you are in Ghazvin and a hundred dollar bill falls out of your pocket, do not bend over to pick it up!" and, "In Mashhad and Qum women get pregnant only after their husbands get tired of sex with *kooni* (homosexuals)".

The practice of *sigheh* (the use of temporary wives) is also rampant. One of my female Muslim friends told me that she was warned to avoid going near any of the major mosques, in order to avoid a confrontation by *mullahs* who might want her to become a "temporary wife." The only way to elude those unwanted sexual advances was to be accompanied by her husband or a chaperone.

Young women who find themselves attracted to young men may conduct a sexual relationship by engaging in any sexual act except intercourse, to avoid pregnancy. Some women also resort to satisfying their sexual desires secretly with other women. Unfortunately, women are severely punished for engaging in any sexual activity outside of marriage: prison, lashing, hanging, and stoning are typical punishments in the Islamic Republic.

The irony is that strict Islamic rules and the total control of women and their sexuality have caused homosexuality to flourish.

There is also the issue of incest. Several of my childhood friends told me about their personal experiences with incest, which their families tried to keep secret. Iranian families, due to a lack of knowledge of birth control, had large families of sons and daughters who were close in age. These families were, for the most part, very poor and inhabited only one or two rooms. The entire family often slept in one bed, or on a mattress on the floor, and during the winter the entire family all slept under one big heavy blanket; this physical proximity could easily lead to sexual intimacies between siblings and cousins. Occasionally, we would hear whispers in the community about a rape occurring within a household. Family members quickly covered up these disgraceful events.

Pepper Pike, Ohio
June 22, 2009

"I don't believe it!" I shouted at the television. "How can this be?"

Roz came into the family room. "Isaac, why are you yelling?"

"I am watching The Daily Show and who comes on to be interviewed, but Ebrahim Yazdi's son!"

"Is there something wrong with that?" Roz asked.

"Yes, there's a lot wrong with that!" I roared. "Yazdi's son is presenting his father as a supporter and leader of Iran's Green Movement. He said his father is presently under house arrest and being ill-treated because of his pro-civil rights, reformist position."

"Well, he was the leader of the Freedom Movement of Iran for a long time," Roz reminded me. "Didn't he join the Front for Resistance created by Taleghani and Mehdi Bazargan?"

"That may be so, but he was and is no saint," I insisted. "In fact, for a long time, he was a confidant of Ayatollah Khomeini. In 1972, Yazdi was named to be Khomeini's personal representative and intermediary to U.S. officials. This was a man who had spent part of the 1960s setting up Young Muslim Student Associations in the United States. Then, in 1977, Yazdi traveled to Najaf, Iraq to conspire with Khomeini. They made arrangements to obtain funds from Libya's Muammar Qadafi. Yazdi next traveled with Khomeini to Neuphle-le-Chateau, France where they were joined by Ghotbzadeh and Banisadr, two anti-Shah organizers who were well-organized, well-trained, and highly committed."

"So, Yazdi was against the Shah. A lot of intellectuals and American-educated Iranian men wanted to see the Shah leave power," stated Roz.

"That's true, but Yazdi disguised himself as a sheep, but he was really a wolf!" I continued. "Yazdi had access to President Carter; in fact, he brought Carter's personal message to Khomeini after the Guadalupe Conference. Carter sent U.S. Air Force General Robert Huyser to Iran to meet with General Gharabaghi, head of Iran's army, and Bazargan; the purpose of the meeting was to persuade the Shah's army to remain neutral. General Huyser clearly announced that it was in the best interest of Iran's army not to get involved, but rather to let the Shah leave and thus allow a peaceful transition to take place. This was the biggest mistake Jimmy Carter made."

"Yazdi disguised his true intentions all along!" exclaimed Roz.

"Of course! Yazdi was no freedom fighter; he was no champion of human rights: He wanted to establish an Islamic republic, with Khomeini in charge. The Americans were fooled, hoodwinked— especially Carter's U.N. representative, Andrew Young; he believed that Yazdi was a saint, similar to Gandhi! Khomeini named Yazdi the Deputy Minister for Revolutionary Affairs." I was very upset and agitated. "His official ministerial duties included forming the Islamic regime's secret service."

"Yazdi is smelling more and more like a rat," said Roz with disgust, "but a rat with a brain. He was a very smart man."

"Wait, there's more. Much more. Yazdi proudly spent time in Yasser Arafat's terrorist PLO training camps in Lebanon. The Libyan government of Qadafi also provided similar training camps. The Shah underestimated the radical Islamic movement. After the victory of the Islamic Revolution, in February 1979, Yazdi handed over the Israeli Embassy in Tehran to Yasser Arafat. Khomeini's son Ahmad and Yazdi welcomed Arafat into the Israeli Embassy on Kakh Avenue," I declared with great anger. "Yazdi was a master of *Taghieh*, lies and deceit."

"He was showing his true colors," Roz acknowledged.

"Absolutely! That same year, 1979, kangaroo courts were formed. Trials of former statesmen, diplomats, politicians, military officials, artists, political activists, and ordinary people who voiced their rejection of the new regime were held without legal assistance and without an opportunity to prove that the accusations against the accused were false. Those courts were a mockery of justice. Many thousands of people were executed, and Yazdi was one of the culprits behind the executions."

Roz was quiet for a few moments, then said, "I remember reading somewhere that Khomeini was heard to say, 'anyone who is against me is against God and should be killed immediately, for he is waging war against Allah. This is our justice.'"

"That's right," I agreed, "and Yazdi was happy to participate in that brand of justice. Khomeini and his dedicated followers, like Ebrahim Yazdi, perpetrated a bloodbath. Who knows how many thousands were executed! Ebrahim Yazdi acted as Prosecutor General and in some instances held televised interrogations of those who had been military and civilian leaders under the Shah. It was Yazdi who was instrumental in creating a "revolutionary justice system" and the establishment of the Revolutionary Guards of the Islamic Republic.

"In 1979, Yazdi resigned from his post as Foreign Minister to protest the US Embassy takeover as "contrary to the national interest of Iran." He resigned to save face, but his statements were merely superficial and self-serving—his public statements against the embassy takeover had the desired effect: Presidents Carter and then Reagan both continued to trust Yazdi; he even managed to set up a "back channel" communication with some supposed *moderate* members of the Islamic regime. Remarkably, President Reagan's National Security Advisor, Robert McFarlane, urged Reagan to negotiate an arms deal with Iranian intermediaries. By 1985, realizing he had been duped, he was urging Reagan to end the arms shipments," I explained.

"If I remember correctly, McFarlane resigned in disgrace, and he attempted suicide a couple of years later," Roz offered. "And that Yazdi character was very clever! All of this information clearly shows that the Islamic Revolution did not happen overnight: It was well planned and organized, beginning in 1963, when Khomeini instigated the first demonstrations. Yazdi was only one of Khomeini's masterminds, but he certainly was one of the most devoted and devious ones," Roz concluded.

"Now you understand why I am so upset about Yazdi portrayed as a hero! When Jon Stewart said on the Daily Show, 'Ebrahim Yazdi is a lovely, wonderful man,' and 'Yazdi is in our prayers,' I became sick to my stomach. Yazdi is out to take care of Yazdi—he is no hero; he is an opportunist. I become enraged when yesterday's terrorist and criminal has been transformed into a reformist and dissident! Yazdi is clever, that's for sure. He knows how to pull the wool over almost everyone's eyes and serve himself up as an old man who is a victim of the Islamic Republic."

I spent the rest of the evening and most of the night thinking about the Islamic Revolution and how, in Iran, *nothing is ever really as it seems!* Non-Iranians discover that Iranian behavior is confusing and impenetrable: Try looking into a mirror that has been broken into many pieces, and then glued back together—a "Persian mirror"— the resulting image is not really your face, but rather a distortion of reality. [Sciolino, Elaine. *Persian Mirrors, The Elusive Face of Iran*. New York: Free Press (Simon & Schuster), 2000]

The mind of the Iranian is filled with confusion; the entire nation is confused. Why? Because to the Iranian, everything is fluid, everything is relative. Even though there is a theocracy ruling the country, there is no real understanding of what is right and what is wrong. Conflicting ideas awash in a sea of expediency send mixed messages. For example, the average Iranian admires a successful person, but at the same time hates him for his success. Iranians love American technology and expertise, yet are taught to hate Americans. *There are endless examples of Iranian ambivalence; Iranians have a love/hate relationship with the West—and themselves!*

I, too, am often confused and ambivalent. The Persian mind is like a broken mirror whose pieces have been glued back together; consequently, every thought is distorted and fragmented. There is always an underlying subterfuge—and, as I've stated previously, nothing is really as it seems.

Pepper Pike, Ohio
July 15, 2010

Recovering from a serious illness, I spend a lot of time just sitting in the sun, without energy. Perhaps I am becoming old, but the heat of the sun feels so good, so soothing. As I watch clouds drift across the hazy sky, I became languid, as heavy as the humid summer air.

A plate of watermelon eaten in the shade of my patio tastes almost as refreshing as the watermelon I ate as a child in the courtyard of our house. A cold glass of ice tea sipped in my Ohio back yard tastes almost as restorative as the glasses of ice-cold rosewater I drank as a boy.

The heat of the Tehran summers brought the neighbors out of their homes. I smile to myself as I ponder one of the paradoxes of the Iranian mind: Build walls to separate yourself from your neighbors, and then spend as much time as possible in the street and on your front steps talking to each other! The women loved to chat and gossip while the children played together in the *koocheh*, and the men enjoyed gathering in small groups to converse about the issues of the day.

The sweltering heat of the Ohio afternoons wraps me in lethargy. I stretch out on a chaise lounge in the shade, listening to *golha* music on my CD player. I read Persian magazines and Persian poetry and drink Persian tea. From time to time, I switch on my favorite Persian radio station that broadcasts "The Voice of Iran" from Jerusalem. I immerse myself in all things Persian.

I pass the humid Ohio evenings time-traveling to the rooftop of my boyhood home. While I spend my summer nights in my air-conditioned house, I fondly recall the sultry Tehran nights when the entire neighborhood migrated to the roofs to sleep in the open air—bedrooms without walls! My parents took their mattress to the rooftop and hung white fabric around it for privacy. As the hours went by, conversations shouted from house to house became whispers in the dark. The exotic rooftop encampments gave the aura of a festival, an open-air holiday.

Pepper Pike, Ohio
December 2010

Several days ago, my daughter Leah and her husband Eric came to share *Shabbat* dinner at my house. (They come often, I'm happy to say.)

"Hi, Dad! What's for dinner?" Leah asked me with a hug.

"Lemon chicken, Persian chicken soup, *sabzi,* and rice," I said with a smile.

"You know I love love love, *tahdig,* Dad. I intend to eat a plateful!"

"There will be plenty for you, don't worry. I make it as good as my mother did," I assured her. *Tahdig* literally means "bottom of the pot," and it refers to the crunchy, crispy layer at the bottom of a well-made pot of basmati rice. The *tahdig* is considered a delicacy and a sign of the cook's prowess.

After Leah and Roz lit and blessed the candles, Eric poured the wine and the *Kiddush* was recited. Then I placed my hands on Leah and Eric's head and offered a blessing. It is also customary for the man of the house to bless his wife and praise her. Instead of my usual blessing for Roz, reciting Proverbs 31:10 (*Eshet chayil*, "A woman of valor"), I read a poem that I wrote especially for her:

> *Love does not have the color of the sea, sky, or mountains—*
> *Like the miracle of God's four seasons,*
> *It is a gift of the Creator.*
>
> *Loving you gives me hope and elevates me,*
> *Your love gives me renewed vision and a new voice.*
> *You are my East, my prayer direction, my rising sun.*
> *You are my friend, my companion,*
> *And my breath of life. Thank you.*

"That was very sweet, Isaac. Thank you," Roz whispered, tears filling her eyes.

"Let's not get maudlin, you two," admonished Leah with a smile. "Tell me again about *Shabbat* in Tehran, Dad."

"Friday mornings, while my mother began to prepare the evening meal, we children listened to the radio. In the afternoon we took naps. When it was almost sunset, my father would tell my brothers and me to get dressed to go to the synagogue—and believe me, we gave him a hard time. Finally, when we were dressed in our best *Shabbat* clothes, we followed him to the synagogue, running in a line behind him, like ducklings or baby chicks, trying to keep up with his long strides.

"My brothers and I enjoyed going to synagogue because it was a very happy place. There was beautiful singing to enjoy and after the service there were raisins, nuts, and cookies to eat. While the children ate the treats and ran around outside, the fathers talked with each other and shared the news of the past week: how was business; which family was sending a beloved eldest son to America to study; whose son or daughter was preparing for marriage.

"As we walked home, my grandfather would go over the Saturday morning Torah portion using simple words, so that we would be prepared for the next day's teaching. By the time we got home the *sofreh* was spread and everything was set out for the *Shabbat* meal: chicken soup prepared with dried lemon, rice, *sabzi*, and *sangak*. Friday night the children who attended Jewish school could stay up as late as they wanted, because Saturday was a day off."

"On Saturday morning you went back to the synagogue, right?" Leah asked. Even though she already knew the answer, she liked to hear me talk about how my life was in Iran.

"Of course. When my brothers and I were very young, my father prepared a quick breakfast of *sabzi*, hard-boiled eggs, fried eggplant and bread for us. By the time we were older, we ate a big breakfast and went to the synagogue later in the morning. On Saturday afternoon we did our homework, while our parents took a nap," I said with a wink.

"Oh, I get it! They weren't "napping" at all!" remarked Leah, blushing.

"Saturday nights my father took us all to the resort area of Shemiran or to a local ice cream shop where we could sit down and enjoy our treat. Jews were very good customers because they spent a lot of money on entertainment. Sometimes Uncle Shlomo took us to the movie theatre on a Saturday night."

"But on winter *Shabbats* you didn't eat ice cream," said Leah, with a shiver.

"No, in the winter we stayed home and listened to the radio and did a lot of homework. We were stuck in the house because of the weather. Winter in Tehran was very similar to winter in Cleveland: It was long and cold and snowy. I remember the beauty of the sun shining on ice-covered tree branches, just like here in Ohio. I remember the muffled sound tire chains made as cars drove down Sheikh Hadi Street. And I recall the delicious smells coming from street vendors' carts: the earthy smell of beets roasting on charcoal fires; the sweet scent of roasting corn; the smoky, tangy aroma of BBQ chicken and lamb *kebabs,* and chicken livers and beef livers cooking," I described with closed eyes. "When I was a boy, if I had some money, I would buy a lamb *kebab*, some *sabzi*, and a large piece of *sangak*, and make a sandwich. If I had enough money, I'd also buy a bottle of beer and really enjoy the day."

"All you think about is food!" remarked Leah.

"No, that's not true," I retorted. "I have many memories that have nothing to do with food. For example, diesel fumes remind me of Tehran."

"Diesel fumes?"

"Yes. Whenever I smell diesel fumes, I think of Tehran. I guess the air was polluted, but we didn't know about pollution then—it just reminds me of home."

"Olfactory memories are very powerful," Leah agreed.

"Definitely. The aroma of bread baking takes me back immediately to my childhood neighborhood. I distinctly remember the smell of our straw and mud roof after we soaked it with water to cool the air inside the house. Even the odor of cow dung is pleasant to me."

"It reminds you of the countryside and living on the Robab's farm, doesn't it?" said Leah.

"Yes, it does. People in the rural areas used to burn dried cow manure as fuel for cooking," I added.

"On that appetizing note, let's eat!" said Eric.

"Maybe we can talk about something else," laughed Roz.

Pepper Pike, Ohio
January 2011

I have had several nightmares lately and the underlying plot has been similar in each one: Someone—a man wearing black clothes, his face covered—invades my home to steal my belongings and I am unable to defend myself. I try to fight with the man, but my arms are weak and useless. I attempt to run after the burglar, but my legs are paralyzed.

After each of those nightmares, I regained consciousness in a cold sweat, with my pounding heart threatening to escape from my chest. And each time Roz calmed me afterwards and told me I was safe.

"What does the dream mean?" I asked her.

"Dreams are symbolic portrayals of what is going on in your subconscious mind, Isaac," she offered. "Obviously you feel threatened by someone or something from your childhood that makes you feel powerless and weak."

"Fear is always right below the surface, and vulnerability has been burned into my brain," I admitted. "But why is the intruder a thief?"

"Because someone is trying to steal something very important from you, my love. The thief in the night is trying to steal your sense of self-worth and your pride. That is what I think," she declared.

"And when do you think I will sleep soundly and have peace?"

"When you accept the fact that you are not inferior to anyone," she assured me.

Pepper Pike, Ohio
March 20, 2011

It is *Purim* once again. Everyone is asking, where is spring? Winter has been so cold and snowy and we are in need of a celebration!

I remember the wonderful *Purim* celebrations of my childhood years in Iran, especially the food. Returning from the synagogue we shared food normally consumed after a funeral: "fruit of the tree," such as dates and apples; "fruit of the land," such as cucumbers; hard-boiled eggs; fried fish and *kookoo sabzi* (spinach omelet). This meal symbolized the intended slaughter of the Persian Jews that happily never came to pass.

To celebrate the empowerment of the Jews and their deliverance from annihilation, trays of pastries and sweets followed the funereal repast. *Halvah,* a dessert made from a mixture of sesame seeds, almonds, sugar and cardamom or saffron, was a family favorite. There were bowls of almonds toasted with sugar. My aunts baked *bamieh*, an oval-shaped piece of dough that is deep-fried and totally drenched with syrup made of honey, rosewater and lemon zest. They also prepared a great supply of *zooloubia* and pistachio-laden *baklavah* pastries.

Suburban Temple
A Lecture to Congregants
March 25, 2011

The Jewish holiday of Purim is observed and celebrated by Jews all over the world. The two days of this holiday celebrated by Persian Jews are paradoxical: The first day is sad and somber while Jews fast to commemorate the *first* decree of the Persian King Ahasuerus (His name in Farsi is Khashayarsha): his decision to annihilate all Jews of Persia—this was the result of the king's minister, Haman. The second day is festive and happy, celebrating the freedom and the right to self-defense of Jews based on the *second* decree of the king, which allowed for the survival of all Persian Jews.

The main characters of that historic event are King Ahasuerus; Queen Esther, who was Jewish; her Uncle Mordechai; and the king's prime minister, Haman. The story starts with the king's highest minister, Haman, convincing the king to sign a decree to annihilate all Jews on the 13th of Adar; the date was selected randomly. Queen Esther, upon the recommendation and insistence of her uncle Mordechai, put her life on the line and intervened to save her people. It was the diplomatic skills of Esther—and her fearless leadership—that is demonstrated throughout the story of Purim.

It must be explained that decrees of the king were irreversible and the date of annihilation could not be changed. Furthermore, the queen was not allowed to visit the king without first being summoned by him; violation of this rule was punishable by death.

Queen Esther first had to unite all the Jews in order to lead them, and then she had to find a way to nullify the king's decree. The queen well understood that *fear is a brother to death.* She knew that allowing fear to dominate the mind and soul makes men paralyzed, half dead. To unite the Jews she asked her uncle to inform them that she was about to violate the internal laws of the palace, and thus endanger her life, by visiting the king uninvited. Mordechai was to advise the Jews to fast for three days and pray for her safety. Esther's fearless and brave decision caused the Jews to unite and collectively reaffirm their trust both in the queen and, more importantly, in God. The Jews complied and fasted for three days.

To cement her position as a trusted wife and advisor to the king, Esther chose the avenue of diplomacy. She hosted two feasts and invited all the king's ministers, particularly Haman, to each banquet. Extending her invitation to include her fiercest and most dangerous enemy indicated her bravery. She removed all fear from her mind and soul.

The king asked Esther to tell him what wishes he could fulfill. She realized that the only way to save her tribe was to obtain their right to self-defense: Even though the king could not reverse any of his past decrees, he could issue a *new* decree. This new decree would give all Persian citizens the right to self-defense, limiting the state's power and eliminating the possibility of civil war between minorities and the majority population.

The day before Esther decided to ask the king for a new decree, she asked her uncle to inform the entire Jewish population about the impending law. She also asked him to again inspire the Jews to unite and collectively pray for her success. While she would fast (This came to be known as the Fast of Esther) she commanded that no Jew should fast, but rather they must remain strong and prepare themselves for self-defense.

Queen Esther, with assistance from her uncle, succeeded both in her diplomacy and in her leadership. When Haman, the minister in charge of annihilating the Jews, and the Persian public observed the crowds of Jews united to defend themselves, they became convinced that a mass killing of the Jews was impossible. Some legends claim that many non-Jewish Persian citizens joined their Jewish neighbors to further empower and support the Jews; their actions made a war against the Jews unlikely. (Other stories claim, however, that the Jews and non-Jews did engage in fighting with each other, with the Jews victorious.)

Some Orthodox Jews believe Mordechai was Esther's cousin and husband, and they believe that Mordechai should get all the credit, arguing that Esther was just following his instructions. A recent book by Dr. Mitra Makbuleh, *Purim, A Mystical Interpretation,* claims that the entire story of Purim in the *Book of Esther* is historically inaccurate and must be interpreted only in its mystical meaning.

At any rate, Esther's tomb in Hamadan (Shoosh or Shooshan) has become a shrine and a holy site with a small synagogue. Jews and non-Jews make a pilgrimage to visit her tomb. The name Esther is popular among Iranian women; my mother's Hebrew name is indeed Esther and a number of my cousins are named Esther. Iranian Muslims and Zoroastrians refer to Queen Esther as "Ester Khanom," Lady Ester. Mordechai was also buried in the area, but no one has found his tomb.

To me, Queen Esther was a great leader and diplomat, and perhaps the first Persian female who realized the power of uniting the citizenry and encouraging them to demonstrate peacefully in public. Esther inspired her people to desire freedom and *unite* to obtain their rights as equal citizens. *They underwent a psychological transformation. She empowered the Jews to save themselves!*

In Iran, the first day of Purim was a day of fasting. We also attended services and read the story of Purim in our synagogues. We broke our fast at night by eating *halvah* and immediately changing our mood from sadness to happiness. Most Jewish schools presented plays about Purim and celebrated the second day of Purim as a festival of singing, dancing, and eating. In the United States (and many other countries, including Israel) it has become a custom to dress the children in costumes, while adults celebrate by drinking to the point of tipsiness.

The most valuable lesson of the story of Purim is to encourage every generation to abolish their inner fears. Esther and Mordechai demonstrated that no king nor his minister could ever annihilate a fearless and united people or community.

Living life without daily fear is difficult for many Holocaust survivors, war veterans, and oppressed peoples. At a recent *Shabbat* dinner in the New York home of a Holocaust survivor, I witnessed the heated arguments between the survivor and her children and grandchildren. She still finds herself living in a universe dominated by anti-Semitic people, like Haman, ready to kill all Jews. Although she left Europe and came to America at the age of twenty-four, her mind and her soul are still prisoners of the Warsaw Ghetto—the place where she lived with her parents during her teenage years. Yes, she left the tyranny of Europe and the Holocaust, but the Holocaust never left her.

When her first son was born, she fought with the rabbis and insisted that the boy not be circumcised or given a Hebrew name, so that he might remain safer. Throughout her sixty-six years of life in America she has been planning her escape from this country, so that she can leave in a minute's notice: She keeps a valid passport ready and maintains liquid assets in gold and diamonds. She has even built many hiding places within her house and in her yard. The paranoia of life in the ghetto and fear of all non-Jews has made her a prisoner within herself, within her mind and soul. She has chosen to live in a suburb away from other Jews and Jewish institutions because she is fearful that "the non-Jews know where the Jews live!" Unlike Esther, she has lost her trust in God. Haman and Esther are at war within her, allowing her only to exist.

I pray for the day that a fearless Esther will rise up and overcome her inner Haman. May she attain a trust in God that gives her strength and inner peace!

A news article appearing on the web page of *Arutz Sheva*, Israeli National News, states on January 9, 2011 that Iranian authorities have downgraded the status of the site known as the Tomb of Esther: Government officials have removed the sign at the mausoleum, in the city of Hamadan, in central Iran, that declared it an official pilgrimage site.

The state-run Iranian news agency *Pars* hints that the fate of the site could ultimately be much worse. It says that Iran has chosen to ignore— for the time being—the "responsibility of Esther and Mordechai for the massacre of 75,000 Iranians, which Jews celebrate at Purim."

The article goes on to say that Muslims should be aware that Israelis have threatened to destroy the Al-Aqsa Mosque in Jerusalem, and if they proceed, Muslims will destroy the tombs of "the lowly murderers" who slaughtered 75,000 Iranians in a single day!

Obviously, Iranian authorities have decided to revise the story of Esther and Mordechai, teaching schoolchildren that the annual festival of Purim is celebrated by Jews to commemorate this "Iranian Holocaust." As a result of this distortion, Muslim Iranians will observe Purim as a day of mourning this year.

On a cable news show, there was a brief story about Purim. The video showed Jews celebrating Purim by waving *groggers* (noise makers) that had the face of Iranian President Mahmoud Ahmadinejad affixed to them, during a reading of the *megillah* outside the Iranian United Nations Mission in midtown Manhattan.

The rabbi presiding over the celebration stated that in every generation there are those who try to overcome the People of Israel. He assured the crowd that as Jews prevailed over Haman, they will prevail over Ahmadinejad, and he will go down!

The rabbi was correct in labeling Ahmadinejad a modern day Haman.

Encino, California
April 2011

The Jewish community in Iran is the oldest, enduring, large Jewish community in the world. What allowed us to survive and keep our faith for over 2500 years? (The Jews of Spain, Western Europe, Eastern Europe, and even Jerusalem did not survive as long.)

During a recent trip to Los Angeles, I interviewed a large number of my Iranian friends, a number of elderly Jewish Iranians, and several American-born Jews of Iranian parents. The questions I asked them included: What type of discriminations did you experience in Iran? Why did you leave Iran? Would you go back to Iran? What makes you proud to be Iranian? If you had a choice, would you assimilate into the American culture or would you hold fast to all Iranian customs and traditions?

The elderly generation responded to my questions very predictably and with great consistency. They all recited many examples of discriminations, especially during their childhood, at work, in their neighborhoods, and during their travels within Iran. "In spite of all the discrimination, we always kept our faith with pride, with our heads held up. If we felt fear, we made sure our children would never feel it." These people left Iran during their mature years, mostly after the 1979 Islamic Revolution, because of fear of a regime based on religious dictatorship—they were certain the country was going to revert to the same anti-Jewish reality that was experienced during the Safavid Dynasty. These Jews came to the U.S. instead of Israel due to the economic opportunities and the stability and strength of America.

The elders all stated that they dream of returning to Iran someday, as visitors, because the nostalgia for Iran is in their blood. They spoke to me of their pride in Persian civilization and history. They explained the paradox of loving Persian culture while disliking the Islamic Republic. It is evident that these immigrants are deeply pained by their ambivalence. "Can we invent a nuclear bomb that discriminates between radical *Shiah* clergymen and other Iranians? I would be the first volunteer to drop these bombs," declared a white-haired Iranian gentleman sitting in a bookstore in Westwood. A UCLA professor having lunch with me in a Persian restaurant in Westwood whispered to me, "We need another Reza Shah to bomb all the clergy and bring back the Iranian Constitution of 1901."

The oldest Persian Jews described how they attempted to assimilate into the American culture and yet maintain their Persian customs and traditions. "We have become a part of the intricate mosaic which is the cultural architecture of America, but we have not lost our heritage. We have taught our children to be proud of being American-Iranian and proud of being Jewish," said an eighty-year-old immigrant.

From my Iranian friends, and other immigrants who are my age (in their early 60s), I received a variety of conflicting messages. It became evident that all their present day views and responses have been influenced by the socio-economic status of their life in Iran. Almost all those who had lived in northern Tehran, in upper class neighborhoods, claimed that they experienced very little or no discrimination; many of them named several Muslim friends that were closer to them than any Jewish friend or relative—but in the same breath they added that they disliked the Muslims who supported the Islamic regime. When I asked these friends of mine why they expressed so much hatred of the regime, they enumerated many instances of discrimination and mistreatment by the clergy, judges, governmental agencies, public agencies, and even some teachers! It became clear to me that my generation of immigrants tries very hard to remember the good and wonderful memories and forget all the miseries and emotional and physical tortures.

Even though I left Iran in 1966, most of my generation left Iran between 1978 and 1980. Leaving Iran after the Islamic Revolution was as natural a phenomenon as swimming is for fish. Survival under the new Islamic constitution was simply impossible. They chose America as their new home because of the strong economy, familiarity with the English language, and pleasant memories of past visits to the United States. Israel was not considered seriously due to its socialist ideology; a deep love of Israel was simply not enough of a reason to build their home there.

As for returning to Iran, my generation gives the unanimous response, "We would return in a heartbeat, if and when the regime changes." When I asked, "What about your children and grandchildren?" they responded that they would love their offspring to visit Iran with them. A number of my friends from Great Neck, New York stated that they would love to return to Iran, with their entire families, when democracy is established there—or even if the Shah's son should rule. "The Jews of Iran need other Jews to marry their sons and daughters. It is our responsibility to go back and rebuild our proud Iranian-Jewish community," said one of my boyhood classmates.

Another childhood friend who now lives in California declared, "I am a proud Iranian. I have taught my children to correctly pronounce their Persian names. I have introduced them to Persian history, art, music, and poetry. Even though assimilation is the path to success in America, our Persian individuality must be protected: To the outside world we are violins in the large American orchestra, yet at home we are the *tar* and the *tanbur* that play Persian music."

I have found that young American-Iranians are somewhat confused. There are frequent conflicts and struggles between the old fashioned Iranian culture and the modern American way of life: This clash of cultures creates adverse reactions among fathers and mothers and sets the stage for difficulties between parents and their children. For example, at what age should dating be acceptable? Is it different when a son goes on a date than a daughter? Should the young people date only Iranian Jews, American Jews, or just good human beings? What professions should the children choose, and should the parents have a say? How far from home should the college be? Should the son or daughter choose the wedding location and the food that will be served, or the parents?

I have come to understand that the majority of our American-Iranian children feel they must have choices and options. They respect both the old and the new, but they demand the freedom to choose the direction of their own lives. And even though they abhor the present conditions in Iran, these young American-born children are not consumed by Iranian politics, as are their immigrant parents.

The young, though they are proud of their roots, could live happily with or without the Persian culture. "I love to eat *chelo kebab*, but if it were no longer available I would be just as happy to eat pasta! I enjoy Persian music, but I also gladly listen to Madonna. I don't particularly like Persian poetry because I find it too flowery and affectatious; I prefer American poets such as Walt Whitman and Emily Dickenson," declared my friend's daughter, Mojdeh. "I abhor the Persian practice of *ta'aroff*, the pretend politeness and exaggerated flattery," stated Manoochehr, another friend's son. "I never know if Persians mean what they say. I just cannot trust Iranians. My father never speaks his mind in a direct way, he always uses metaphors and I have to figure out what he really means," said Mahtab, the daughter of yet another friend. "My greatest problem with Iranian culture is the extremely high expectations for the children. It seems like my parents are never satisfied with their own achievements, let alone those of their children. We are never good enough! And they try to live their lives through us," lamented Mehryar.

While in Los Angeles, I was invited to the home of Shahra'm A. (his grandfather and my grandfather had been part-owners of a donkey in Esfahan). Shahra'm wanted me to have *chelo kebab* for dinner and spend time with his brother Shokroallah A., who was visiting from Tehran. Shokroallah had an import business and a wholesale fabric store in the Tehran Bazaar.

The reunion with Shokroallah was very moving. Suddenly I felt as if I were at home on Sheikh Hadi Street. We spoke in the Esfahani dialect, as Persian music played in the background and Persian food cooked on the stove. We talked for hours. Finally lunch was served. I asked Shokroallah, "When are you going to move to the U.S.?"

"Isaac Joon, I am very happy in Tehran with my friends and family. My business is good, the Muslims respect me, and the Jewish community needs me. I still love Tehran."

"What will happen to you when the government finds out about your travels abroad?" I asked him.

"I pay enough to the right people and feed enough hungry mouths!" he responded, with his usual arrogance. "My Iranian Muslim neighbors come to me to help support the poor widows and orphans. I pay respect to the *mullahs* and *akhoonds*, and even one of the *ayatollahs*. I pay my dues and I know my limitations. In return, they ignore my frequent travels to the United States, Europe, and even Israel. I have a special visa sheet that is not attached to my passport."

"How can you tolerate the lies against Israel, and the way they treat women and the Jewish community?"

He responded impatiently, "Talk is cheap. It's all politics and posturing. And as for women, the Islamists treat our Jewish women with more respect than their Muslim women—and Jewish women are not required to wear the filthy black chador. Also, our Jewish boys do not get drafted, since we pay the government not to take them. As far as the Jewish community is concerned, I serve on the Anjoman (the Tehran Jewish Federation), and I deal with Jewish issues daily. I promise you, we are not allowing the crazy Islamic radicals to squeeze us. Yes, we had to accept the Islamic constitution and the limitations imposed on all non-Muslims, but look, we live a better life in Iran than some of you here in America. We observe Jewish laws and holidays, and we attend Jewish services. We keep our heads down and do our business as usual. We have less intermarriages and divorce than you American Jews do. So what if we have no say in the government, the courts, and the media? The only things I miss are the musicians and artists who have left the country. The most important thing is the fact that our Jewish sons can find Jewish girls to marry and establish Jewish homes. Listen, the Muslims are busy killing and torturing each other, while leaving us alone. We Jews cannot demand democracy."

"So, you are a very important man in Tehran?"

The Kourosh Boys. (left to right) Hooshang, Behrooz, David, Isaac, Ebi, Feridoon (behind Ebi), Bijan, David, Mani, and Benji. (Leah's wedding, December 22, 2008.)

"Oh, yes. I am needed in the Jewish community to solve problems with the Muslims who run the regulatory offices. Do you know how many times I've posted bonds for Jewish families who have gone on vacation to the Caspian Sea, allowing their wives and daughters to swim in improper clothing? How many times have I told them that Iran is not America, that their women must be fully covered! And how many times have I received calls from the chief of police about Jewish families who serve hard liquor at parties in their homes? I collect bond money from the families, pay the penalties, write apology letters, and get the offenders freed. If I leave Iran, my community, especially the young men, will not know what to do, whom to pay, and how much to pay."

Late in the afternoon, as I was leaving Shahra'm's house, I hugged Shokroallah and asked, "So, when will I see you again?"

"When I am able to buy a house in Beverly Hills similar to the one I have in Tehran, and when I can get the same respect from my fellow Jews in America as I get from my Muslim friends in Tehran."

I asked him to give my regards to my many Muslim friends and former neighbors in Iran.

Los Angeles, California
June 31, 2011

I met with Hossein Mohammadi while visiting Los Angeles. He recently returned from a trip to Iran where he visited friends and relatives in Tabriz and Tehran, as well as several towns and villages. Many Iranians to whom he spoke voiced their intense dislike of the Supreme Ayatollah's regime, and many people also expressed anti-Islamic feelings. Not one of the people he met praised the quality of life in Iran! In fact, one of the farmers Hossein talked to, spoke earnestly, with the understanding of anonymity. "I yearn for the days of peace, security, prosperity, and happiness that we enjoyed under the Shah!" declared the farmer. Hossein was shocked.

A group of well-educated Tehrani professionals, and their wives, joined Hossein for dinner one evening. Without exception, the erudite dinner guests offered their disgust with the regime. "We never supported this heartless, conniving government," they declared vehemently. "The *mullahs* and *akhoonds* should go back to the mosques and allow the educated youth to run the country!" The wives, none of whom wore a *chador*, passionately stated, "religion must remain a personal and private matter. No *Zeinab's sister* (female enforcers of *hejab* laws) should have the right to beat us and humiliate us if we refuse to wear the *hejab!*" Hossein asked them, "What are you doing about your dissatisfaction?" After a long silence, a response came: "We have no choice! We must *besoozim mo besazim*—we must burn and survive! We must resign ourselves to the way things are."

Hossein concluded that the moderate and liberal Iranians are not yet ready "to put their money where their mouth is"; ***they are as yet unwilling to speak up publicly.*** The overwhelming majority of disenchanted citizens are not yet willing to pay the price for liberty, human rights, and the freedom to pursue happiness.

Pepper Pike, Ohio
November 25, 2011

Two days ago, on November 23rd, I received a book in the mail from my dear friend Bijan. *Veiled Romance – A Persian Tale of Passion and Revolution*, a novel written by Simon Sion Ebrahimi, is a page-turner. I read it in one day. Although the author claims that all the characters are fictitious, I found the story to be almost identical to the experiences of two Iranian women who told me their imprisonment sagas shortly after the 1979 Islamic Revolution. I have concluded that Ebrahimi's book is as truthful as the real experiences of Ja'net N. and Rashel E. who are presently living in Los Angeles and New York with their families.

Ja'net, six months pregnant, was arrested by the Revolutionary Guards while hosting a party for friends and relatives. What was her crime? She was taken to Evin Prison for listening to Persian music and dancing with her hair, arms, and lower legs exposed—in her own home!

Evin Prison is notorious for torture, rape, hangings and executions. On the first night of her imprisonment, Ja'net's guard—a filthy, malodorous man who proclaimed he was a deeply religious Muslim— tried to force himself on her. The guard declared that allowing him to have sex with her would make her a better person, perhaps even save her soul! While in prison, Ja'net studied the Quran in both Arabic and Farsi. She came to the conclusion (as I have) that women's rights, democracy, and human rights cannot be achieved through the strict practice of Islam demanded by the Islamic leaders of Iran. She realized that Islamic laws, for the most part, are in direct contradiction with democratic laws and human rights.

Rashel's story is also heartbreaking. She worked at a prestigious bank in northern Tehran until one of her colleagues, a gray bearded conservative Muslim, tried to rape her when they were alone in her office. When Rashel's co-workers came to her rescue, the attacker claimed that Rashel had seduced him with her exposed arms and uncovered hair. She was arrested and served over six months in jail before she was freed. Her husband paid a large ransom to influential *mullahs* and Revolutionary Guards in order to secure her release. To this day she is silent about the details of her treatment in Evin Prison.

The more I contemplated the plight of those caught in the web of Iran's legal system, the more depressed I became. The prisons in Iran are staffed by sadistic thugs who have no concept of human rights. The most radical and conservative Islamic clergy and their followers use Quranic verses to serve their own interests: the subjugation of Iran's people, especially the women. Millions of followers have never read the Quran in their native language (Farsi) and have no understanding of the actual meaning of the verses written in their holy book.

I am often overcome by the depth of suffering borne by the people in my ancestral homeland. Who will lead them on the path to democracy, modernity and freedom? Perhaps Iran's courageous women will show the way.

Pepper Pike, Ohio
December 5, 2011

Suffering is relative. An insupportable stab in the heart for one person might be shrugged off by another person as a mere flesh wound. What conditions must be in place to cause a person to be assailed by perpetual mental pain? Certainly other people in other places and times have endured more injustice and discrimination than I experienced in my motherland. Certainly others have been in greater peril. But however insignificant my distress might have been, it is folded into my psyche and kneaded into my soul. I can attest to the fact that injustice crushes the spirit and distorts the way one sees the world.

It comes down to this: My own heart and soul are held captive in my homeland. Even though I experienced great joy and happiness in Iran, I realize I have also been damaged by the discrimination I encountered there. I understand that anger is the sister to fear, and fear is a brother to death, but an intellectual understanding in my mind does not seem to overcome emotional trauma. My *heart* must heal, somehow.

As I become older, the memories of my birthplace become more vivid and alluring than ever before. I long to return to Iran. There are so many friends I want to see before I die—so many unfinished conversations that need to be completed. I need to see the place of my birth and revisit all the familiar places from my childhood. I realize now that I tried to leave my past behind, but it never left me.

Perhaps I will be forever stuck between Tehran and my present life, somewhere between memory and reality. Somehow I must make peace with the ghosts that haunt my nightmares. My mind is in turmoil. I have unfinished business. There are loose ends to tie up and unresolved matters that need to be settled before I can experience peace. *The more the years go by, the more I think of Iran. It is as if time and distance mean nothing: the heart wants what the heart wants.*

I am still trying to leave Iran.

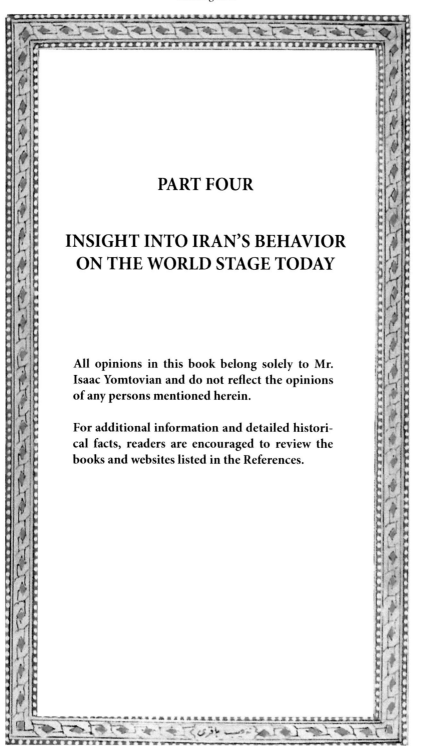

PART FOUR

INSIGHT INTO IRAN'S BEHAVIOR ON THE WORLD STAGE TODAY

All opinions in this book belong solely to Mr. Isaac Yomtovian and do not reflect the opinions of any persons mentioned herein.

For additional information and detailed historical facts, readers are encouraged to review the books and websites listed in the References.

Do not reveal to a friend
every secret you possess.
How do you know if at some time in the future
He may become an enemy?

Nor inflict on your enemy
every injury that is in your power,
As he may some day become
your friend.

—Sa'adi Shirazi

A tyrannical man cannot be a sultan,
As a wolf cannot be a shepherd.

A padshah who establishes oppression
Destroys the foundation of the wall
of his own reign.

—Sa'adi Shirazi

WHY DID THE 1979 ISLAMIC REVOLUTION OCCUR?

I am often asked to discuss present day Iran, its policies and actions on the world stage. The following is my attempt to enlighten the reader and help him or her to better understand the Islamic Republic of Iran: How it became the entity it is today and why it acts the way it does. The beliefs of conservative Islam, controlled and manipulated by Iran's clergy, have created an insular, isolated regime that has taken Iran backward in time, to the days of the Safavid Dynasty. During the Safavid Dynasty, *Shiah* Islam became the official religeon of Iran and the Islamic laws were strictly enforced. (See page 325, discussion of Najes)

My writing is based on growing up among religious, socially conservative Muslims who comprise at least eighty-five percent of today's Iranian population. Almost all of today's rulers came from the class of people with whom I grew up. Also I have kept in close touch with what is happening now in Iran—through the media, discussions with scholars of Iranian affairs, and attending a large number of lectures on the topic of the Islamic Republic of Iran.

How and *why* did the Islamic Revolution occur? Hopefully, the following material will help the reader understand the complex religious and political influences that ultimately shaped the regime we see in Iran today: The events, within their historical context, emphasizing how British and Russian domination, the power of the clergy, the impact of the discovery of oil, the repercussions of the White Revolution, the influence of the United States, and the Shah's indecisiveness all converged in Iran's history to bring about the perfect storm: the creation of the Islamic Republic.

I begin with a brief history of the modern era and some of the most important facts and milestones. The following facts are the basis of conspiracy theories [see pages 320-322] that are strongly believed by many Iranians, including my Muslim Iranian friends. (I have presented the information as bullet points, in chronological order.)

•In **1857**, the Treaty of Paris marked the end of the hostilities of the Anglo-Persian War. In the one-sided treaty, the Persians agreed to withdraw from Herat, Afghanistan, to apologize to the British ambassador when he was reinstated, to sign a commercial treaty, and to cooperate in suppressing the slave trade in the Persian Gulf. The British agreed not to support and shelter opponents of the Shah in the British Embassy. The British were given the status of "masters."

•On August 31, **1907**, Great Britain and Russia signed a decree that divided Persia between them. The central government of Persia was consequently weakened to the point that Persian soldiers had to take orders from the Russians and British. Foreigners were granted the right to exploit Persia's natural resources: oil, minerals, etc. Iran, for all intents and purposes, became a colony of the Imperialists. The Russians joined the British as "masters."

•It must be mentioned that in **1907**, the average life expectancy in Iran was thirty-three years; infant mortality was among the highest in the world; malnutrition and unhygienic conditions were common, and typhoid, malaria, cholera, and trachoma were widespread; famine was rampant; fewer than 1% of the population was literate. Conditions such as these do not ensure the survival of the government in power. Iran was in need of a powerful "master."

•In **1915**, Iran became a battleground. The Germans and Turks were on one side, and the British and Russians were on the other. Under the shameful Anglo-Iranian Treaty of **1919** (the year my father was born), Iran became a British protectorate. During this troubled time, a power vacuum existed: there was little law enforcement or police protection provided. This lawless environment enabled the clergy to obtain a stronghold; the clergy began its rise to power, becoming increasingly prominent in the lives of the people of the country.

•On February 21, **1921**, the British General Edmund Ironside declared that Reza Khan (who later became Reza Shah), a dedicated servant of Britain, should be appointed the Minister of War. In **1923**, Ahmad Shah Qajar, the reigning monarch, left Iran for Europe and Reza Khan Pahlavi became prime minister.

•On October 31, **1925**, the Iranian Parliament voted to end the Qajar Dynasty and replace it with Reza Shah (the Pahlavi Dynasty); the transition was peaceful. The Anglo-Iranian agreement was denounced and Russia lost much of its power in Iran. At this time, the French military was invited by the new king, Reza Shah, to build an Iranian army, navy, and air force. Belgium was invited to run the customs bureaucracy and the Swedes were invited to train and run the police force. The banks remained in the hands of the Russians, British, and Turks. Iran was managed and operated by foreigners. The administration of the country was out-sourced.

•Beginning in **1926**, Shah Reza Pahlavi imported French teachers to establish a modern Iranian school system; the French Alliance also established Jewish schools; French became the third language of Iran, after Farsi and Arabic. He also revitalized the system of government and introduced many modern amenities: road construction, buses, trains, radios, cinemas, and telephones. The number of modern industrial plants increased dramatically. Reza Shah was a staunch enemy of the clerics and the Safavid-style control they had over the population. Under Reza Shah, Iran started to taste self-governance and independence.

•In **1931**, Reza Shah refused to allow British Imperial Airways to fly in Iranian airspace; instead he gave the concession to German-owned Lufthansa Airlines—a symbolic gesture to let the British know they did not control Iran. However, this decision came back to haunt him later on. Reza Shah was not a Nazi; he also invited the French and Italians to do business in Iran. Reza Shah was especially impressed with German discipline, work ethic and the quality of German manufactured goods. He was also impressed by the Swiss culture and education system; he sent his son, Prince Mohammad Reza, to be educated in Switzerland.

•The Trans-Iranian Railroad was begun in **1927**; it linked the Caspian Sea to the Persian Gulf. It was completed in **1938**. This was one of the greatest accomplishments of Reza Shah and allowed him to establish a strong central government.

•In **1932**, Reza Shah Pahlavi cancelled the Anglo-Iranian Oil

Concessions and revised it into a better agreement, much more favorable to Iran. The cancelled agreement gave Iran 16% of net profits from oil operations; the new agreement asked for 21%—and the Shah was successful in securing that amount. The new agreement did not please the British.

•In **1935**, Reza Shah wrote to the League of Nations insisting that his country be referred to as "Iran" and not "Persia". This was another attempt on his part to regain Iranian prestige and pride and make a statement that Iran was seeking a place among nations as a free country. Reza Shah planned to free Iran from the British and Russians. (A year later, in 1936, my father entered the Iranian Army.)

•During Reza Shah's reign, the Women's Awakening Movement (**1936-1941**) came into existence. This movement wanted to eliminate the wearing of the veil, but it met heavy opposition from the clerics; Reza Shah later gave women the option to wear or not wear the veil. The modernization of Iran became his obsession.

•Reza Shah was the first Iranian monarch in 1400 years who paid respect to Jews; he prayed in the synagogue of Esfahan while visiting the Jewish community there. The Jews were impressed with Reza Shah and considered him to be second only to Cyrus the Great. Reza Shah's reforms opened new occupations to Jews and allowed them to leave the ghetto. *The "box" for Jews became much larger.*

•On September 1, **1939**, World War II began. About two years later, on August 23, **1941**, the Russians and the British invaded Iran once more. Why? Because when the Germans attacked Russia, the Allies suspected Reza Shah of collaborating with the Germans. Therefore, in the summer of 1941, the Allies insisted that Iran break its ties with Germany, but the Shah refused. Britain and Russia invaded under the pretext of securing a supply route to Russia. The British became the "masters" again. (Lufthansa Airlines lost its right to Iranian airspace.)

•Reza Shah was forced by the Allies to resign on September 16, **1941**. His son, Mohammad Reza Pahlavi, replaced him on the throne. Iran became, for all practical purposes, a colony of Britain and Russia.

•After World War II, the United States and Britain withdrew from Iran, as promised. The Soviet Union remained. Desperate to relieve his country of the Soviet occupation, Mohammad Reza appealed to the United Nations for assistance. President Truman sent a letter to Stalin insisting that the Soviets withdraw or face American forces. At the time, the US was the only country with nuclear weapons, and so Stalin withdrew his troops. This solidified the alliance between Iran and the United States. Now the Shah had only two masters rather than three: the British and the Americans.

Obviously, the desire for oil was the prime incentive for foreign powers to seek control of Iran. To understand the role that oil played in de-stabilizing Iran, ultimately resulting in Ayatollah Khomeini's takeover, it is necessary to begin at the beginning.

•The first place that oil was discovered in the Middle East was Iran. In 1901, an Englishman, William Knox D'Arcy, secured what became known as the D'Arcy Concession; this document offered Shah Qajar a large amount of cash for complete rights to search for, obtain, and ship out for sale petroleum, for sixty years. The Shah accepted this shameful deal. By **1911**, a British company, the Anglo-Persian Oil Company (APOC) was producing oil in Iran, robbing the country and raping its natural resources.

•Dr. Mohammad Mossadegh became the leader of a movement to expel Britain and nationalize the Iranian oil industry; Mossadegh eventually was elected prime minister. In May **1951**, Iran's oil industry was nationalized and the National Iranian Oil Company was founded (NIOC); Mossadegh expelled the British from Iran. The British placed an embargo on Iran and tried to cause a revolution to get rid of Mossadegh, but their efforts failed. The British tried very hard to convince President Truman to topple Mossadegh, but Truman refused. Finally, in **1953,** the British persuaded President Eisenhower to get rid of Mossadegh by claiming that he was a communist. The British and the Americans intelligence agencies masterminded a coup d'état that took place on August 19, **1953**; this coup removed Mossadegh from power and gave total authoritarian control to the Shah. Iran was no longer a constitutional monarchy. From then on, the Iranians no longer trusted the British or Americans and consider them to be the "Great Satan." [Source material and additional information regarding the nationalization of oil can be found at http://www.iranchamber.com/history/oil_nationalization/oil_nationalization.php]

•In **1954**, a consortium of eight of the largest oil companies signed an agreement with the National Iranian Oil Company (NIOC). This made the rape of Iran legal.

•In **1957**, more oil companies entered Iran: Irano-Italian Oil Co. and the Iran Pan-American Oil Company. This created competition and allowed Iran to have some right of negotiation.

•On July 31, **1973**, NIOC took control of all Iranian oil resources. Freedom at last!

•OPEC met in Tehran on December 22nd and 23rd, **1973** (shortly after the Yom Kippur War) to set the price of oil; the price increased dramatically. (William Simon, U.S. Secretary of the Treasury, called the Shah a "nut" and blamed him for the oil crisis.)

[In the review and presentation of information relating to Oil History in Iran and the roles of the British, Russians, and Americans—as well as the fall of the Shah—I used the following sources: *Answer To History*, by Mohammad Reza Pahlavi, the Shah of Iran. My notes from lectures and interviews by Dr. Abbas Milani, as well as his book, *The Shah*, were also used.]

Other political factors besides Iran's oil and the presence of foreign influence led to the eventual overthrow of the Shah: The Shah's noble attempt to modernize Iran, known as the White Revolution, greatly contributed to his downfall and the subsequent establishment of an Islamic government. The White Revolution was not one event, but rather a series of changes implemented by the Shah and his administration over a relatively short period of time, **from 1962**

through 1975. These noble attempts at modernization and progress included the following nineteen very progressive reforms:

1. Land reform

2. Nationalization of forests

3. Sale of State-owned enterprises to the public

4. Workers' profit sharing of 20% of net corporate earnings, and the establishment of a minimum wage and the right of workers to unionize.

5. Voting and political rights for women

6. Formation of the Literacy Corps

7. Formation of the Health Corps

8. Formation of the Reconstruction and Development Corps

9. Establishment of Houses of Equity

10. Program for the nationalization of water resources

11. Program for urban and rural reconstruction

12. Modernization and decentralization of the administrative offices of government

13. Employee and public ownership extension

14. Price stabilization

15. Free education and free daily meals, K-8th grade

16. Free nutrition for infants

17. Establishment of national social security

18. Fight against land and house speculation

19. Fight against corruption

The architect of the White Revolution was actually the United States, though the Shah was given credit as being the implementer, and it became his most important accomplishment. The grand intent of the Shah's White Revolution was to create a modern state and bring Iran from the 15th century into the 20th century.

Gradually, the Shah replaced his British and Russian bosses with American advisors. He also included experts from Italy, France, and even Israel. By **1967**, shortly after the Six Day War, the Shah felt secure enough to really push his agenda. It was obvious by **1973** that the Shah was feeling secure in his power and was confident enough to act independently of other Middle Eastern countries: He did not back the **1973** embargo of Israel, but rather sold oil to Israel during that time. He also decided that oil should be valued as a commodity—and that the price of oil must go up! The Shah was instrumental in forming OPEC and instigating higher oil prices. During the Nixon years, Iran was the most influential country in the Middle East, except perhaps for Israel, and it was certainly the most prosperous. *Money poured into Iran in amounts never before experienced: there was an explosion of wealth. On the down side, the economy did not have the capacity to process the excessive wealth, and that created enormous problems.* The high point of this era was the sending of thousands of Iranian students to foreign universities, with the Iranian government paying for the students' education.

The first eight of the White Revolution's tenets were implemented very quickly and became very successful. However, in my opinion, the speed of progress exceeded the capacity of the people to accept change. The rural and urban citizens had not been prepared by the government to understand the importance of the Shah's improvements. The golden years of the Shah's reign began with the mandates of the White Revolution—and ended with its shortsighted and misguided implementation.

When the 9th law of the so-called revolution, the Establishment of Houses of Equity, was proposed, significant opposition among the population began to grow and the seeds of an Islamic revolution were planted. Why? Because over five centuries, ever since *Shiah* became the official religion of the country, the clergy and their supporters had been in control of small villages and towns and the courts: The implementation and the interpretation of Islamic laws had been solely in their hands. The new edict shook the clergy to their core; their legitimacy was threatened.

When the Shah established non-religious "Houses of Equity," he in effect took away power and funds from the clergy. This act was perceived as an assault on the religious community and caused the unification of all the opposition leaders. As a result of the Shah's attempt at reform, many powerful, well-organized and well-funded groups were established: the Islamic Brotherhood (which originated in Egypt); Islamic Student Centers; Association of Islamic Students, for students in Iran and students studying in the West; and the Muslim Students' Association. While the Shah and his supporters were in a rush to pass more laws and implement more improvements and modernization as soon as possible, the clergy initiated the formation of many more organizations, which were operated by well-educated Muslim doctors, engineers, lawyers, and other professionals, to resist the intrusion of the new laws into their sphere of influence and power. All attempts to modernize Iran were interpreted as Westernization of a Muslim country.

Even the implementation of the 7th and 8th decrees (formation of the Health Corps and the Reconstruction and Development Corps), which on the surface seemed innocuous enough, caused great repercussions among the populace: Imagine the introduction of thousands of young, urban men into conservative, heretofore self-contained communities! The people who lived in rural areas, especially the elders, did not know how to relate to these unfamiliar "city boys." The rural population was not properly prepared for change.

After all, these young men were not *mahram* (a family member) and village women were not allowed to interact with them; also many of them did not even know how to perform *namaz* (pray). These young interlopers were not taught to respect Islamic traditions (a number of them were Jews, Christians, and Baha'is), and the people in the towns were not prepared in advance for the invasion of these government reformers. There was much turmoil and confusion; husbands, community leaders and local clergymen were insulted.

It became obvious, albeit too late, that the Shah's most desirable plans and good intentions to improve the lives of his countrymen would not be successful solely by passing legislation and shipping truckloads of city boys to distant towns and villages!

The 11th law established a program for urban and rural reconstruction; this program also met with resistance. The men in rural communities were not used to having decisions made for them in Tehran, and they resented the fact that bureaucrats living far away were empowered to tell villagers what projects should be undertaken. By and large, the rural people saw no need for intervention of any kind; they were happy with the way things were.

The 12th law mandated modernization and decentralization, attempting to bring about an administrative revolution. This program was intended to resolve internal public problems and teach the citizens to accept all the new revolutionary changes. This well-intentioned plan "repaired the eyebrows, but blinded the eyes" of the people it was meant to help. It was pushed too quickly, and thus it was doomed to failure.

The 13th law, employee and public ownership extension, added tons of salt to the open wounds of the remaining supporters of the Shah's government; the law impeded their ability to create jobs and maintain economic stability. This tampering with the economy was actually the introduction of socialism, and it resulted in skyrocketing stock prices and inflation because of rampant speculation. Commodities and goods experienced out-of-control prices.

The 14th law, price stabilization, was not the straw that broke the camel's back, but it certainly bent the camel's back! Again, this plan was ill-designed in a hurry and with no understanding of proper execution. The Shah and his Western advisors (including some Western-educated Iranians) and the uncaring members of Parliament neglected to take the time to study their plans and analyze the consequences. When scores of young, inexperienced, zealous young men were given the power to inspect and monitor prices of goods in the *bazaar*, in the streets, and in the neighborhood shops, the immediate reaction was one of resentment and hatred.

When told that they were not allowed to raise their prices, many of the *bazaaries* rioted. Proud Muslim businessmen were treated like criminals, without respect. These same Muslims had been strong supporters of the Shah's father and the Pahlavi Dynasty, but now they were leaning towards those who were forming an opposition movement. In the meantime, the law engendered huge corruption and high inflation—the exact things the law was intended to curtail. The lack of stability caused chaos.

The 17th revolutionary law established national social security and had a large impact on the clergy and the Islamic centers; it weakened the need for Islamic *zakat* (charity) and assured families economic security without help from the clergy, the mosques, or other devoted Muslims. This was a stab into the heart of the clergy.

The two most damaging revolutionary laws—the ones that broke the camel's back—were numbers 18 and 19: the "Fight Against Land and House Speculation," and the "Fight Against Corruption" mandates. To begin with, the most corrupt and effective speculators were the Shah's family, extended family, and closest friends—also his parliament members, his ministers, and all the wealthy families in his social circle! In effect, these two laws were in direct conflict with the Shah's strongest supporters. Members of the Shah's family, his closest personal friends, and all the established land developers became criminals overnight. Mistrust between friends and families began to destroy the regime from within.

[Sources of material pertaining to the White Revolution include: wikipedia.org/wiki/White_Revolution; also www.iranchamber. com/history/white_revolutionwhite_revolution.php]

Iran became more and more dependent upon the West, relying on their technology and advisors. The migration of non-Muslim foreigners into Iran was overwhelming: Westerners flooded the cities, hotels, restaurants, theatres, nightclubs, resort areas, bazaars, and residential communities. Westernization became fashionable. Frequent trips were made to Paris and London. The demand for foreign goods and luxury items got out of hand. The ports in south Iran were overwhelmed by the arrival of large freighters bearing foreign goods. The internal road systems could not provide adequate transportation for goods and people. The country was spinning out of control.

The Americans were total strangers to Islam and ignorant of the principles of the Quran and Shariah Law; the Shah's corrupt administration and a weak body of legislators, with no understanding of the impact of their actions, doomed the White Revolution to total failure. By **1977-78**, it was clear that most of the Shah's attempts at modernization had totally backfired. He rescinded some laws and enacted new ones, causing even greater confusion among the people. *The collateral damage to the country's social and economic institutions was astounding.* The well-organized opposition groups were ready to assert themselves, especially the radical Islamists.

In my opinion, the Shah was an intelligent, well-educated man who was a fairly good administrator. Unfortunately, he was not a leader with the heart of a lion—he was gutless and allowed himself to be manipulated and controlled by foreign powers. These foreign powers, especially the Americans and the British, kept him on a very short leash during his entire reign. When the Shah finally tried to loosen their grip, he was removed from power.

Late in his reign (1974), the Shah suffered from cancer and kept his illness a secret; soon the Israelis discovered his "secret" and agreed to keep quiet. In 1977, the Shah underwent chemotherapy, radiation, and other treatments and his strength and capacity to make decisions was greatly impacted; by this time, his cancer was public knowledge in Iran. He should have stepped down from his responsibilities. Instead, he selfishly clung to power and became more and more isolated from his people. His illness caused him to neglect his duties and he relied on America to advise him and save his regime. The Americans, however, worried about protecting their own interests and provided little support.

The Shah operated in a state of panic from 1977-1978, replacing one prime minister after another. In August 1977, he replaced Abbas Hovyda—a competent and loyal administrator who had been with the Shah for many years—with Jamshid Amoozgar. Amoozgar inflamed the already angry clergy by reducing subsidies formerly paid to them. In August 1978, Amoozgar was replaced with Sharif Emami. November of 1978 saw yet another change in the post of prime minister: General Gholam Reza Azhari replaced Sharif Emami. A mere one month later, on December 29, 1978, Shahpur Bakhtiar replaced General Azhari as prime minister.

In spite of the Shah's erratic style of governing, President Carter declared on December 31st, 1977 that, "Iran, because of the great leadership of the Shah, is an island of stability in one of the most troubled areas of the world." A few days later, on the 7th of January 1978, major riots erupted in Tehran. The situation continued to deteriorate until finally, on September 8, 1978, marshal law was declared; Iran's intellectuals solemnly referred to that day as "Black Friday". Ironically, the Shah had been trying to appease the intellectuals for years. The edicts of the White Revolution were designed, he thought, to gain the favor of the intelligentsia who desired a modern country and a constitutional monarchy.

The Shah became increasingly paranoid and was gripped by fear of the clergy (the "blacks") and terror of the communists (the "reds"). He began to drown in his own fantasies of conspiracies and intrigues. The people of Iran had loved the Shah's father, but they were tired of the son's arrogance and remoteness.

The clergy and the other opposition groups began to fill the vacuum created by the Shah himself. Even the intellectuals were losing trust in him. The clergy took advantage of the chaos in the government and the unrest of the citizenry. They promised to repair the country and preached a message of economic prosperity, hope, justice, and Islamic morality. Meanwhile, the intellectuals and liberals, who sought democracy and human rights, underestimated the power of the clergy and the deep-rooted influence the clergy had on Iranian minds and hearts.

The passive behavior and weakness of the Shah emboldened the clergy. When he ordered his military leaders to sit back and allow the demonstrations to get out of control, he thought he was avoiding civil war, but in reality, he guaranteed the death of his officers and the destruction of his army and his country. Not one of his foreign advisors stepped in to assist him in his decision-making. Nothing but tragedy ensued.

On January 16, 1979, the Shah left Iran. On January 23, Mehdi Bazargan, an intellectual and a scholar, declared the establishment of the Islamic Republic of Iran; in February, he was appointed by Ayatollah Khomeini to head the provisional government. Bazargan had been involved for many years in the movement to establish a democratic government; he was a leader of the religious movement that blended nationalism and reform in politics, society and religion. He advocated "Islamic liberalism" and was adamant about limited government, individual rights, the rule of law, and democracy. [For additional source material, *The Shah* by Abbas Milani. Palgrave Macmillan, 2011. Also, Milani's lecture videos: webjournal.us/ show/Abbas+ Milani, and www.bing.com/videos/watch/video/ abbas-milani/17wm18exq; also, charlierose.com]

As head of the lame-duck government, Bazargan appealed for calm and reason amid the revolutionary fervor that culminated in the takeover of the American Embassy in Tehran in November of 1979. He resigned when Khomeini endorsed the embassy siege, in which 52 Americans were taken hostage. His resignation underlined a terrible, new reality: *The Islamic fundamentalists were displacing the intellectuals, who had been in control of the opposition movement until January 1979.* In my opinion, **the clergy, led by Ayatollah Khomeini, hijacked the revolution!**

If the military had fully supported Bazargan and many of the intellectuals against the radical Islamists, Iran would have become a much more liberal nation. Bazargan could have saved Iran and allowed freedom to blossom. He could have created an Islamic democracy—a democracy with an Islamic flavor.

Andrew Young, the U.S. representative to the United Nations, was relieved that the coup had taken place and that Khomeini was to be the head of the new government. Mr. Young was quoted as saying that the Ayatollah was a saint! (I felt that he should have moved himself and his entire family to Iran to enjoy the saintly persona of Khomeini.) President Carter thought that Khomeini, being a man of God, would surely institute laws providing human rights for his people. Carter was very wrong.

THE CONSPIRACY THEORIES BELIEVED BY MANY IRANIAN MUSLIMS

As I mentioned earlier, Mohammad Mosaddegh was appointed prime minister in 1951. The CIA was instrumental in the overthrow of Mosaddegh on August 19, 1953; this allowed the Shah to reign as an absolute monarch and became the genesis of the anti-Americanism. The Iranian *ayatollahs* have managed to maintain their power by perpetuating the following conspiracy theories; according to them, all of Iran's internal troubles—economic failures, prostitution, alcoholism, drug addiction, and **especially the anger and unrest of Iran's youth**—are caused by the direct interference of the British and Americans. The following "theories" blame foreigners for every evil in Iran today.

Conspiracy Theory #1. *The oil companies, known as the "Seven Sisters", and the American industrial-military complex controlled the Shah, the Iranian military, and Iranian industry.*

Since 1953, when President Eisenhower saved the Shah's rule and defeated Mosadegh's National Revolution, Iran became the defacto enemy of America. The Shah became a puppet of America and incapable of making any decision without approval of the West. This "theory" underscores the premise that the Americans forced the Shah to develop and implement his White Revolution, which attempted to give the people of Iran secularized education, thus taking power away from the clergy.

The Iranian clergy also contended that the modernization of Iran created a better market for American goods; it was, therefore, in the best interest of America to make Iran sell more oil—and borrow more money from the West—in order to buy more goods that Iranians did not need. More and more American companies coming to Iran meant more and more American influence, which the clergy detested. According to the clergy, the British and Americans sought the downfall of Iran.

In the meantime, Iran became the major military power and economic powerhouse of the Middle East. When President Jimmy

Carter's weakness as an international leader became known, the Shah's opposition realized their opportunity had come: As soon as the clergy recognized Carter's passion for human rights, they knew they had to make their move soon, before Iranian citizens developed a taste for such freedoms.

Conspiracy Theory #2. *The oil companies forced the increased oil prices and oil embargo of 1973 so that (a.) they could make more profit; (b.) Iran would earn much more revenue, allowing the country to purchase more American weapons at artificially inflated prices, and (c.) American companies would obtain more contracts in Iran, causing an influx of even more American advisors and spies.*

As proof of this theory, Dr. Ebrahim Yazdi wrote in his book, *Final Attempts in Last Days*, about Nixon and his administration initiating the sale of an endless supply of jet fighters, tanks, radar equipment, and other modern weaponry that Iran did not need. Yazdi claimed that in 1977, between 50,000 and 60,000 American military technology experts and specialists lived in Iran. He contended that these foreigners did not respect Islam and introduced Western corruption and immorality to Iran. Iran was becoming Westernized and the clergy was gradually losing its hold on the population; a way of life that had endured for over 500 years for the Iranian clergy was being threatened.

Furthermore, Yazdi claimed that Israel was America's partner in controlling the Shah and the Iranian economy. If Iran would dare oppose the wishes of the oil companies, Yazdi declared, then Israel and America—with their worldwide control of the media and financial institutions—would make sure that any Iranian opposition would be defeated. It was constantly reiterated that the Shah and the people of Iran were the servants of America, Israel, and the oil companies. *The Protocols of the Elders of Zion*—an untrue, anti-Semitic booklet first printed in Russia in 1903, described the Jewish plan for world domination. (The Islamic clergy continues to propagate the ridiculous content of that book, using it to keep the hatred of Israel alive in the hearts of many Iranians.)

Conspiracy Theory #3. *The Shah was mentally ill and incapable of* *making decisions.*

In 1976, the United States published documents indicating that the Shah had physical and psychological problems; this strengthened the position that was held by the clergy and was construed to be proof that the Shah was a puppet of the West.

Unfortunately, these conspiracy theories are deeply rooted in the minds of some of my friends who support the Islamic Republic of Iran—while enjoying the "good life" in America.

AYATOLLAH KHOMEINI AND *SHIAH* BELIEFS: THE DOGMA BEHIND THE CLERGY'S POWER

Understanding the behavior of today's leaders in Iran requires study of the foundation of Islamic beliefs according to Iranian *Shiah* thinking. The word *Shiah* means "follower" and is used to refer to a particular religious sect of Islam. The word *Shiite* refers to an individual who adheres to the tenets of the *Shiah* religion; they are followers of the first Imam, Ali, who was the cousin and son-in-law of the Prophet Mohammad.

There are a number of branches of *Shiah*. The official Iranian sect is based on *Shiah Ali Asna Ashari*, which means the followers of Imam Ali and the Twelve Imams. The word *imam* is defined as "divinely guided leader." Eleven of the twelve *imams*, including Imam Ali, have already lived, and their lives are well documented. None of the eleven Imams died from natural causes: one was killed with a sword, and the rest were poisoned.

The final or the Twelfth Imam is referred to as *Imam Mehdi*, the Absent Imam; he is expected to arrive sometime in the future to save the world. The significance of this absent *imam* is very great since the belief in his coming to the world shapes the beliefs and behaviors of the Iranian *Shiah*—and greatly contributed to Ayatollah Khomeini's ability to seize political power. [See, *The Twelfth Imam*, by Joel C. Rosenberg]

The term *imam* is very restricted in its use within the *Shiah* sect, but is freely used in the *Sunni* tradition to denote any recognized religious leader. This messianic view is the cornerstone of the success of the Islamic Republic.

While awaiting the coming of Imam Mehdi, a time known as the "Period of Absence," *Shiites* are guided by the following specific principles:

1. The *Ummat*, meaning all people, communities, governments, and countries that are Believers, must live under the laws of God (Allah) as recited by the Last Messenger (the Prophet Mohammad) and written in the divine book, the Quran. The supreme leaders—the successors of the *imams*—present the interpretation of the *Shariah* laws; these leaders are called *ayatollahs* and *olamas*. Therefore, during the "Period of Absence" the **decision of the Supreme Ayatollah is accepted to be Allah's divine decision.**

The success of Ayatollah Khomeini was partially due to the recognition of him being an Imam, which qualified him to be the earthly representative of Allah. Thus the *Umma* (Iranian population) accepted that Khomeini was divinely guided and they were obligated to follow him. Some of Khomeini's followers went so far as to believe that he was indeed the Mehdi!

2. Since the *Ummat* (the people) are not as learned as the *Olama*, they are considered to be *faghieh*, unable to make major decisions, and must rely on the wisdom of the *Ayatollahs* and *Olamas*. All governments of the world must be Islamic and must be led by a Supreme Ayatollah. This form of government regards the citizens of a country as children, *faghieh*, while the father is the *valie*, the leader.

Ayatollah Khomeini was declared the Supreme *Valie*; his learned assistants were declared *Olamas*, and the Iranian population was declared to be *Faghieh*. The place of residency, or country, of the *Faghieh* is called *Velaiate Faghieh*.

3. The Supreme Leader, the *Ayatollah*, must approve all major

political decisions—including who is qualified to be a candidate for any political or public position. This concept was demonstrated by the outcome of the 2009 election: Even though the people did not elect Ahmadinejad, the Supreme Leader (now the Ayatollah Ali Khamenei) declared him the president of the republic. Ahmadinejad is subordinate to the Ayatollah.

4. The founding precept of the Islamic Revolution is the uncompromising battle between the *mostazeafin* (the oppressed) and the *mostaberin* (arrogant oppressor, as manifested by the West). This worldview divides the globe into two factions: the righteous and the infidels.

Ayatollah Khomeini promised to fight the *mostaberin*, beginning with the Shah. Once the Islamic Republic was established, the fight was extended to the other *mostaberin*: the West. Using Khomeini's logic, Iran needed an Islamic revolution to save the souls of its population.

5. To legitimize war against an enemy, the Supreme Leader must first demonize the enemy so that Islamic laws will allow him to declare *Jihad*, a Holy War, against the enemies of Islam. (Jihad is translated to mean "exertion in the service of God"; *jihad* can be declared against an individual, i.e. Salman Rushdie, or a country, i.e. Israel.) To fight against the United States and Israel, traditional methods of warfare will not work: suicide bombing and non-traditional weapons must be employed. (Quran, Sura 2:154, "And do not say that those who are killed in Allah's cause, 'They are dead.' Indeed they are alive but you do not perceive it.)

Even the use of nuclear weapons is not ruled out. Mr. Rafsanjani, an influential member of the Islamic Republic's Supreme Committee, indicated that if Iran were to drop nuclear bombs on Israel, the Israelis would be almost totally annihilated. If Israel were able to retaliate, then four, five—maybe ten million Iranians would be killed. Rafsanjani declared that ten million *shaheed* (martyrs) would be acceptable if the Zionist Satan were destroyed.

Numerous verses in the Quran propose and sanction the killing of nonbelievers. Here is a sampling:

Sura 2:191, 193, "And kill them wherever you come upon them and expel them from where they expelled you, as persecuting people to sway them from Allah's religion is graver than killing. But do not fight them at the Sacred Mosque, unless they fight you; then kill them; this is the recompense of the nonbelievers. And continue fighting them until there is no more persecution and Allah's religion prevails, but if they desist from unbelief (convert to Islam), then there should be no hostility except to evildoers."

It would be foolish to think that Iran will not use nuclear weapons if such weapons are available.

WHAT IS *NAJES*, AND HOW DOES IT IMPACT THE WORLDVIEW OF CONSERVATIVE MUSLIMS?

I described my personal experiences with *Najes* in the first section of this book, "My Childhood in Iran." *Najes* is an insidious brand of institutionalized discrimination, sanctioned by the conservative Muslim clergy and *it has been deeply ingrained into the psyche of Iranians.*

The words *Johood, Kalimi,* and *Yahoodi* refer to a Jewish person. Of those three words, *Johood* has the most derogatory connotation. The concept of *Najes* (impurity) has its origins with the *Shorut* (conditions or restrictions) developed and implemented in the year 717 CE during the reign of Umar II who brought his anti-Jewish feelings from Arabia. *Najes* was politicized during the Safavid Dynasty (1502-1736 CE); at that time *Najes* became sanctioned by the government and became the law of the land. By the late nineteenth century, the orthodox *ulama* stipulated more than fifty different types of *Shorut* that the Jewish community had to observe. [For additional information please refer to an article by Mina Hakim-Bastanian concerning minorities in Iran: hhtp://www.

iranian.com/BTW/2006/Book/index.html]

Here are some of the restrictions:

-Jews were forced to pay a separate and additional tax called *jaziyeh*.

-Jews were denied the right to open shops in the bazaar.

-Muslims were not allowed to purchase goods from Jews.

-Jews were not permitted to testify in legal matters.

-Jews were not protected by law in criminal cases.

-A Jew could only inherit a portion of family assets; Jews who converted to Islam obtained the right to inherit *all* family assets.

-Jews were not allowed to walk in crowds and/or in the middle of the road.

-There were special laws regulating the clothing of Jews.

-There were laws that regulated the living arrangements of Jews: They could only reside in a ghetto in small, unostentatious homes with low ceilings; no Jewish home could be painted white, etc.

-There were laws restricting Jews' speech, such as limiting the volume of their voices when singing, praying, or even talking.

-Jews were not allowed to name their children names that were considered to be "Muslim."

-Jews could not use public baths.

-Jews were forbidden to read the Quran.

-Jews were not allowed to hold pubic office.

-There were laws regulating Jews' movement: Jews could not cut through a mosque, from one street to another (but a donkey or a camel was allowed); Jews could not own a donkey or a horse, greatly inhibiting their ability to do business; Jews were not allowed in certain Muslim religious cities (such as Qom).

-Jews were not allowed to walk in the rain: Raindrops might splash off a Jew and land on a Muslim, resulting in the Muslim becoming impure; rain dripping off a Jew might end up in the groundwater, thus contaminating it.

The greatest poets and scholars of Persian literature wrote disparagingly of Jews: Rumi used the metaphor *Johooda'ne'h* in his poetry to describe someone as being "like a *Johood*," that is, being like a dog. Ferdosi referred to *Johoods* as "enemies," "Satan worshippers," "dishonest," and "liars." Nezami described *Johoods* as "snakes," "dogs," "cowards," and "deceitful." The poet Saadi wrote in chapter three of his *Golestan* that only contaminated well water should be used to wash *Johoods*, no matter whether they are alive or dead; Saadi also states that a house is worth ten *dinar* as long as a *Johood* lives in it, but the moment the *Johood* dies and leaves the house, it becomes worth one thousand *dinar*. Shams-i Tabrizi, the spiritual instructor of Rumi, described Jews as cowardly, deceitful liars—in his book about love!

Obviously, the writings of such learned, respected men exerted (and continues to exert) a great influence on the hearts and minds of Iranians. [This information was written in an article by Mahmood Kavir, *Shofar* Magazine, vol. 369, November 2011; published by the Shofar Foundation, Inc.] In spite of their treacherous writings about Jews, I have used the poetry of some of the aforementioned poets in this book: Because I dearly love Persian poetry, I must try to ignore the duplicity of Persian poets.

After 1920, when Reza Shah came to power, those restrictions were not enforced. However, some of these *Shorut* are still practiced in villages and small towns and condoned by local clergy. (For example, I was not allowed to disembark a bus that made a stop in the town of Qom.)

When Khomeini came to power in 1979, he was asked how the Jews were going to be treated. He informed the Jewish leaders that since they were the "People of the Book" they would be tolerated, but not equal to Muslims. Jews were warned that any mention of Zionism was a crime; Zionism was forbidden. Travel to Israel was not allowed unless a Jew could prove he was going there on a religious pilgrimage.

Generally speaking, Jews in Iran were told, "Don't worry! You will be well treated." But Jews can only hold low-level offices in the Islamic regime and Jews, as a separate ethnic group, have one representative to speak for them in the government. This representative, however, is merely a messenger who receives information from the government and disseminates information to the Jewish population; he has no influence in the decision making process and has no voice when it comes to making laws and regulations. Jews, though "protected" by the government, are second-class citizens and are not equal to Muslim citizens.

TRUTH AND DECEIT— CAN THE UNITED STATES TRUST THE ISLAMIC REPUBLIC OF IRAN?

A total lack of respect for the truth is inherent in Iranian culture. That is a terrible thing to say, but it is so.

Truth has no value to most Iranians, especially the government and religious leaders. I am reminded of another Mullah Nasruddin story, and although it is an ancient tale, it underlines *the twisted logic of the Islamic Republic:*

One day, Mullah Nasruddin's neighbor asked the mullah if he could borrow his mule. Mullah Nasruddin was not inclined to lend the animal to that particular man, so he answered, "I'm sorry, but I've already lent the mule to someone else." All of a sudden, the donkey could be heard braying loudly behind the wall of the courtyard. "Mullah, I can hear the donkey behind the wall!" the neighbor exclaimed. "Who do you believe," the Mullah replied indignantly, "the donkey or your mullah?

Thus Iranians are told that they must believe the clergy at all costs—even if doing so is contrary to common sense and contrary to the truth!

Ta'aroff is the sanctioned, deeply ingrained practice of lying in social and business situations. Business owners also practice deception when it comes to pricing their products or making deals. In fact, to be deceitful is a sign of being *zerang,* smart and sensible; to be truthful and honest is to be *saadeh* or *haloo* (stupid or simple-minded). Success, wisdom and cleverness in Iranian society are measured by the degree of deceitfulness, cheating and lying that are used to attain one's goals. A *bazaari,* a devoted Muslim businessman in the bazaar, is praised when he proves to his colleagues that he is more dishonest than they, and he is respectfully called *Zirak,* a "Wise Guy." It is no great leap to understand that Ahmadinejad's success is measured by his skillfulness in deceiving the West.

The role of the Islamic theocracy is to dissimulate, to hide its true intentions from the West. Iran's government will lie whenever it feels there is something to be gained from doing so: Underhandedness and double-dealing are the accepted methods of diplomatic engagement known as **Taghieh**, lying to one's enemy. The Quran clearly states (Sura 3:28), "The believers should not take the unbelievers for allies; and whoever does this has deprived himself from Allah's blessing. You should guard yourself against them in devotion to Allah, and Allah cautions you directly." Therefore, entering into treaties or agreements with Iran is foolish!

Perhaps another cautionary tale, attributed to Mullah Nasruddin the 14th century sage, says it best: "A man came up to Mullah Nasruddin and declared, 'I notice that every time you tell a different person about the fish you caught, you vary the size of the fish. Why?' The Mullah replied, *'I never tell a man more than I think he will believe!'"* In the Mullah's world, lying was raised to the status of art; it was up to the listener to beware. And so it is today.

The United States and other Western countries must remember that an authoritarian theocracy is the same as fascism: The population must do as it is told. There is no morality or compassion, only the will of the *ayatollah.* Dissenters are executed. The State exists, not for the welfare of its citizens, but rather for the perpetuation of the

State—and in the case of Iran, the State has the domination of other countries on its mind.

Iran abhors the imperialism of the Western nations, but paradoxically has great pride in its own history of empire. The fact that Iranians—never foreigners—have always defined Iran's borders is another source of great national pride. Iran also looks to its history of empire to justify its political interest in many of its neighbors: What is now Afghanistan was once part of the Persian Empire, as were parts of present day Pakistan. I am sure that Iran would like to annex these territories again.

When Iran looks over at southern Iraq, it sees three of the holiest *Shiah* cities—Najef, Karbala, and Basrah—which at one time belonged to Iran. Since those cities share the same values and religious beliefs as Iran, why shouldn't they become, once again, "independent" territories under the "protection" of Iran? As was practiced by the kings of ancient Persia, a government would be appointed in the protectorate that would swear loyalty to the ruler in Tehran, and be subordinate to Tehran.

Then there is Lebanon, a country in which the majority of people practice the *Shiah* faith and where there are many important *Shi'ah* shrines and schools. *Hezbollah* was organized and is financed by Iran. Obviously, Iran already has a strong influence in Lebanon and is maneuvering to control Lebanon completely.

What about Tajikistan? The people there speak Farsi and also share culture and values that are similar to Iran's. Azerbaijan? It is presently carved into portions: the Russians control one portion, the other is controlled by Iran. Muslims who do not want to remain under Russia's thumb populate the Russian-controlled section of Azerbaijan. What about the area around Bukhara, the capital of Uzbekistan? Why shouldn't Iran claim all these territories that have a Persian-Muslim population and should rightfully belong to a Muslim nation?

What about Kurdistan? Today it is divided into three parts: Iranian, Iraqi, and Turkish, but originally it was all part of the

Persian Empire—and Iranian nationalists think Kurdistan should once again belong entirely to Iran. The Kurds, who are *Sunni* Muslims, don't want to be controlled by Arabs, Iraqis or Turks— but they wouldn't mind coming under the auspices of Iran, with the freedom to rule themselves.

Looking to the Persian Gulf, Iran sees many little islands that presently are sheikhdoms. These sheikhdoms are becoming more and more nervous lately due to the political unrest and public demonstrations of their people and the fact that Iran claims that these islands, especially Hormuz, Abu Musa, Greater Tunb Island and Lesser Tunb Island belong to Iran. Even Dubai and Bahrain have large Iranian populations.

Iran's fingers are presently in the affairs of all the aforementioned countries. Iran feels it has a legitimate right to claim any or all of them, in order to re-establish its pre-World War One borders.

Add to all the previous information the fact that Iran is striving to develop nuclear weapons, and you have a very dangerous situation. Iran is determined. The regime will not negotiate in good faith with the West over the issue of nuclear weapons because Iran will not allow itself to be dominated by a foreign power—the Persian ego (and the Islamic religion) will not allow it! I can't emphasize enough: The governments of free people must keep a close watch on Iran. Iran is capable of de-stabilizing the entire region and causing even greater chaos than the Middle East is presently experiencing.

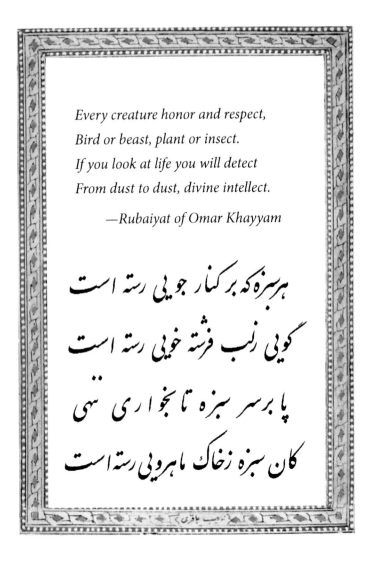

Every creature honor and respect,
Bird or beast, plant or insect.
If you look at life you will detect
From dust to dust, divine intellect.

—*Rubaiyat of Omar Khayyam*

هر سبزه که بر کنار جویی رسته است

گویی ز لب فرشته خویی رسته است

پا بر سر سبزه تا بخواری نهی

کان سبزه زخاک ماهرویی رسته است

IN MY OPINION

It is possibly dangerous, and certainly not politically correct, to make generalizations about the followers of the Muslim religion. However, I have formed my own opinion about Islam and have divided Muslims into four types: (1) Those who have embraced modernity while practicing Islam. They have decided to live in peace with non-Muslims and have embraced the universal laws of morality and decency. They are moderate Muslims. (2) Those who have embraced the mysticism and spirituality of Islam, known as *Sufis*. They are peace loving, humble, and tolerant individuals. (3) Those who run away from Islam, yet do not accept conversion into any other religion. They are secular humanists and intellectuals who are ashamed of the radical members of Islam and are tolerant of non-Islamic religions. Their children embrace Western values and do not necessarily practice Islam. I consider most of the Muslims living in Western countries to be in this category. (4) Those who accept Islam literally and submit themselves to the interpretation of the Quran and the *Shariah Law* as dictated by their Islamic leaders. This faction has, unfortunately, influenced how the non-Muslim nations of the world view Muslims as a group.

In my opinion, Iran under the present regime will never give up its position on strict *Shariah Law*, the use of *Taghieh* (lying to one's enemies) in all negotiations, and the idea of destroying the "Great Satan" and his followers.

Obtaining nuclear power has become a religious obligation; it is the will of Allah, as stated in the Holy Quran. Also, the use of *jihad* against the enemies of Allah is a religious obligation and a sacred duty.

Can the West use military and/or economic intervention to bring about the downfall of the Islamic regime? Such attempts would be entirely useless because martyrdom and suffering are holy and are integral elements of the *Shiah* sect. One need only observe the self-inflicted beatings during the month of Moharam to understand the role that physical discomfort plays in the hearts and minds of the faithful.

To save the world from a nuclear holocaust, the moderate Muslims, Arab and non-Arab, must speak up and stand against radical regimes and their followers. The West must assist all moderate Muslims to set aside their fear, for failure to oppose the Islamic Republic now will only result in a greater peril: Iran with nuclear capabilities.

Meanwhile, we in the United States must stop apologizing for our past actions. We must also stop extending our hands in friendship to a regime that reads such overtures as a sign of weakness. If we compromise in our negotiations with Iran, we are strengthening the Iranian leaders in the eyes of the Iranian people.

The United States, unlike the British and the Russians, has never invaded Iran: Contrary to Iranian conspiracy theories perpetuated by the regime, the United States has never been an oppressor (*mostakberin*) of Iran. In fact, the United States has been instrumental in bringing much industry to Iran, as well as bringing advanced agricultural practices and state-of-the-art agricultural machinery. The United States has also helped with the construction of infrastructures throughout the country and has modernized the Iranian military, especially the navy and air force. In addition, secular education, healthcare, and many social programs have been positively influenced by American assistance.

The majority of the Iranian people love Americans and the American goods, technology, and life-style. If Iranians could freely apply for American visas today, tomorrow Iran would be empty! Therefore, it is in the interest of the United States (and Arab and other Muslim countries) to empower and support the Iranian youth and the Iranian opposition groups, both in Iran and abroad, in order to bring a secular, democratic regime back to Iran.

How can this empowerment be accomplished? One way to help bring about change would be to donate a meaningful amount of money to Iranian television stations in the United States that are operated by people who oppose the existing government of Iran. At the present time, there are at least twenty-four Farsi television stations in the United States that broadcast to many countries in the world—including, of course, Iran. These stations have very limited budgets and most of the commentators, journalists, and scholars who work for the stations receive no compensation or salary. Helping to finance the Persian radio and TV stations in the United States and elsewhere would be a cost-effective and successful way to defeat the existing regime in Iran.

A little financial help goes a long way. For example, during the Iranian election protests of 2009, one Persian television station in Los Angeles raised $10,000 to purchase small video cameras to be used by the demonstrators. In this way, people in the streets of Tehran could broadcast to the world the images and sounds of the opposition marches. One of the donated cameras was used to document the death of Neda, a beautiful Iranian woman who was shot down by a soldier of the infamous Revolutionary Guard. This image reached the entire world and was shown on most television stations. People who oppose the regime should be encouraged to make video documentation of human rights violations and the officials who perpetrate these violations. Clerics who violate Islamic laws should be exposed. Satellite phones, Internet connections, and other technology should be donated to the opposition.

The American and European Iranians who oppose the Iranian regime have very limited resources, but they are anxious to free their country. The Free World must assist the various dedicated groups so that they can continue to support their comrades in Iran.

It will be extremely difficult for the people of Iran to resist the power of the totalitarian regime, but they must stop being obedient followers; their "herd mentality," practiced for so many decades, must be overcome—Iranians who follow the Supreme Ayatollah with blind faith have abdicated their obligation to think for themselves; they must be guided by their liberal peers.

Women in particular have suffered under Iran's Islamic regime. Women are encouraged to wear the *hejab*; they are not equal to men under the law regarding civil rights; they are raped and tortured when arrested as political prisoners. The Iranian women living in the Diaspora are the ideal role models for the women of Iran: Communication and exchange of information between women can create a mass movement to enhance the lives of the sisters, mothers, and daughters who are presently oppressed. I believe that women are the key to obtaining freedom in Iran; they must stand firm and demand equality under the law.

Encouragement and financial assistance to opposition groups from the democracies of the world, along with assistance from Iranians living abroad, will bring about the collapse of the present regime. Also very important, as I have written many times in this book, are the voices of moderate Muslims, from all countries in the world, raised in an outcry of protest against radical Islam. This international outpouring of support will generate a hurricane within Iran—and it will be unstoppable! No longer will Iran's young people be debased, imprisoned and held hostage by a regime that they do not want.

GLOSSARY

This glossary has been prepared to assist readers to understand the essence of each story; it is not necessarily linguistically correct and should be only used as a guide for clarification of the text.

To clarify the background of the individuals mentioned in this book, their religious affiliation is included. Please note those names followed by a "p" are Persian names.

MUSLIM NAMES IN THIS BOOK

Abdollah, Abbas, Ahmad, Ali, Akbar, Amir, Amjadi, Azimi; Badeie; Danesh (p); Esmaeil; Fakhri, Fallah, Farshid (p), Fazlollah; Gholam Ali, Gholam Hussein; Haajar, Habib, Hassan, Hussein, Husseini, Hajj Habib, Houman; Islami; Jalaal; Khalghi; Maheen, Mahmood, Majid, Maseud, Mehdi, Mohammad; Robab; Shahrokh (p), Shekholislami; Touran (p).

JEWISH NAMES IN THIS BOOK

Abi, Aharon, Ariela, Asher; Behrooz (p), Bijan (p); Chaim; David, Dilmani, Dilmanian; Ebrahim, Elias, Elyahu, Enayat, Eshrat, Ezat, Ezi, Ezra; Fereidoon (p); Gohar (p); Hertzel, Homa (p), Houman (p); Iraj (p); Jaleh (p), Jila (p); Kamrava; Leah, Lida (p), Lili (p); Malihe, Manoochehr (p), Mansoor, Manzal, Mazal, Michael, Misha, Mojdeh (p), Monir (p), Morad (p), Mousa; Nazarian, Nejat (p); Omidvar (p); Rashel, Refouah, Ronica, Ronit, Roslyn, Ruben, Ruth; Saeid, Sarah, Shahnaz (p), Shahram (p), Shamsi, Shemuel, Shokri, Shoshana, Shoshi, Soleiman, Soraia (p); Tishbi, Torkan; Yashar, Yosef, Yousef.

FARSI, HEBREW AND ARABIC WORDS AND PHRASES:

agha (Farsi) – mister; father

aftabeh (Farsi) – a metal pitcher used for washing parts of the body

ajil-e shab-e yalda (Farsi) – a combination of nuts, raisins and pumpkin seeds eaten during the celebration of Shabeh Chelleh.

akhoond (Farsi) – a Persian name for a Muslim cleric, commonly used in Iran; *akhoonds* are responsible for leading religious services in a community; *akhoonds* lead the prayers in the mosques, deliver religious sermons and perform religious ceremonies, such as birth rites and funerl services; they also teach in Islamic schools; they commonly dress in religious attire. Their coat is called *ghaba*, and *amameh* is their headcovering.

Al–Shahada (Arabic) "The Testimony" – "There is no god but God, Mohammad is the messenger of God." This is one of the five pillars of Islam.

aragh (Farsi) – a clear, colorless distilled alcoholic drink that may be flavored; empty bottles may be tied onto lemon trees, positioned so that blossoms are inside the bottle, causing a lemon to grow inside it!

ayatollah (Arabic) – A high-ranking Shiah cleric who is an expert in Islamic studies, such as jurisprudence, ethics, and philosophy; they usually teach Islamic studies in universities. There are only about 70 *ayatollahs* with the title "*Grand Ayatollah*" in the world.

azan (Arabic) – Islamic call to prayer, especailly at noon.

baba (Farsi) – an honorific title for "grandfather," and "father."

baleh (Farsi) – yes

band andazoon (Farsi) – "The Beautification" – This is a celebration held a few days before a wedding; it is attended by the women in the bride and groom's families. The purpose of the party is to remove hair from the bride's face and body. It may include getting manicures, facials, and massages. Gifts are given to the bride, and the objective is to have fun and beautify the bride and prepare her for the wedding night.

bar mitzvah (Hebrew) and ***bat mitzvah*** (Hebrew) – the Jewish

338

coming-of-age rituals; *bar mitzvah* literally means "son of the commandmant"; *bat* means "daughter." Boys at the age of 13 (12 or 13 for girls) become obligated to observe the commandments. The *bar mitzvah* ceremony formally and publicly marks the assumption of that obligation, along with the corresponding right to take part in leading religious services, to count in a minyan (minimum number of people needed to perform certain parts of the religious services), to form binding contracts, to testify before religious courts, and to marry. A Jewish boy automatically becomes *bar mitzvah* upon reaching the age of 13 years, and a girl upon reaching the age of 12 years. No ceremony is required to confer these rights and obligations.

bazaari (Farsi) – is a name given to the merchants and store owners of *bazaars*, the traditional marketplaces of Iran. These men, mostly importers, are wealthy, conservative Muslims and are said to be the class of people who helped make the 1979 Islamic Revolution occur. The *bazaari*, united in their resistance to dependence on the West and the spread of Western ways, are traditionalists and have close ties with the *Shiah* clergy.

bochary (Farsi) – a coal burning stove, or a kerosene heater.

caravansary (Farsi) – an inn for travelers, with a central courtyard for their animals; these *caravansaries* were found along trade routes and at religious shrines.

chador (Farsi) – an outer garment or open cloak worn by many Iranian women and female teenagers in public places. A *chador* is a full-body-length semicircle of fabric that is split open down the front, with a head-hole in the top. This cloth is tossed over the woman's or girl's head, and then held closed in front; it has no hand openings, and no buttons or clasps, but rather is held closed by her hands or by wrapping the ends around her waist. Muslim women wear solid black *chadors*.

chakeram (Farsi) – literally, "we are very obedient to you," or "we are very much your servant." It is a word used to express Persian etiquette (*ta'aroff*).

deezi (Farsi) – a traditional lamb stew made with lamb shank, tomatoes, beans, and fresh herbs and spices.

doogh (Farsi) – a yogurt-based beverage popular in Iran and was consumed in ancient Persia. It may be flavored with mint or cucumber.

Ey pedar sagg! (Farsi) – an insult, "son of a bitch." It can also be used to describe a naughty child, as in "you rascal," or "son of a gun."

Erev Shabbat (Hebrew) – the eve of the Sabbath, all of Friday prior to sundown.

Es,hagh (Farsi) – Isaac's first name, in Iran.

Fadaieh shoma! (Farsi) –"May I die for you!" A phrase that expresses Persian politeness and verbal etiquette (*ta'aroff*).

Farsi – is the most widely spoken Persian language; the spoken language in Iran. Persian has at least 110 million native speakers, holding offical status in Iran, Afghanistan and Tajikistan. For centuries Persian has also been a prestigious cultural language in Central Asia, South Asia, and Western Asia, with a long history of literature before the invasion of Arabs brought Islam to Persia. Books on science, literature and philosophy that were written in the Persian language using the Hebrew alphabet were saved from destruction by the Arab invaders—they thought the books were religious texts and spared them. Some of the famous works of Persian literature are the *Shahnameh* of Ferdowsi, the works of Rumi, the *Rubaiyat* of Omar Khayyam, and the poems of Hafiz and Saadi.

gaz (Farsi) – the traditional name of Persian nougat, originating in the city of Esfahan; *gaz* is the sweet sap found on the angebin plant that is combined with pistachios, rosewater and egg whites; modern versions of *gaz* may use sugar and corn syrup as a substitute.

Ghaabele shoma niest! (Farsi) – "It is not worthy of you!" – This phrase is used in several situations: when you thank someone for something he or she has done for you; when you ask about the price, or fare, or cost of something; when you thank someone for a gift. This phrase is an expression of formal politeness, or *ta'aroff*.

ghanadi (Farsi) – a shop that sells candy and cakes

Ghorbonat beram! (Farsi) "May I be your sacrifice!" – A phrase that expresses Persian politeness and verbal etiquette (*ta'aroff*); used when greeting someone.

Ghorbane shoma! (Farsi) "May I be your sacrifice!" A phrase that expresses verbal etiquette (ta'aroff) when greeting someone.

golha (Farsi) – literally translated, means "flowers." *Golha* is the traditional, classical Persian music.

golpar (Farsi) – Golpar seeds are used as a spice in Persian cooking; these seeds are slightly bitter. Golpar seeds are usually sold in a powder and are often sold as "angelica powder." The powder is sprinkled over beans and potatoes and is used in soups and stews. It is often sprinkled over pomegranate seeds.

gondi (Farsi) – Persian meatballs, typically served in a bowl of hot chicken soup, are unique to the Jews of Iran; it is traditionally served on *Shabbat*. *Gondi* are made from ground lamb or chicken, cooked chickpeas or chickpea flour, grated onion, and dry lemon. *Gondi* (in chicken soup) are accompanied by bread and raw green vegetables (see *sabzi*)

haft seen (Farsi) – literally translated, "the seven S's" – is the traditional table setting, called *sofreh hahft seen*, for Norouz, the Iranian spring celebration that marks a New Year. The seven kinds of food each symbolize life, health, wealth, abundance, love, patience, and purity: *sabzeh*, wheat or lentil sprouts represent rebirth; *samanu*, a creamy pudding made from wheat germ is regarded as holy; *seeb*, the apple symbolizes health and beauty; *senjid*, the dried fruit of the lotus flower for love; *sir*, garlic is considered for medicinal purposes and represents health; *somagh*, sumac berries represent the color of the sunrise and victory of good over evil; *serkeh*, vinegar represents old age and patience. There are other things that may be placed on the *sofreh* (tablecloth): a book to symbolize wisdom, such as the Quran and/or poetry books of Persian poets; a few coins to represent prosperity; a basket of painted eggs to represent fertility; an orange floating in a bowl of water to symbolize the earth floating in space; a flask of rosewater for its cleansing power; a brazier for burniing wild rue, an herb whose smoke wards off the evil spirits; a pot of hyacinth or narcissus; a mirror, which represents the images and reflections of Creation; candlesticks, to symbolize enlightenment and happiness.

hajj, hajji (Arabic) – The pilgrimage to Mecca, the *hajj*, is obligatory for any Muslim able to make the journey. *Hajji* or *Hajj* used before the name of a man or woman tells that he or she has made the pilgrimage.

halal (Arabic) – literally means "lawful," is used to designate any object or action which is permissible to use or engage in, according to Islamic Law. The term is used to designate food permissible to eat, according to *Shariah* (Islamic Law). The opposite of *halal* is *haraam*.

halva, or *halvah* (Arabic) – literally means "sweet," is used to describe two types of desserts: a dry, powdery flour-based product made from flour, typically semolina, which is sauteed in clarified butter, to which sugar and saffron is added; and a moist or gelatinous halva to which rosewater is added.

hanukiya (Hebrew) – a type of *menorah* (candelabra) that is used in the Jewish celebration of Hanukkah. A typcial *menorah* holds seven candles and a *hanukiya* holds nine candles.

haram (Arabic) – literally means "forbidden" and is used to refer to anything that is prohibited by the words of Allah.

hanna bandoon (Farsi) The application of *hanna* or *henna* is an ancient practice which occurs a day or two before a wedding and is part of the beautification of the bride. The bride-to-be is surrounded by female family and friends and henna designs are applied to her hands and/or body; this is followed by dancing, eating, and celebrating.

hejab (Arabic) literally means "curtain" or "cover," and refers to both the head covering traditionally worn by Muslim women and modest styles of dress in general. By law, women in the Islamic Republic are required to observe *hejab* by concealing the shapes of their bodies and covering their hair in public places and in front of men who are *na-mahram*, not closely related to them.

imam (Arabic) is an Islamic leadership position, often the worship leader of a mosque. The word *imam* is also used to describe a Muslim leader of the line of Ali, held by *Shiah* to be divinely appointed, sinless, infallible successors of Mohammad; thus it can describe any of the various rulers who claim descent from Mohammad and who exercise spiritual and temporal leadership over a Muslim region. The belief in the 12th Imam is one of the most important tenets of the *Shiah* sect and impacts all aspects of the beliefs of radical Islamists.

jahel or ***jaahel*** (the word has Arabic roots, but is used as slang in Farsi) – a hoodlum, a thug; a person of low moral character.

jihad (Arabic) is an Islamic term that translates as "struggle": The struggle to attain personal spiritual perfection within the Muslim faith, and also the struggle against evil within the world; the latter definition has been interpreted to condone and encourage the goal of extending Islam throughout the world. *Jihad* appears 41 times in the Quran.

joon, or ***jaan*** (Farsi) – literally means "life"; is used as a term of endearment; it is used with affection and attached to a loved one's name.

Johood (Arabic?) - In Iran, a word for "Jew" that has a derogatory meaning and is used as an insult.

Kaddish (Hebrew) means "holy"; it is a prayer recited in the Jewish religious service whose central theme is the magnification and sanctification of God's name. The word *kaddish* is often used to refer specifically to "The Mourners' Kaddish" which is part of the mourning ritual in Judaism; "saying Kaddish" unambiguously denotes the ritual of mourning, and along with the *Shema* and *Amidah*, is one of the most important and central prayers in the Jewish liturgy.

Kalimi (Arabic) – In Iran, the offical government word for "Jew."

Khak bar saram! (Farsi) – literally, "Dirt on my head!" It can also be defined as "Shame on me!" or "Woe is me!"

khakham (Hebrew) – a learned or wise Jewish man, sometimes used to mean "rabbi."

khoresh fesenjoon (Farsi) – Persian chicken, pomegranate and walnut stew.

kibbutz (Hebrew) –literally means "gathering," or "clustering"; plural, *kibbutzim*. It is a collective community in Israel that was originally based on agriculture. *Kibbutzim* began as utopian communities, a combination of socialism and Zionism.

Kiddush (Hebrew) – literally, "sanctification," is a blessing recited over wine or grape juice to sanctify the Sabbath and Jewish holidays.

kippah (Hebrew) – is a cap worn by Orthodox Jewish men to fulfill the requirement held by some orthodox halachic authorities that their head be covered at all times; it is worn at times of prayer by Conservative and Reform men (and less frequently, women).

koocheh (Farsi) – a narrow alley or street; the high walls of the buildings on both sides of the *koocheh* provided relief from intense sunlight; this was an efficient and ancient form of urban design in Persia.

korsy (Farsi) – a contraption used to keep people warm in the winter; it consisted of a large, bulky cotton blanket placed over a low, square table; under the table was placed a metal bowl or tray that contained hot coals. To use the *korsy*, family members sat around the table and placed their legs under the blanket to soak up the heat from the coals. Many families congregated around the *korsy* to eat their meals and sip their hot tea from small glasses. In between meals, the men of the house sat around the *korsy* to read their newspapers; children burrowed under the blanket to nap or do their homework. At night, people could sleep around the korsy.

Lida (Farsi) Isaac's youngest sister's first name, in Iran.

Lydia – Isaac's youngest sister's first name, in America and Israel.

mahram (Arabic) – In Islamic Shariah Law, *mahram* is an unmarriageable kin with whom sexual intercourse would be considered incestuous, a punishable taboo. Current usage of the term covers a wider rane of people and mostly deals with the dress code practice of hejab. A woman's male *mahrams* fall into these categories: Permanent or blood *mahrams*; In-law *mahrams*. Theoretically, a Muslim woman's *mahrams* form the group of allowable escorts when she travels. Except for the spouse, being *mahram* is a permanent condition; that means a man will remain *mahram* to his ex-mother-in-law after divorcing her daughter. One is *ghayr mahram* (non-*mahram*) to one's ex-spouse. One must not stay with a *ghayr mahram* in seclusion where none of their *mahrams* is present.

matzah, matzo (Hebrew) – plural, **matzot** – an unleavened bread traditionally eaten by Jews during the week-long Passover holiday, when eating *chametz* (bread and other food which is made with leavened grain) is forbidden according to Jewish law. *Matzo* is eaten by Jews as an obligation during the Passover Seder meal.

megillah (Hebrew) – A scroll of the Book of Esther, read on the festival of Purim.

mezuzah (Hebrew) – is a piece of parchment contained in a decorative case which is afixed to the doorposts of a Jewish home. It is a constant reminder of God's presence and His *mitzvot* (commandments). The words of the *Shema* are written on the tiny scroll; the prayer must be written by hand by a scribe.

mitzvah (Hebrew) – A commandment of the Jewish law and/ or the fulfillment of such a commandment; a worthy deed, a meritous or charitable act.

mokhlesam (Farsi) – A word used to convey respect to someone: "I am your humble servant," or "I am indebted to you." It is used to express *ta'aroff*—formalized Persian politeness and etiquette.

morshed (Farsi) – literally means "one who guides" - a storyteller who chants from memory the ancient Persian sagas, especially the *Shahnameh* (The Book of Kings).

mullah (Arabic) – literally means "master," or "guardian" and is generally used to refer to a Muslim man who is educated in Islamic theology and sacred law; it is the title given to some Islamic clergy or mosque leaders, most of whom have memorized the Quran. The title has also been used in some Iranian Jewish communites to refer to the Jewish religious leadership.

Mullah Nasruddin – a Sufi figure, sometimes believed to have lived during the Middle Ages (around the 13th century) and considered to be a populist philosopher and wise man, remembered for his funny stories and anecdotes. He appears in thousands of stories, sometimes witty, sometimes wise, but often the butt of a joke. A Nasruddin story usually has subtle humor and a pedagogic premise. As generations go by, new stories have been added, others modified, and his stories have spread to many regions. His stories deal with concepts that are timeless, like Aesop's fables; they are full of folk wisdom and have become a part of the folklore of a number of nations and cultures (Turkish, Persian, Arabic Azerbaijani, Kurdish, etc.)

Muslim Students' Association – or Muslim Student Union, of the U.S. and Canada, is a religious organization, established in 1963, that is dedicated to establishing Islamic societies on college campuses. Today the membership is made up of mostly American-born Muslims. Some of their fund raising, recruiting, and propaganda have caused controversy in recent years.

Najes (Arabic) – literally means, "impure," "filthy," "unclean" – There are numerous rules or laws governing which animal, people, or substances are *najes*. Some things that are *najes* are: bodily fluids, such as urine, blood, sperm, sweat, feces; dogs; pigs; liquor and wine; unbelievers, that is, non-Muslims. [See the section on Najes in Part Four of this book.]

namaz (Farsi) – literally means "prayer"; it is one of the most important of the five pillars of Islam. A Muslim is obligated to pray five times each day. The *Shiah* ritual of *namaz* follows a number of prescribed chronological steps.

nanvaie, noonvaie (Persian) – bakery

Norouz, or ***Norooz, Nowrouz*** – (Farsi) – Literally means "new light" and is the name of the Persian (Iranian) New Year; it marks the first day of spring and the beginning of the year in the Iranian calendar. It is celebrated on the day of the vernal equinox, which usually occurs on March 21st. *Norouz* was originally a Zoroastrian festival. The Jewish festival of Purim is probably adapted from the Persian New Year celebration. There are many traditions that are observed during *Norouz* [See "*haft seen*"]. In Iran, the Islamic Republic attempted to suppress the holiday following the revolution because the *ayatollahs* considered *Norouz* a pagan holiday and a distraction from Islamic holidays, however they were unsuccessful.

olama or ***ulama*** (Arabic) – refers to the educated class of Muslim legal scholars who are arbiters of *Shariah Law*. In a broader sense, the word is used to describe the Muslim clergy who have completed several years of Islamic studies.

Pedar sagg! (Farsi) – derogatory, literally means "Son of a dog!" or "Son of a bitch!"

Pesach (Hebrew, Yiddish) – is the Jewish holiday of Passover; it is also known as the Feast of Unleavened Bread. The holiday lasts for eight days and commemorates the Exodus of the Jews from Pharaoh's Egypt; in commemoration of the Exodus, no leavened bread is eaten for eight days; a *seder*, the traditional ritual meal which follows the *Haggadah* (the ancient text that sets forth the order of the *seder*) is celebrated in Jewish homes the first two nights of the holiday. *Pesach* is celebrated in the spring, and begins on the 15th day of the month of Nisan in the Jewish calendar.

Quran (Arabic) – the Muslim holy book, the Koran; it is the central religious book of Islam.

Rosh Hashanah (Hebrew) – literally means, "head of the year"; it is the Jewish New Year and is the first of the High Holy Days, or *Yamim Nora'im* (Days of Awe). It is observed the first two days of the month of Tishrei, and occurs ten days before *Yom Kippur*, The Day of Atonement. It is believed that a person's fate for the coming year is decided during the High Holy Days.

sabzi (Farsi) – a traditional serving of green vegetables (such as scallions) and herbs (such as basil, mint, and tattagon).

salaam (Arabic) – literrly means "peace," often used in Iran as a greeting.

salavat (A prayer in Arabic) as in, "send a *salavat*"; a prayer to Allah that is offered in times of distress, or when thanking

God in gratitude—almost a relfex (similar in intent to a Catholic making the sign of the cross on his chest).

sangak (Farsi) - literally means "little stone"; it's the name of the rectangular or triangular Iranian whole wheat, sourdough flatbread. The bread is traditionally baked on a bed of small hot stones in an oven.

saraaf, saraafi (Farsi) – private Jewish or Muslim shops, located near the bazaar in Tehran, which perform some of the functions of a bank: the exchange of currency from *toman* to dollars; sending money out of Iran, *but leaving no paper trail* (*havaaleh*); lending money, with interest, with only a handshake (no paper trail). *Saraaf* is the person providing the service; *saraafi* is the place of business, usually a small storefront.

seyad, or *sayed* (Arabic) - a title given to male, direct descendants of the Prophet Mohammad; *saadat* is the title given to a female whose lineage can be traced to the Prophet Mohammad.

Shabbat (Hebrew) – literally means "rest" or cessation"; the seventh day of the Jewish week; *Shabbat* begins at sunset on Friday evening and ends Saturday night when three stars are visible in the sky. On *Shabbat,* Jews remember that God created the world and then rested from His labors (Genesis 2:2). *Shabbat* is considered the most important of the Jewish holidays—even more important than *Yom Kippur* or the other High Holidays— because it's observance is commanded in the *Torah*. There are three main rituals during the *Shabbat* observance: lighting the *Shabbat* candles; saying *Kiddush* over wine; reciting *HaMotzi* over the *challah* (bread).

Shabeh Chelleh (Farsi) – literally means "night of forty"; is the winter solstice celebration which has been celebrated since ancient times and had great significance to the Zoroastrians since it marks the eve of the birth of Mithra, the Sun God. It is a time of great joy. It is celebrated on or around December 20 or 21, on the longest night of the year, on the last day of the

Zoroastrian month Azar. The first day of the new month, known as *Khore rooz*, belongs to the Zoroastrian God, Ahura Mazda, the Supreme Wisodm. It is a social occasion when family and close friends get together; it is obligatory that fresh fruit (especially watermelon) be served to observe the ancient custom of invoking the divinities to request protection of the winter crop. Activites common to the celebration include eating, reading poems out loud, including verses of the *Shahnameh*.

shah (Farsi) – king; sovereign; the title of Iran's monarchial rulers before the 1979 Islamic Revolution.

Shahnameh – (Farsi) – literally means "The Book of Kings."

Shariah Law – (Arabic) –literally means "A path to life-giving water," and is the moral code and religious law of Islam; it is the law of the Quran. It is a discussion on the duties of Muslims and is divided into several branches that deal with ritual worship, transactions and contracts, morals and manners, beliefs, and punishments. What the clerics in Iran call an Islamic society and government denotes an underlying model that has brought about huge upheavals in the political, cultural, legal and ideological structures of Iranian society. It is significant that public opinion has not simply accepted these laws, and even the courts have not implemented them to the full because they fear public anger. Women have been in the forefront of demonstations against archaic punishments and misogynist laws.

shater (Farsi) – a baker

shelosheem or sheloshim (Hebrew) – literally means "thirty"; the first 30 days following the burial, including the days of *shiva*, are called *shelosheem*. Most restrictions that applied to mourners during the seven-day *shiva* period are lifted during *shelosheem*; mourners are allowed to leave their house and begin to work again; however, they should severly limit social engagements during this time, and certainly avoid festive outings where music is played. Mourners do not shave or cut their hair during this time. One is still mourning, but during *shelosheem* the laws allow for gradual re-entry into everyday life. After the completion of the *shelosheem*, if mourners are mourning anyone but a parent, spouse or child, the official mourning period ends. In the case of parents, children or spouse, the period of mourning extends for eleven months.

Shema Yisrael (Hebrew) – are the first two words of the Torah (Hebrew Bible) that is the centerpiece of the morning and evening Jewish prayer services. The first verse encapsulates the monotheistic essence of Judaism: "Hear, O Israel: the Lord is our God, the Lord is One." Observant Jews consider the *Shema* to be the most important part of the prayer service, and its recitation is a *mitzvah* (religious commandment).

Shiah*; *Shiite (Arabic) – The branch of Islam that recognizes the Prophet Mohammad's son-in-law Ali, and his descendants as the rightful successors of Mohammad. A *Shiite* is a member of the *Shiah* sect. The *Sunni* Muslims do not accept this belief.

shiva (Hebrew) – literally means "seven"; *shiva* is the first stage of mourning. After the burial, the immediate mourners return to a home called the "*shiva* house," to begin a seven day period of intense mourning. This week-long observance is called "sitting *shiva*" and it is an emotionally and spiritually healing time when the mourners stay together and accept short visits from loved ones who come to comfort them. Mourners should ideally not leave the *shiva* house at any time; others must take care of any errands or outside commitments for them. To be seen during the day in public is inappropriate at this time.

shofar (Hebrew) – a Jewish instrument, usually made from a ram's horn; it makes a trumpet-like sound and is traditionally blown on *Rosh Hashonnah*, the Jewish New Year.

sigheh (Arabic) – a temporary marriage; a *Shiah* practice that allows couples to marry for a period of time of their choice, from a few minutes to ninety-nine years, by reciting a verse from the

Quran. *Sigheh* is sometimes used to "legitimize" extramarital affairs or prostitution; it has also become a practical method of dealing with the Islamic regime's crackdown on couples who are dating.

sofreh (Farsi) – literally means "tablecloth" – Very often a *sofreh* was spread over Persian carpets on the floor, or over a *korsy*, and the food and utensils were arranged on it.

sofreh abolfazi (*sofreh*, Farsi; *abolfazi*, Arabic) – a meal in one's home to thank God for answering a prayer.

sofreh aghd (Farsi) – a wedding meal

sofreh haft seen (Farsi) – the traditional setting of the Norouz table

ta'aroff (Farsi) – a complex system of formalized courtesy that is common in Iran and elsewhere in the Middle East. Some English translations of *ta'aroff* phrases used in Iran are as follows: "May your shadow never be shortened (become less)," which means "May your friendship and kindness continue"; "May we (my family) remain under your shadow," which means "May your friendship and kindness towards my family continue"; "May your children grow under your shadow," which means "May you live to see your children reach adulthood"; "May your steps be upon my eyes," which means "You are welcome to my home/place of business"; "Thank you, it is not worthy of you," is a polite response to "How much do I owe you?" or in response to giving a gift.

taghieh (Arabic) – a permitted Islamic lie; according to *Shiah* tradition, dissimulation is permissable, if not compulsory, to defend one's faith.

tahdig (Farsi) – literally means "bottom of the pot"; is a specialty of Iranian cuisine consisting of crisp rice taken from the bottom of the pot in which the rice is cooked.

tefillin (Hebrew) – are two small black boxes with straps attached to them; Jewish men are required to place one box on their forehead and tie the other on their arm each morning, except *Shabbat* and holidays. *Tefillin* are biblical in origin and are commanded within the context of several laws outlining a Jew's relationship to God. The text inside the two boxes is hand-written by a scribe and consists of Exodus 13:1-10, 11-16 and Deuteronomy 6:4-9, 11:13-21.

toman (Farsi) – is a superunit of the *rial*, the official currency of Iran. At the time the author lived in Iran, 1 American dollar equalled 8 *toman*; 1 *toman* always equals 10 *rials*.

tonbak (Farsi) – a goblet shaped drum from ancient Persia that is still used today.

tootoon (Farsi) - tobacco

Torah (Hebrew) – is the name given by Jews to the Five Books of Moses (Genesis, Exodus, Leviticus, Numbers and Deuteronomy) that begin the Hebrew Bible, known commonly to non-Jews as the Old Testament.

velayat-e fageh (Arabic) – the rule of Islamic jurisprudence; it refers to the Islamic Republic's supreme leader, the *ayatollah*, who has ultimate authority in the absence of the *Shiah's* Twelfth Imam. (The Twelfth Imam was said to have disappeared in the ninth century, and faithful Muslims believe he will return one day.)

Velesh kon! (Farsi) – Leave him alone!

Waay bar man! (Farsi) – Woe is me!

Yad Va'Shem (Hebrew) – is Israel's official memorial to those Jews who died in the Holocaust: The Holocaust Martyrs and Heroes Remembrance Authority.

Yahudi (Hebrew) – word for "Jew"; Persian Jews use this word when speaking to each other or refering to Jews; *Yahudi* does not have the derrogatory connotation of *Johood* and *Kalimi*.

Yom Kippur (Hebrew) – known as the Day of Atonement, is the holiest and most solemn day of the year for Jews; it is one of the Jewish High Holy Days. Jews observe a fast. The Yom Kippur service builds in intensity throughout the day, culminating with the final *Ne'ila* service. During the final hour of the day, all who have fasted and prayed together gather strength from their friends and cry out for the gates of forgiveness to remain open. The cathartic moment, which occurs when nighttime has descended, is punctuated by the blowing of the *shofar*, as all congregants exclaim, "Next year in Jerusalem!"

Yomtoubian (Farsi) Isaac's family's last name, in Iran.

Yomtovian (Hebrew) Isacc's family's last name, in Israel.

zakat (Arabic) – mandatory charity

Zarathushtra (ancient Persian) – a prophet and founder of the Zoroastrian faith; there are no confirmable sources of information about his life or when he lived.

zerang (Farsi) – slang for "smart," "sensible"

zirak (Farsi) – slang for "a wise-guy"

Zoroastrianism (ancient Perisan) – the religion of the followers of Zarathushtra; the three tenets of Zoroastrianism: Good Thoughts, Good Words, Good Deeds.

REFERENCES

Books

Ali, Abdullah Yusuf, translator. *The Qur'an.* Elmhurst, New York: Tahrike Tarsile Qur'an, Inc., 2009.

Aslan, Reza. *No God But God: The Origins, Evolution, and Future of Islam.* New York: Random House, 2005.

Daniel, Norman. *Islam and the West: The Making of an Image.* Oxford: Oneworld Publications Ltd., 1993.

Ebrahimi, Simon Sion. *Veiled Romance - A Persian Tale of Passion and Revolution.* Los Angeles, 2011

Hamilton, Jordan. *Crisis.* (in Farsi) Toronto: Omid.

Hakakian, Roya. *Assassins of the Turquoise Palace.* New York: Grove Press, 2011.

Hinnell, John R. *Persian Mythology.* New York: Peter Bedrick Books, 1985.

Kavir, Mahmood. *Shofar Magazine,* Vol. 369, November 2011. Great Neck, New York: Shofar Foundation, Inc.

Keddie, Nikki R. and Hooglund, Eric. *The Iranian Revolution and the Islamic Republic.* Syracuse: Syracuse University Press, 1986.

Lieber, Rabbi Moshe. *The Pirkei Avos Treasury: Ethics of the Fathers.* Brooklyn, New York: Mesorah Publications, Ltd., 1995.

Majd, Hooman. *The Ayatollah Begs To Differ.* New York: Doubleday, 2008.

Majd, Hooman. *The Ayatollah's Democracy.* New York: WW Norton, 2010.

Makbuleh, Mitra Ph.D. *Purim: A Mystical Interpretation.* Irvine, California: T.R.E.E. Publications.

Milani, Abbas. *The Shah.* New York: Palgrave Macmillan, 2011.

Moreen, Vera Basch, translator. *In Queen Esther's Garden: An Anthology of Judeo-Persian Literature*. New Haven & London: Yale University Press, 2000.

Pahlavi, Mohammad Reza. *Answer to History*. New York: Stein and Day Publishers, 1980.

Parsa, Bahman. *Iran: The Land of Civilization*. Tehran: Katab Sara Publishers, 2000.

Petrochevski, Ilya Povolovitch. *Islam in Iran*. (translated from Russian to Farsi by Karim Keshavarz.) Tehran: Payam Publications.

Putnam, Robert D. and Campbell, David E. *American Grace: How Religion Divides and Unites Us*. New York: Simon & Schuster, 2010.

Rosenberg, Joel C. *The Twelfth Imam*. Tyndale House Publishers, 2010.

Rosenberg, Joel C. *The Tehran Initiative*. Tyndale House Publishers, 2011.

Saberi, Roxana. *Between Two Worlds: My Life and Captivity in Iran*. New York: HarperCollins, 2010.

Sarshar, Houman, editor. *Esther's Children: A Portrait of Iranian Jews*. Beverly Hills, California: The Center for Iranian Jewish Oral History, 2002.

Sciolino, Elaine. *Persian Mirrors: The Elusive Face of Iran*. New York: Free Press (Simon & Schuster), 2005.

Shahbaz, Hassan, editor. *Rahavard Persian Journal*, vol. XI, No. 38, Spring, 1995. Los Angeles.

Shahery, Josef, editor. *Shofar Magazine*. (in Farsi) Great Neck, New York: Shofar Foundation, Inc.

Sullivan, William. *Mission To Iran*. (in Farsi) Toronto: Omid.

Yassavoli, Javad, book designer. *The Fabulous Land of Iran: Selected Works of Iranian Photographers*. Tehran: Farhang-Sara Publications,

1997.

Yazdi, Dr. Ebrahim. *Final Attempts in Last Days: Untold Stories of the Islamic Revolution of Iran.* (in Farsi) Tehran: Ghalam Publications.

Zidan, Dr. Ahmad and Dina Zidan. *The Glorious Qur'an.* Cairo: Islamic Inc. Publishing, 1993.

Websites

Aslan, Reza. *No god but God, lectures and interviews*: You Tube (accessed March 26, 2011).

Britannica Online Encyclopedia. *Iran: The White Revolution.* http://www.britannica.com (accessed April 24, 2011).

Ganji, Manouchehr. *The realization of economic, social, and cultural rights: Problems, policies, progress*: Document – United Nations (accessed April 3, 2011).

History of Iran: Oil Nationalization. http://www.iranchamber. com/history/oil_nationalization/oil_nationalization.php (accessed April 15, 2011).

History of Iran: White Revolution. http://www.iranchamber. com/history/white_revolutionwhite_revolution.php (accessed April 22, 2011).

Majd, Hooman. *The Ayatollah Begs to Differ, lectures and interviews*: You Tube (accessed April 2, 2011).

May 26, 1908: Mideast Oil Discovered – There Will Be Blood. http://www.wired.com (accessed April 16, 2011).

Milani, Abbas. *Video lectures and interviews*: webjournal.us/ show/Abbas+Milani (accessed April 17, 2011).

Milani, Abbas. *Video lectures and interviews.* http://www.bing.

com/videos/watch/video/abbas-milani/17wm18exq (accessed March 30, 2011).

Milani, Abbas. Videos lectures and interviews. http://www. charlierose.com (accessed March 18, 2011).

Ramazani, R.K. *Iran's White Revolution: A Study in Political Development.* http://www.jstor.org/stable/162585 (accessed May 5, 2011).

The Iranian Oil Fields Are Nationalized. http://www. historytoday.com (accessed April 15, 2011).

ADDENDUM

EXPOSING FEAR

In the past, most Muslim Iranian families living in America have proudly displayed a picture of the Prophet Mohammad and his cousin Imam Ali.

In the home of Muslim friends (left to right) Roslyn, Isaac's wife; Shahnaz, Isaac's sister; Ruben, Isaac's brother; Soraya, Isaac's sister; Lydia, Isaac's sister; Ezat, Isaac's mother; and Homa, Isaac's sister. On the wall is a picture of the Prophet Mohammad and his cousin Imam Ali.

Recently, however, it seems that these families deny their commitment to Islam and even declare themselves to be Zoroastrians! It is now expedient for many Muslim Iranians to try and distance themselves from Islam rather than make an effort to renounce and reject the Islamic Republic of Iran. They are disgusted by Iran's Islamic government, yet too fearful to speak out against it.

Many of my friends, Jewish and Muslim, who encouraged me to write this book have asked me to change their names in the text and remove their photos. Although they remain supportive regarding the factual events presented in this book, they are fearful and anxious about this project: They are worried about the reaction of the Islamic Republic and the "representatives" of that government who may be lurking in the United States of America. My friends have given me examples of individuals who talked or wrote negatively about the policies of Iran and were later found physically beaten or harmed financially. My friends also referred to the book *Assassins of the Turquoise Palace*, by Roya Hakakian, a book which documents the assassination of hundreds of Iranians living outside Iran. Perhaps my friends' fear is well founded? Or maybe their fear is unfounded and they are cowered by memories of pain and humiliation they endured in Iran?

Many of my friends also expressed concern that being mentioned by name in this book would negatively impact their relationships with their Muslim or Jewish colleagues, business associates, friends and neighbors. I am, therefore, very proud of all those who gave me permission to use their photos and real names, for they have truly "left Iran" and are free in mind and spirit. Several Muslim clerics and scholars of Islamic subjects who were asked to review this book reacted with anger and hostility; most of them refused to write their opposing views and opinions. Clearly, the Islamic Republic has succeeded to intimidate most Iranians living outside of Iran.

It is my belief and conviction that only through true dialogue and honest discussions we, the lovers of Iran, will succeed to heal our past wounds and unite to remove the fear and oppression of the Islamic Republic. We must remember that fear is the brother of death.

This book can be the catalyst of new hope and courage.

BOOK REVIEWS

Isaac, I reviewed your book and I am proud to know you all over again! Your book is very entertaining and informative. Your memories of Iran are mesmerizing. As a devoted *Shiah* Muslim Iranian I especially enjoyed reading about your family's relationships with Iranian Muslims. I certainly agree with most of your observations and conclusions; however, I have significant disagreement with your claim that the Holy Quran advocates violence, hatred, the superiority of Muslims over all other people, and the ultimate domination of the world. I also disagree with your inference that Iranian Muslims have made little contribution to a civil and peaceful world, human rights, ethics, art, literature, science, etc.

I think you should stop complaining so much about the brutality of the Holy Quran and Muslims. Take a look at the Shechem story in the Bible: How Jacob's two sons (Shimon and Levi) deceived the people of Shechem, slaughtered the king and prince, and then murdered the entire population of the city, taking all of their belongings. The barbarism of Shimon and Levi was worse than the forced conversions and killings condoned by the Prophet Mohammad and his cousin, Imam Ali.

The concept of *Jihad* is misunderstood and wrongly practiced by radicals. The majority of Muslims all over the world condemn *Jihad, Jihadists,* and terrorism. However, you are right to demand that moderate Muslims speak up.

In Iran, Islam has not yet achieved the adoption of modernity and moderation. Many of the Ayatollah's laws are unacceptable in today's world. I am convinced that an overwhelming majority of Iranian Muslims prefer revisions of the *Shariah* Laws to include civil and human rights.

Thank you for allowing me to read your manuscript.

Parviz Tabrizi, Psychologist and Scholar of Iranian History

My dear friend, Isaac Yomtovian, gave me permission to read his new book which is actually an autobiographical accounting of his birth and upbringing as a Jew in a predominantly Muslim country.

Many of his recolloections remind me of my own observations as a non-Jew who observed the degree to which the masses can be ignorant and cruel. This cruelty was possible because of the over 1400 years of brutal brainwashing that Iranians suffered at the hands of Arab invaders—brainwashing that continues up to this date. We as Iranians are faced with two opposing identities, one the Iranian/Persian identity of which we are proud, and the other the imported Arab (Islam) identity which has been hammered into our heads for over 1400 years. We have to decide once and for all as to which one we want to be.

The part of this book which is somewhat at odds with my own recollections and studies is the section that gives reasons for the existence of the present regime in Iran. A brief study of history of Iran during the last 200 years shows that the people of Iran have disposed of four monarchs (Shahs): Mohammad Ali Shah, Ahmad Shah, Reza Shah and Mohammad Reza Shah. One should ask why the people didn't like their Shahs. (The first two were from the Ghajar Dynasty and the last two were from the Pahlavi Dynasty.)

Iran is the only country in the region that has gone through three revolutions during the last 150 years. The 1906 Revolution promised to bring constitutional monarchy and the rule of law, only to be totally ignored by the rise of Reza Khan to power; he founded a new dynasty. There is no question that Reza Shah was at heart a patriot, but unfortunately he also was initially under the influence of the British. He had sworn to uphold the constitution and the law of the land, but the first thing he did was to ignore the constitution. The invasion of the Allies in 1941, resulted in the exile of Reza Shah, and the revolution of 1979 deposed his son, Mohammad Reza Shah, whose rise to power with help from the CIA is well documented in this book.

In a constitutional monarchy the Shah is supposed to be a ceremonial figure, but in Iran he became the governing body. This resulted in abolishing political parties, rigging elections, and closing down the opposition newspapers. The Shah himself negotiated major deals with major powers; he appeased the mullahs at every opportunity and even built a mosque in the middle of our university in Tehran. He also claimed that he dreamed that his reign would be saved by this and that Arab Imam.

The vacuum that this father and son created in the political arena by silencing all the critics with brutal force, left the mullahs to preach freely their warped and murderous message—and when the revolution came, only the mullahs were organized enough to wrestle the power and take the country back to where it is now.

This book is well written, and for the most part well documented. Highly recommended.

M. Valadbeigi

[Dr. Valadbeigi is a Muslim and a scholar of Persian music; he was an anti-Shah activist and spent three years in the Shah's prison in the late 1960s. —Author's note]

From generation to generation: (upper left) Great-Grandfather Agh Baba Yomtov; (upper right) Grandfather Elyahu Yomtoubian; (lower left) the unshaven brothers, Hertzel, Isaac, and Ruben observed shelosheem, the period of mourning for their father, Ebrahim Yomtoubian, (photo lower right) in April 2006.

ABOUT ISAAC YOMTOVIAN

His name is Isaac, *Pesare' Ebram Johood*, son of Ebrahim the Jew. His father's father was Eliyahu. His great-grandfather was Aghbaba, who was the son of Shelemo, who was the son of Yehazghel.

Isaac's parents were both born in Esfahan. The Jewish community of Esfahan traces its roots back 2,500 years to ancient Persia. After their marriage, his parents moved to Tehran's Jewish ghetto in 1942.

On August 19, 1948, shortly after the birth of the State of Israel, Isaac was born in Tehran, Iran in a modest house near Pahlavi Street, a stone's throw from the Marble Palace of Mohammad Reza Shah Pahlavi. The house in which he was born was located in a new Jewish neighborhood outside of Tehran's Jewish ghetto, known as *Mahaleh*.

Isaac attended a Muslim public elementary school because his father was unable to afford the tuition to the private Jewish school. During the six years of elementary school, Isaac was taught Qur'an, *Shariah Law*, and Islamic history. His first four years of high school were completed at the private Jewish Kourosh School; the last two years of high school were completed at a private Muslim night school where he majored in mathematics. During the six years of high school, Isaac worked in his father's fabric store located in South Tehran, in a modest, very conservative, religiously observant Muslim neighborhood. Isaac befriended many Muslim young people and Muslim families, learning their beliefs, traditions, and way of life. From time to time he lived in the homes of his Muslim friends.

In 1966, Isaac was accepted into a number of universities in Tehran, but he chose to emigrate to Israel and join Kibbutz Gan Shmuel. He volunteered in the 1967 Six Day War and subsequently attended the Technion Israel Institute of Technology, Department of Civil Engineering. He remained active in the Zionist movement and worked in the Israeli Department of Defense, Survey Office.

In 1971, Isaac was offered a scholarship in the Department of Water Resources Research of the University of Nebraska in Lincoln,

Nebraska, where he obtained a Master of Science degree. In 1974, he attended the post-graduate program of the Agricultural Engineering and Civil & Environmental Engineering Department of Cornell University in Ithaca, New York. During this period he remained active in the Iranian Students Association.

In 1976, Isaac joined his older brother in Minneapolis, Minnesota and worked for private engineering firms in St. Paul and Minneapolis. In 1978, he opened his first engineering firm, Enviroscience, and married Roslyn Kaplan, MD. In 1988, he and his family moved to Cleveland, Ohio. In 1990, Isaac obtained his Executive MBA from Case Western University and expanded his real estate development projects in Ohio and New York.

Isaac has served as an engineering and construction arbitrator, and is registered with the American Association of Arbitrators. He has completed Leadership Cleveland, and has served as the president of several Rotary Clubs, as well as on the boards of several charitable, educational, and religious organizations.

Mr. Yomtovian has published technical engineering articles in professional journals on the subjects of civil and environmental engineering, the privatization of public assets, and toxic and hazardous waste control and management. In addition, he has written articles for the local media on the subjects of Iranian Jewish life, Iranian culture and civilization, and the Islamic Revolution of 1979. *The Chagrin Valley Times, The Cleveland Jewish News,* and *The Sun Newspapers* have published his views on Jewish holidays in Iran, as well as stories about his life's journey from Iran to Pepper Pike, Ohio.

Isaac is a frequent guest speaker for various educational and religious groups in the Cleveland Metropolitan area. His unique, first-hand experience and knowledge of Islam, Iran, and Jewish history makes him a desirable speaker and lecturer on these timely subjects.